THE COMING
MATRIARCHY

THE COMING MATRIARCHY

How Women Will Gain the Balance of Power

Elizabeth Nickles
with Laura Ashcraft

SEAVIEW BOOKS

NEW YORK

Authors' Note

Throughout *The Coming Matriarchy* the names of the interviewees have been changed to protect their privacy. The names of the experts have remained unchanged.

MANUFACTURED IN THE UNITED STATES OF AMERICA.

FIRST EDITION.

Seaview Books/A Division of PEI Books, Inc.

Library of Congress Cataloging in Publication Data
Nickles, Elizabeth.
     The coming matriarchy.

     Bibliography: p.
     1. Women—United States. 2. Power (Social sciences) 3. Women—Employment—Social aspects—United States. I. Ashcraft, Laura. II. Title.
HQ1426.N53   305.4'2'0973   80–54519
ISBN 0–87223–686–2   AACR2

For the women in my family.

E. N.

Contents

Contents

Acknowledgments

There are many voices in this book, and a large number must remain anonymous. First, thanks to all of those who opened their lives and their souls for the sake of this book.

The wide range of experts who offered their valuable professional insight helped shape the book, each in his or her unique way. It is possible and natural, however, that any of them may disagree with certain points made in the book, and Ms. Ashcraft and I take full responsibility for the thesis, which may not necessarily reflect the views of these individuals, and for any errors or weaknesses that may have inadvertently occurred.

Market Facts, Inc., made possible the cornerstone of the book and offered the immeasurable contributions and unfailing assistance that are hallmarks of the firm. A special debt of gratitude is owed to Omar Bendikas, vice president, Susan Clark, study director, and David Hardin, chairman.

Dr. Roy Grinker, Jr., not only contributed his professional time and analysis, but also reviewed the entire manuscript from a psychiatric point of view. His guidance and clarification deserve special thanks. Clinical psychologist Porter Bennett also offered insight and illumination on numerous points.

Gloria Esdale and Lynn Rosener of S.R.I. International provided key information. A special debt is owed to Ms. Rosener for her painstaking explanation of alpha and beta leadership styles.

Mitchell S. Fromstein, president of Manpower, Inc., shared his extensive expertise in current trends concerning today's working women.

Marilyn Moats Kennedy, Dr. Brenda Solomon, Dr. Linda Keller Brown, Dr. Robert Blattberg, Sheila R. Coin, Dr.

Arlene Kaplan Daniels, Lillian Deitch, Dr. Sid Levy, Arlene Cohn, Courtney Brady, Ann Ladky, Kay Riegler, Will Hokin, Marion Howington, Dr. Thomas Murphy, and Dean Richard Thain each made contributions that were extremely important to the book. Helen McLane made available the unique survey of women holding corporate offices compiled by Heidrick and Struggles, Inc.

Carol Zheutlin's editorial suggestions and enthusiasm helped define the issues and clarify the concept.

Bonnie Zeitlin searched out hundreds of articles used in the background research. Janet Peper deserves not only appreciation but a medal for her incredible patience and intelligent reading and typing of the manuscript.

For any book to take that leap from idea to reality, there must be those who believed in it before it happened. So my deepest gratitude is offered to Charles Sopkin, not only for appreciating and valuing the concept, but for his confidence in our work. Also, there could have been no more positive and constructive support than that of Tamara Asseyev, who helped in more ways than could ever be adequately listed on a printed page, and who guided this book from conception to completion with skill and sensitivity. In this, Alex Rose was her partner.

For the personal support that makes it all worthwhile, my friends and family were extraordinarily patient, understanding, and enthusiastic. Sanford Bredine and Dale Ashcraft were not only head cheerleaders, but also offered many important insights. Laura Ashcraft and I thank them for bearing with us for so long.

Most of all, I wish to express my admiration and appreciation to Laura Ashcraft, my partner and research collaborator, who also made countless creative contributions. Without her professionalism, talent, and friendship, this book would literally not have been possible.

—ELIZABETH NICKLES
January 1981

Introduction

Revolutions are not what they used to be. Take the Industrial Revolution, for instance. Even as it happened, you could tangibly account for it. Anyone could look at a piece of machinery that did the back-breaking labor of three, ten, or twenty people, give or take a few horses, and be able to comprehend the events and changes of the time.

Today, things are more complex. Developments are less easily categorized, defined, and explained because society is more fragmented, change more multifaceted. Now a new kind of revolution is in the making, but it has not been easily identified, perhaps because it is paradoxical. It is obvious yet hidden. Conscious and unconscious. Far-reaching yet individualistic. A revolution of choice, a revolution of need. It is aggressive, yet ambivalent. And it is happening in a way that is largely intangible, because it is an *attitudinal* revolution—involving the motivations and emotions of hundreds of thousands of American women.

Women are changing in ways that will collide with and forever alter the comfortably familiar contours of our social and economic topography. They are assuming characteristics associated with leadership—becoming more aggressive, independent, authoritative, decisive, and goal-oriented. Young women are growing up still better prepared for leadership roles through early conditioning, diversification of role models, education, broadened opportunity, and life-style modifications. All this is concurrent with the massive migration of women into the work force, our principal forum of prestige, status, and power. These changes have already made hairline fractures in the balance of sexual power. Ultimately they will alter it permanently.

In the past twenty years, the percentage of American women who are employed has mushroomed from 33.4 percent in 1960 to 52.2 percent in 1981, with the greatest increases among women who traditionally have had the strongest motivation for staying home—those with school-aged children. Socioeconomists have called this the single most outstanding phenomenon of this century, and have compared it with developments like the invention of electricity and the advent of nuclear power. We are already feeling the effect of this phenomenon. But still more immense changes await us in the future.

With women still facing many serious disadvantages in the power structure, it may be difficult to imagine where the force will come from to push them to equality, much less matriarchy. Yet it is already coming from within the women themselves, from fundamental changes in their values and attitudes combined with inescapable social and economic forces. Four key factors will launch and perpetuate new dynamics in the sexual balance of power:

• The escalation and continuation of the economic and social dynamics that have drawn women into the work force, establishing employment as a financial and psychological necessity and redefining the perceived value and social status of women in our capitalistic system.

• The emergence of a new psychographic profile of women that is eclipsing the norm of the traditional housewife. This new, uniquely motivated and aggressive type of woman will scuttle interests of domesticity for those of outside self-gratification.

• The failure of women, men, and their institutions to

adapt to the changing needs of women, causing this new breed of woman to avoid or short-circuit those institutions and initiating a restructuring of the socioeconomic system as we have known it.

• The fact that women's basic leadership styles will be increasingly more effective and appropriate than men's in dealing with and solving the complex issues and problems of the times.

As a result of these and other factors, we can anticipate tremendous changes in role modeling, parenting, and basic conscious and unconscious formative experiences, which will perpetuate such forces once they are set in motion. More importantly, they will inevitably cause us to adjust the development of our psychological foundations to permit flexibilities and alternatives that were previously neither acceptable nor plausible.

What are the possible consequences of tipping the balance of power in favor of women? A redefinition of sexual roles; the breakdown of the traditional family structure; a rearrangement of the home as we know it; new systems for childrearing; new value and reward systems for both men and women; new foundations for sexual relationships; expanded technologies to fill the domestic void left by women who are no longer tenders of the hearth; political distributions that reflect the shift in women's power; ultimately, perhaps, a revision of our capitalistic system. All could occur.

The term "matriarchy" does not mean that women will hold every political and industrial office, nor does it imply an end to femininity or doomsday for masculinity. It is not a matter of simple role-reversal, but of role diversification, offering each sex a broader spectrum of options and opportunities. Women, however, will be in the better position to hold—and will be more strongly motivated to achieve—power, assuming power is defined as the capability of exerting influence, based on the control of desirable resources in social and economic relationships.

I did not randomly come to these conclusions. In fact, four years ago, when I began talking to women about their jobs and themselves to learn how their work affected their lives, their goals, their relationships, their families, and their futures, I had few preconceptions. But as I talked to more and more women, it became clear that, for most, work involved vastly more than putting in time for a paycheck. I saw that having a job changes a woman, often drastically, and I detected vast differences between women who worked outside the home and those who did not.

Over the next several years, I interviewed almost a hundred women to learn as much about them as I could. Any time I encountered a woman became an opportunity to learn more about her.

For instance, at two o'clock one blizzardy, subzero morning I was groggily jockeying for prime position along the airport luggage conveyor. Out of the corner of one half-closed eye, I noticed a young woman hefting my baggage, and that of a hundred other passengers, off the lift truck. She was in her early twenties and wearing an airline maintenance crew uniform. Even at two in the morning I was curious enough to call her aside and ask a few questions. She was twenty-two years old, a college graduate working the night shift full-time on the baggage detail. The following week, I met this woman at the airport again, and we spent two hours talking, enough for me to get to know her and begin to understand how she felt, who she was, how she was changing, where she was going.

The women I spoke with in these years had much to say. Bus drivers, corporate executives, artists, beauticians, secretaries, homemakers, entrepreneurs—all poured out their lives as if I were a long-sought touchstone. One women whispered, "I feel like I'm burning my soul."

Common denominators began to surface. Most of the employed women felt their jobs had altered their lives in many ways. I heard the pride shimmering in women's voices, the (often newfound) self-assurance that comes with knowing your professional skills are worth something to society and to yourself. I also heard the tortured stories of how jobs had changed some women in intrinsic ways that ultimately led to shattered traditions and relationships, broken homes and hearts.

The interviews exposed the flaws in the smooth surface of the female role we have known for so long. More significant than a group of interesting individual stories, the interviews began to reveal a process set in motion.

But did these patterns carry through on a broader scale? While personal interviews provided an interesting, qualitative base from which to speculate, they were in no way statistically valid. I needed a quantitative, unbiased picture of attitudes, motivations, and behaviors of both working and nonworking women across the country. The only problem was that none existed. Even if I had crisscrossed America and spoken to a hundred thousand women, or polled them at random, the result would not necessarily be representative of a valid national cross-section.

Laura Ashcraft, a professional marketing researcher and officer of the American Marketing Association, recommended applying consumer research techniques. She outlined a research plan involving a mail survey and commissioned Market Facts, Inc., one of the country's top research firms, to provide a nationally projectable survey sample. It is this national projectability that enables the research upon which this book is based to be representative on a national basis, without polling every woman in the United States. Market Facts maintains a mail panel of over 100,000 households across the country that constitute a statistically accurate microcosm of the population. Each household is categorized and filed on a computer in such a way that we were able to tailor a nationally projectable sample of 2,400 women with characteristics matching key national demographics. Included were working and nonworking women, white-collar and blue-collar workers, and managers and employees of every level.

Ashcraft and I put together a detailed four-page questionnaire that was mailed to this sample. Questions in this survey—as in the personal interviews—were designed to pinpoint the basis of the attitudes and behaviors of those women who worked outside the home and those who did not. Whether a woman worked or not, we structured our questions to reveal in-depth information about her background, her role models and expectations as a child, her views of the appropriate role of a woman, her personal, social, and economic self-image, her past, current, and future expectations. If she had a job, we went on to probe her feelings about her work, her relationship with her family and husband or male companion, if any, the problems and benefits of her job, and her career and personal objectives.

The responses to our mail survey were tabulated by a computer, which compared various individual traits and patterns, then sorted responses into groups according to various common denominators. Ashcraft spent several months analyzing these data.

The result is the first in-depth, nationally projectable profile of how American women feel about their work and their lives, and how work outside the home—or lack of it—impacts on their lives and behaviors. The trends and patterns that emerged form the nucleus of this book. We believe that this survey offers statistical documentation of an emerging attitudinal movement among American women. Women are changing as a result of their employment. And we believe that as greater numbers of women join the work force, these changes will be increasingly pronounced. This phenomenon will be the catalyst for the forces that, combined with the economic impact of working women, will make possible the emergence of a matriarchy.

The in-depth interviews which are included illustrate some of the people behind the statistics. They are women of many backgrounds—white-collar, blue-collar, "pink"-collar, lower-class, upper-class, white, black, single, married, young, older. Because of the significance of the white-collar area as the predominant instrument of growth and change for the working woman, a larger proportion of the personal interviews have been concentrated in that area. But the common link across the board is attitudes that cut across occupational and demographic strata.

This book focuses on attitudinal change, but also encompasses many other social, cultural, biological, historical, and political issues. The following chapters, in dealing specifically with the primary thesis of the book, may exclude various aspects in relation to certain points for reasons of scope. But in exploring the issues, we have tried to go straight to the source—the actions, words, motivations, and attitudes of the women themselves.

Nothing stays the same forever, and as people change, so must their world.

E. N.

THE COMING
MATRIARCHY

CHAPTER 1

The Facts of Life

No matter how accomplished she may be as a homemaker, how fulfilled her life as a mother, how gourmet her cooking, how selfless her volunteer work, how beloved she is as a friend, lover, wife, mother, or daughter, there is one inescapable fact about a woman who does not earn her own living. She is dependent. Usually on a man. She may or may not enjoy and feel justified in this, but the fact is that not much has changed since she was a little girl under Daddy's roof, buying candy with the allowance he gave her. Even as a married woman, a contributing member of the household, she may refer to her allotted money as her "allowance." Psychologically as well as financially, a woman who does not work for pay must rely on someone else to supply her needs. She may feel like an equal partner. She may be told she is an equal partner. But she is not, and she never really can be.

The wage earner will always hold the power, because we live in a capitalistic society, where an individual's status is based on economic productivity. When women—or men—do not contribute directly to economic production or earn money, they lack power and the avenues to acquire it. Like it or not, the absolute currency in America is the dollar.

Certainly there are other, human values. The woman who is not employed has much to offer in many respects and may be revered as a wife, a mother, and a person. But she can never gain the broad-based power of an individual who works outside the home, because the capitalistic system implies certain things that exclude her from the foundation of the power structure.

Our society is organized to facilitate its primary objectives—profit, competition, and technological development—by splitting into two segments: productive, meaning income-producing, which receives first priority; and domestic, which provides support services for the productive sector. The goal of industry becomes efficiency and productivity, while the home seeks to meet family needs and provide the impetus for earning and achievement. Parenting, child-care, and housewifery have lesser status, because they do not contribute to economic productivity, are unpaid, and control fewer resources than paid work. Any skills that are not directly transferrable to the productivity sector outside the home—such as being a good mother—acquire a second-class image. Individuals outside the work force (meaning, traditionally, women) achieve status via marriage to someone with status. And so it evolves that we find some women being applauded for "good" marriages to doctors, lawyers, and men with big incomes, while others, newly divorced after twenty years as homemakers, are cast adrift by society and unable to get jobs.

It is not my intent to disparage or devalue the contributions of women who do not work outside the home. In this book, I refer to women who are employed as "working" women for brevity and convenience. Of course the homemaker works—as hard as or harder than her employed counterparts. The point is that her work is *perceived* differently, and as a result she perceives herself differently. Paid employment, or lack of it, has a significance of its own, powerful enough to alter the psychological makeup of a woman, as well as society's perceptions of her status and contributions.

Equate, if you will, any typical marriage with the following business relationship. Jerry and Elise open a store. Each has something to contribute: He has the money; she has the know-how. They agree to be partners for life. They say they are equal in the relationship. Certainly they feel equal. But since Jerry is the source of the financing, he owns all the stock in the company, plus the land it sits on. Of course, the office lease is in his name, too. Jerry is the executive. He handles the clients and controls the money and the payroll, from which comes Elise's well-deserved paycheck. Elise, meanwhile, runs the store, handles the phones, keeps records, and manages the day-to-day shopkeeping. In return, she gets her salary from Jerry, a Christmas bonus, paid sick-leave, and a comforting sense of security. Things roll along smoothly for ten years. The "partnership" prospers. Then one day Jerry experiences a midlife crisis and impulsively decides to liquidate the company and ship himself out to Pago Pago on the proceeds. He gives Elise an engraved watch and a letter of recommendation. She is stunned and terrified. She cries. She threatens. So what? She has no real control. As Jerry reminds her, it was his money, wasn't it? All she can do is watch her "partner" hula off into the sunset while she dusts off her resumé and hits the help-wanted ads.

Anyone who thinks that a traditional male wage-earner/female housekeeper relationship is an equal partnership is fooling himself or herself. It is only equal as long as the person who controls the finances agrees that it is equal. When men controlled the money by being the primary or the sole wage earners, an unquestionable social and economic patriarchy existed—and a psychological patriarchy, too, because an entire set of unconscious and conscious behaviors and responses went along inextricably with that control.

Clinical psychologist Porter Bennett elaborates: "Money is much more powerful than mere buying power that one could put on the balance sheet. The power is often denied—we pretend it's not there, but it *is* a very strong controlling factor in most households. That control may be silent, but it is *there.* It influences decisions, and it also sets a tone—who comes to whom when it comes to decision making, for instance. It is also a source of punishment. Withholding the money, however politely, helps establish the power structure."

One housewife had yearned for years to change her particular way of life by going back to school so that eventually she could qualify for a job that required the education. Her husband had always paid lip service to her ambitions but offered no concrete support, and since the couple could not easily afford the college courses, the situation seemed benign. One day, the woman mentioned to her grandmother that she had these dreams. . . . The grandmother rose to the occasion, depositing $2,500 in the couple's joint account specifically to pay the tuition. Joyfully the woman told her husband that now she could get her degree, and before long, the job. They celebrated. Three days later the husband casually mentioned that he'd withdrawn the money and used it to buy four Krugerrands—which he had stacked for safekeeping behind the piano.

Porter Bennett points out that while the Krugerrands may or may not have been a sound investment, the fact remains that the husband took the money without his wife's consent or even knowledge. "He established the old control," says Bennett. " 'It's our money, but *I'll* decide what to do with it.' The woman's decision to go back to school was very threatening to the general power structure. So he moved the power structure back on familiar ground."

It's the golden rule: He (or she) who has the gold, rules.

One woman, now divorced and working, echoed these sentiments when she recalled, "I had to ask for everything I bought: 'May I go buy this?' He never asked me if *he* could buy anything. He bought at will. I had to have *permission.*"

But the balance of power is beginning to teeter as a result

of the unprecedented influx of American women out of the home and into the work force, and the social, psychological, and economic impact of this phenomenon. We are now on the edge of a socioeconomic revolution that will forever fracture the status quo and may permanently alter the balance of power between American men and women.

But before we can look forward, we have to look back.

Roots of Change

Before industrialization, in the time of European agrarian society, men and women worked side by side, each contributing his or her fair share of labor to the necessary tasks. Society was structured around family units, with households representing separate economic units, mingling domestic and economic activities. The household itself was a self-sufficient entity, providing most of its own food, shelter, clothing, and entertainment, and often, as in the case of barter, its own means of commercial exchange. Households contributed to their community on a cooperative basis, by performing complementary tasks that enabled the group as a whole to function. Far from segregating women into a domestic existence, this system resulted in men and women sharing economic and home responsibilities, and women working outside the home, independent of their husbands. Records of eighteenth-century guilds, for instance, show that they almost unanimously consisted equally of male and female members.

When industrialization emerged in England, the early factories at first incorporated and mobilized the family system, with entire middle-class and lower-class families—men, women, and children—working together for one employer. This trend continued until the establishment of child-labor laws in the mid 1800s, when many women who had been working alongside their husbands and children migrated back into the home to care for those children. These women, along with those of the upper class, who had never worked outside the home, became buttonholed into lives that were home-centered. The home and the workplace became increasingly segregated, and the function of parent and worker more distinctly divided by sex, according to the capitalistic mold. This became popularized as the "natural" way of life, leaving any variance open to derision.

The formation of male-dominated trade unions about this time further divided the sexes by excluding the remaining women in the work force from large segments of industry via sheer force of policy. These unions concentrated on obtaining wage, training, and other benefits solely for men, leaving women the crumbs of lower paying, dead-end jobs. Such unionization policies were paralleled in the United States.

As early as 1922, F. Y. Edgeworth noted that "the pressure of male trade unions appears to be largely responsible for that crowding of women into comparatively few occupations, which is universally recognized as a main factor in the depression of their wages."[1]

As a result, women who did not work outside the home were relegated to nurturing roles and had few skills that were transferrable to the industrial sector of the economy, while working women were clustered in "women's jobs" in the service-oriented areas, the economy's version of "housekeeping" jobs, which reflected the nature of their duties at home: sewing, cooking, child-care, teaching, and so on. Clerical work, a male stronghold in the 1800s, became women's territory as organizational growth opened up newer and more mobile opportunities for men, while office-machine technology offered women more attractive working conditions than farm or factory situations.

This job segregation remains a fact of life to this day. Women are still crowded into "job ghettos" where they can realistically find attractive work, creating a vicious circle of low pay and meager opportunity and devaluing many of the careers available to women.

By the turn of the century, one more nail had been driven into the coffin of equal opportunity for women in the form of "protective legislation." By 1908, maximum-hours legislation for women had been upheld on the federal level; however intentioned, this served, in effect, to minimize job competition by women and segregate them still further from the economic mainstream, so that there was no chance of them forming an economic power base.

The result was a patriarchal system, with men in control not only of the system itself, with its inherent money, status, and power, but also of the women tied to that system by their apronstrings. This segregation became ingrained into social attitudes. Although it was recognized that some women, commonly known as "poor things," eccentrics, or spinsters, worked out of necessity, women in general who attempted the crossover from domestic to industrial roles risked the censure and humiliation of being branded "unfeminine," traitors to their "natural" role in life.

During World War I, many American women filled in for the men occupied on the battlefield. But after the war, they slipped back onto the merry-go-round of domesticity or "women's jobs." Social tradition was not yet ready to support a system change, and men opposed it, since women presented a threat to their own jobs. Also, no vehicle was pervasive enough to glamorize such a change until World War II, when women again found themselves stepping into men's shoes to do their jobs. Between 1939 and 1943 the American labor force was 75 percent married women, most of whom had children still at home.[2] A major difference, in addition to a general modernization of attitudes, was that the media were now sufficiently powerful to romanticize the experience on a large scale, and interest in the media was widespread enough to enable this viewpoint to flourish. Women, and society in general, were able to see that the concept of a woman earning her own money outside the home made sense. Women's realization that others like themselves were working and also raising families successfully was a powerful incentive. This experience was a groundbreaker, because for the first time the working woman became not only socially acceptable but a figure to be glamorized.

Consider, for instance, the popular movies of the period. Between 1942 and 1943 at least four glorified the working woman: *They All Kissed the Bride* starred Joan Crawford as a female executive; *Take a Letter, Darling* went one step further, with Rosalind Russell actually hiring a male secretary; *Woman of the Year* featured Katharine Hepburn as a feisty columnist; *Tender Comrade* extolled lady welders whose husbands were fighting men. Joan Crawford herself, in several roles as a working shopgirl, became a heroine to so many women who could identify with the situation that the image catapulted her to stardom. The autonomous woman striving to achieve her aspirations, as personified by Katharine Hepburn, Irene Dunne, Bette Davis, and Barbara Stanwyck, replaced the previous images of child/women (the early 1900s), women ready to drop their jobs for men (the twenties), and women struggling for survival (the Depression years).

This unprecedented break with the traditional image of women indicated the emergence of new attitudes about and by women. The honeymoon was over rather quickly, however, when men returned from the war to their jobs. There was an enthusiastic attempt to again relegate women to the nether land of one-dimensional caricatures, highlighted by the trend in the 1950s toward reaffirmation of male dominance. The "New Look" catapulted skirts down to nonfunctional lengths; the "baby boom" confirmed the desirable status of maternity on a broad scale; and domesticity, sweetness, and sex appeal were considered the most admirable characteristics, as portrayed in the movies by Doris Day and Marilyn Monroe.

After the war, most of the younger women left the world of work and went back to the world of bottles and diapers—but a new seed had been sown, and would germinate. Most of those over forty-five, who had no immediate, urgent need to return to a domestic existence because their children were grown, stayed in the labor force. In fact, during the baby boom from 1946 to 1960 the growth in labor-force participation took place almost entirely among older women. Before the war, and lacking the experience gained during the war period, these women would have been psychologically unprepared to make such a choice. That they chose to stay and work reflected new attitudes. After 1962, as the birthrate declined and the baby-boom children grew, the younger women, having had a taste of paying jobs and finding them attractive, viewed the return to work as a positive alternative to their diminishing home responsibilities.

For the first time, American women found themselves with a viable choice. Many chose to exercise their options and went back to work; others stayed home. Overall, the postwar era found large numbers of women spilling back into the work force. Of the total increase of 25 million women in the female labor force from 1947 to 1978, 10 million represented population growth, while 15 million could be accounted for by increased participation of women.[3] These women found work in newly opened fields of technology and in an expanding base of traditional women's jobs in education and personal services. Most of these jobs were narrowly defined in terms of what a woman's role could be, and there was little reason for psychological conflict. There was no question as to what a woman's primary job was—a job for which she did not receive a paycheck. Still, the first wedge had been driven to unsettle the patriarchal structure that had been so stable for so long.

In the fifties and sixties, economic pressure continued to spur previously employed women who had dropped out to return to the labor force, joined by younger newcomers. Inflation, college expenses, and the material desire for "extras" like appliances, cars, and clothes were all incentives.

As more women became employed, employment became more socially acceptable. At the same time, the women's movement brought about a new stress on self-fulfillment and personal liberation. In the early sixties, this movement emerged with the somewhat confining perspective of a protest against the "feminine mystique" that kept housewives tied to suburbia. By the late sixties, however, it had broadened in issues and emphasis to address women as a social caste and had become a widespread, populist force for changing attitudes of and towards women. As women's perceived options grew, so did their propensity to join the work force.

With the combination of these economic and social factors, there were now more reasons than ever for women to work outside the home, and precedents were established which removed key psychological and legal barriers to their employment.

The validation of women's right to work was reflected by significant legislation in the 1960s and early 1970s that guaranteed women protection against sexual discrimination—regardless of type of employment—in working conditions, hiring and firing policies, and fringe benefits, among other issues: the Equal Pay Act of 1963; Title VII of the Civil Rights Act of 1964 (which also established an enforcement agency—the Equal Opportunity Employment Commission); Executive Orders 11375 and 11478. Other key legislation for women's rights included the Education Amendments of 1972; the Women's Educational Equity Act of 1974; the Equal Credit Act of 1974; and the addition of equal-rights amendments to sixteen state constitutions. Such legislation signaled the widespread acceptability of women working outside the home, and although noncompliance was to remain a thorny issue, the success of highly publicized women's class-action suits represented the backbone of new status for the working woman and the roots of her support system. In 1973, American Telephone and Telegraph, in a landmark decree, agreed out of court to pay $38 million in back pay and salary adjustments to women employees and to upgrade the jobs of 50,000 women.[4]

By the end of the seventies, a widespread change in women's attitudes toward work had occurred. A study called "Women of the Eighties" conducted for the Newspaper Advertising Bureau showed that most housewives felt that working women were more likely to lead a richer, more interesting life, while only a third of the working women felt positively about the housewife's role.[5] Only eight years earlier, a similar study had found both working and nonworking women each viewing their own situation as favorable, and preferable to the other's. Clearly, working women had come to be more highly regarded than housewives. This reversal is a major benchmark, since it signifies the breaking down of traditional role definition, and it opened the way for women to assume authority and power without the degree of social censure they once had to endure.

All this is reflected in sheer numbers. Between 1950 and 1970, the female population age sixteen and over grew by 52 percent—but the female labor force grew by 117 percent. The number of employed married women tripled between 1940 and 1970, with the biggest growth where you'd least expect it: in the childbearing bracket of ages twenty-five to thirty-four,[6] women who had previously had the most reason to stay home.

In the past twenty years, the number of women entering the work force has outstripped men two to one, while the work rate of married men, for instance, has actually fallen more than 10 percent since 1947.[7]

The numbers suggest the stirring of an attitude, a new and independent point of view that gathered speed for three decades.

From 1960 on, we can track a strong, steady increase in the female working population: from 33.4 percent in 1960 to 41.9 percent in 1974.[8] Between 1964 and 1971, employment gains between men and women were fairly even. Then, in the 1970s, women streaked ahead as they poured into the labor market. Between 1971 and 1978, employment of men fell by 100,000, while women gained 100,000. The fastest growth continues to be in women under forty-five. Younger women without children no longer see work as an either/or option in relation to marriage, but as an independent choice. By 1977, 60 percent of all women in their twenties were employed.[9] In 1980, over half of all women over age sixteen were working outside the home, accounting for 42 percent of the total work force in America.[10] According to the U.S. Bureau of Labor Statistics, 90 percent of the girls and young women now in school will work outside their homes in their lifetimes.

The trend is expected to continue. Projections indicate that by 1990, 52 million women will be working or seeking employment, including two-thirds of all married women under age fifty-five and half of all working mothers of children under age six.[11]

Women are pouring into the work force because of many motivations that will be discussed later, but the result and/or concurrent event has been massive changes in life-style that are making traditional roles and value systems obsolete.

Social Shifts

More women than ever before in our history are relying on themselves instead of Prince Charming. Work is the vehicle that permits this.

Becoming a housewife is no longer the all-American girl's dream. According to our survey, only 16 percent of women under age twenty-five plan to be housewives and do not desire a career.

Women are marrying later, or not marrying at all. Today 49 percent of all women aged twenty to twenty-four are still single, compared to 20 percent in 1960. And, in 1979, the median age of a woman's first marriage was 22.1 years, two years older than the median age at the height of the baby boom.[12] In deferring marriage, women gain experience as self-supporting, responsible, independent individuals that they might have missed in the rush to the altar. This experience sets the tone for their later lives. Many women continue on this track: The number of female-headed households in America has doubled to over 8 million since 1960.[13]

As more women earn more money in higher levels of responsibility, they can afford to live better and to express a self-concept to a greater degree. This life-style may or may not include marriage, but marriage is no longer the automatic resolution. When she earns an income, remaining single does not sentence a woman to a lifetime of living with her parents or going home to a pathetic "single girl" apartment with a bed that drops out of a closet and an ironing board that doubles as a dining room table.

Living with a man without marriage is an option for today's women that was socially unacceptable even fifteen years ago, but that allows a woman a new kind of self-sufficiency. In the last ten years, the number of unmarried couples living together more than doubled to 2.7 million.[14]

When an unmarried woman lives with a man and offers an economic contribution, she is more likely to keep her finances separate and view herself as a distinct entity rather than an extension of her partner.

Beyond true love, the propensity to marry often depends on the attractiveness or necessity of a set of anticipated tradeoffs, or gains, contributed by each person. If these gains are decreased, the propensity to marry will drop accordingly. The concept of the self-sufficient woman and the growing acceptance of a wide variety of life-styles offer more encouragement toward independence, fewer perceived rewards from marriage. Juanita Kreps has described this as a shift in the marriage payoff. One study by Kreps indicates that the mutual gains from marriage have declined, particularly in light of lowered fertility and childbirth statistics, and predicts that these factors will encourage a continued decline in the marriage rate.[15]

The declining birthrate is certainly one of the social forces freeing women from the nurturing role and permitting more time to work outside the home. Children, however loved, are no longer an economic advantage, and, given the escalating costs of raising a child, individuals and couples are becoming more discriminating about bearing them, so as to permit the highest quality of life-style for the entire family. Women are now having fewer children and planning them more carefully. The impact of this was seen after the end of the baby boom, when women swept back into the work force in large numbers. Birth control and abortion now offer women still more control over the maternal role.

Women who choose to have children are waiting longer after marriage to do so. In 1960 only 24 percent of all young married women aged twenty to twenty-four were childless. By 1978 this figure was 41 percent.[16] The National Center for Health Statistics reports a recent upsurge in the trend toward later childbearing: From 1975 to 1978 there was a 37 percent increase in the number of women aged thirty to thirty-four who had their first child.[17] For women thirty-five to thirty-nine, an increase of 22 percent was cited.[18] This delay in or abstinence from childbearing offers women a chance to gain footholds in the social and power structures outside the home that are difficult, if not impossible, to establish when a woman's life revolves around children. When child-rearing comes later in life, the woman's position is more secure, has more tenure, and is less likely to be lost or sacrificed as a result.

Even women who do have children are no longer staying home. In fact, the opposite seems to be true. Since World War II, while the number of employed women in this country has more than doubled, the number of employed mothers has increased *tenfold!* By 1979, 54.1 percent of all mothers of children under eighteen were in the labor force or seeking jobs—compared with 28.3 percent in 1950 and a mere 9 percent in 1940.[19] This exodus from the nursery is especially true of mothers of very young children. The year 1980 brought 5.5 million working mothers of 7 million preschool children—43 percent of all married women with children under six—into the forefront as the fastest-growing segment of the work force.[20] The U.S. Department of Labor refers to these events as "one of the most striking demographic changes that has taken place in the World War II era."[21]

Is it any surprise that the traditional American family is an endangered and rapidly vanishing species? Today only 7 percent of all American families have fathers who bring home the bacon and mothers who are devoted exclusively to caring for the children.[22]

This can mean great advantages in the pursuit of career success. In *Passages*, Gail Sheehy notes that married women who are career succcesses tend to devote about seven years to their careers before marriage, and that such types also tend to defer childbearing until age thirty. She points out that a significant number of the visible female superachievers, such as Margaret Mead, did not begin having children until age thirty-five and over.[23] A major social trend toward later childbearing could easily lead to a parallel growth of the most successful group of working women, which we call the Pacesetters—the most independent and aggressive, and least domestically oriented, of all women. Certainly it will mean that more women will have one advantage they never had before in the power structure: freedom from the ties of young children at home, and hence freedom to participate more singlemindedly in the economic power arena.

Today the head of the family is often a woman. Female-headed households have almost doubled since 1960, and women currently head 25 percent of all households.[24] Three-fourths of the increase of the past ten years was due to divorce or separation rather than death of a husband. In 1940 only 0.8 million American women were divorced. By 1960 the figure had inched up to 1.7 million. In 1970, 2.7 million women were opting for divorce. And within another 8 years, the number of divorced women had mushroomed to 5.3 million.[25] Divorces are up 96 percent since 1970. At that time, the U.S. Census Bureau reported 47 divorces per 1,000 married adults. As of a decade later, divorces have almost doubled: 90 per 1,000.[26] Married couples now constitute just over 60 percent of all households. Predictions call for the slide to continue.[27]

Although there is a small incidence of alternative household styles such as role reversals, males raising children, three-generation clusters, and communal living arrangements, basically two kinds of households are emerging as the growing nontraditional social segments: non-family and female-headed. Non-family households have surged 66 percent since 1970, and today one out of every four households consists of a person living alone or with non-relatives. The U.S. Census Bureau predicts this could increase to one out of every three households by 1990.[28] In a speech to the American Marketing Association, the former director of the U.S. Census, Vincent Barabba, cited the fact that more women are staying single longer as a major factor behind the growth of the non-family household.

The economic picture for women is also undergoing some radical revision, reflecting the demise of the "little lady" who is dependent on an "allowance" from her husband and the emergence of the woman as a significant factor in the marketplace, in her own right.

Women currently control the spending of some half a trillion dollars and bring home $390 billion in paychecks. From a base of practically o twenty years ago, we now find 21 percent of all working wives with their own separate checking accounts and 20 percent with their own savings accounts. A total of 50.3 percent of all American stockholders are female.[29] There are 14 million women carrying their own life insurance, an increase of 90 percent since 1970. A total of 13 million are holding their own credit cards (American Express, up 171 percent in the last five years; air travel cards, up 52 percent in the same period).[30] Women controlled about 15 percent of new-car purchases in the early 1960s, 20 percent in 1971, and 40 percent in 1979.[31] In the coming matriarchy, women may guard their financial trappings fiercely and refuse to relinquish them even if they choose to marry.

One aspect of women's increasing financial control is linked to the fact that women are even now outliving men, resulting in control of a growing share of America's financial resources for a longer period of time by women who survive their spouses. The number of widows is increasing rapidly, while the number of widowers is declining: Widows increased from 9.6 million in 1970 to 10.5 million in 1979, while widowers decreased from 2.1 million to 1.9 million in the same period. Millionaire widows increased from 11,000 in 1960 to

36,000 in 1972, while those with assets between half a million and a million dollars rose from 17,000 to 56,000.[32] These figures indicate the tip of a very large and growing iceberg, which is being filled in from the bottom by women whose financial attitudes are increasingly independent and aggressive.

The shift in traditional social and economic structures is opening up new opportunities for women and loosening the grasp of the patriarchy. As these opportunities increase, the social and economic quicksand that has drawn women into the work force will pull more strongly than ever. The situations we see emerging in the eighties are unlikely to change, except to become more acute.

The Whirlpool Effect

A close examination of why women work offers insight into some of the major forces that guarantee they will continue to be pushed further from the traditional axis. These motivations combine to form a "whirlpool effect," which is pulling them into the labor market and keeping them there.

Our survey reveals that almost all women work primarily for one of two reasons: money and "self." (See the table "Who Is Motivated by What?" at the end of the chapter.) If a woman is working for money, she can't afford to quit. And if she's working for "self," she can't afford to quit either.

According to our survey, 46 percent of all working women feel money is their primary job motivation. As a nurse with a young family wrote, "I have to work. Bills come due—I have no choice."

Half of all women who work full-time work mainly for income, while a third of all part-timers put income first (the part-timer figure is probably lower because these women are more likely to be married to husbands earning incomes).

The majority of these money-motivated women work not for pin money, savings, or an occasional splurge in the sportswear department but for reasons of basic economic necessity. This has never been more true than in times of double-digit inflation. When the Gallup Organization conducted a national poll for *Redbook* magazine in fall 1979, one in three women claimed to have left the home to go to work because of inflation, and 50 percent of those polled said they took their jobs because of the current economic crunch.

For the 19 million women who are self-supporting or heads of households, work is survival. Even if a woman is married and her husband has a job, work is more often than not a necessity. According to the 1973 U.S. Census, three-fourths of all women who work either have no husband or a mate whose income falls below $7,000 a year.

Monetary motivations of working women can lead to a pattern that has been charted by economists, known as "the entrapment syndrome," which is, in effect, the ball and chain of dollars and cents. The variations on entrapment are many, but the theme is all too familiar, and the result is an enforced long-term commitment to work.

Research on the buying behavior of wives has revealed that working wives often enter the labor force to achieve specific, short-term goals, like the purchase of a car or piece of furniture, that have been catapulted out of reach by inflation. The family or couple then becomes addicted to the improved standard of living made possible by the woman's paycheck. When the short-term goal is reached, neither husband nor wife is willing to give up the two-paycheck life-style, and so the woman becomes "entrapped" in the working world.

Another variation on entrapment: A newlywed couple begins their life together with optimistic—and unrealistic—

visions of the traditional marriage roles their parents enjoyed. She plans to work for only a short time, till they get their feet on the ground, or build a "nest egg" before starting a family. However, the two paychecks allow the couple great discretionary income and luxuries that are difficult to give up. Installment-plan purchasing often becomes a way of life —but if they "buy now," the wife must continue to work if they are to "pay later." As the couple becomes more dependent on both paychecks, they put off starting a family "just one more year" until the wife reaches the "now or never" late twenties or early thirties. At this point, some couples opt to give up childbearing rather than their accustomed life-style—and the wife's income. Others plan for the wife to go back to work after the child is born or in school. In either case, the woman is back on the job before long.

The American Dream, with the implicit desire to attain an ever-higher standard of living, is also alive and well, with a woman's job often providing the means to this end. Almost half of all working women, according to our survey, feel that a critical impact of their job is that it helps provide the wherewithal for a better home or apartment in a better location than would otherwise have been possible. The price of a new home doubled in the seventies to a national average of about $65,700, and mortgage rates have kept pace, skyrocketing into the double digits as of this writing. Among families who wish to own their own home, these facts are enough to propel the wife back into the job market to help accumulate that all-important down payment, and the same motivation will help keep her there until the mortgage is paid off.

There is no end in sight to the economic factors that are applying increasing pressures to our checkbooks and our way of life. Futurists predict that the United States faces a prolonged period of severe, spiraling inflationary paralysis, with consumers struggling to provide even basic needs, which could last until the middle of the twenty-first century.[33] Given this chilling prospect, women will not be able to afford the luxury of abandoning the work force, even if they choose to do so.

Psychic Income

Marilyn Moats Kennedy, founder and director of a career-planning consulting firm and author of numerous articles and two books on power, office politics, and career strategies, sits alertly in her sunny fourth-floor office. The phone jangles maddeningly and the office is awash in clutter, but Kennedy remains unruffled. She is smiling, sharing an experience that is common to all employed women—she has just gotten paid.

"Money is a great dignifier," Kennedy explains. "You are finally able to play in the league in which you have been told that all the good things happen. We used to celebrate when our husbands made X number of dollars, but now you can do it for yourself. Let me tell you, when that royalty check arrived today I was not one bit a better person—you notice that it didn't miraculously clean my house, it didn't get my articles written, it didn't suddenly make me more beautiful, I'm not going to rush out and buy myself some wonderful trinket—but it was a reaffirmation that, indeed, what I wrote, somebody would want."

For many women, the internal rewards of a job are as great as or greater than the paycheck. Our survey discovered that 48 percent of all working women are motivated primarily by the "self" reasons: self-respect and the intrinsic interest of the job. For these women, the job provides the fulfillment and self-actualization that many women have come to feel is their right. Other studies have shown that most working women claim they would choose to continue to go to their jobs even if they received the same amount of money for staying at home.

It is impossible to totally segregate the financial aspects because we cannot avoid the conclusion that the paycheck is worth something psychologically as well as monetarily. We also noticed that many women who must work for financial reasons often internalize that fact, accept it as a condition of life, and then move on to stress other motivations. "Yes, I must work to support myself, but, given that, I work for self-respect."

For those motivated by "self" reasons, the rewards of a job are measured in the most personal terms. The fact that almost half of all working women rank these reasons as being more important than money underscores the significance of a job as a vehicle for self-actualization.

Dr. Roy Grinker, Jr., attending psychiatrist at Michael Reese Hospital in Chicago and training and supervising analyst at the Chicago Institute of Psychoanalysis, explains: "What the working field singularly provides for some women is the capability to get back from the work some good feelings about themselves. The bottom line is pride, prestige, self-esteem, self-confidence. Of course, these things depend a great deal, also, on a woman's parents, husband, and environment. But the situation of working—even more than the job itself—helps the woman develop, characterologically and in terms of her own self-esteem. Work provides money, but it also provides a tremendous amount of opportunity for positive reinforcement."

In our survey, we saw it written on the pages of almost every working woman's questionnaire. Whether she worked full-time or part-time, interest and pride in her job responsibilities shone through the handwritten comments. Descriptions of jobs were glowingly detailed; the feeling of involvement and self-esteem was obvious.

A medical secretary does not just help out around the office; she "takes blood pressure, weight, age, medications, does X rays, takes EKGs, mounts monitor electrodes on patients, types office consultation reports, does stress tests."

A teacher doesn't just teach; she is "responsible for the education of 150 teenagers every day."

From a school bus driver: "I drive vans, minibuses, and big buses for several schools. I know over eighty-five routes, including special children, problem children, and regular schools."

An assembly line solderer: "I read blueprints to correctly assemble and wire a rapid action switch. My work must pass NASA performance specifications."

And so it goes.

No matter how small or great their actual financial need to work, women who work for "self" reasons get from the job itself what money cannot provide. The job makes a woman feel like an individual in her own right, a member of the mainstream.

"I am a more interesting person because of my job and the fact that I meet people. My job gives me a different perspective on the world and makes me interesting to my husband and children. My self-confidence has increased. And I have more to offer," wrote a librarian.

A teacher concurs: "My job makes me feel good about myself."

And, from a factory worker: "I feel I am contributing to society, not just looking on."

The fact that self-respect is on the rise can be seen in the fact that thirty years ago only one-quarter of all married women worked—and most were probably those who needed jobs to make ends meet. Today half of all married women are employed, and in spite of economic conditions, which may have been a stimulus, only 43 percent of the wives we surveyed named income as their primary motivation. The vast majority of the others work for "self" reasons.

We can see the flip side of self-respect in the fact that today we find housewives apologizing, however needlessly, for staying home: "I'm *just* a housewife."

"Self" motivations were particularly evident when a woman's husband earned enough money to enable her to make the choice to work or not purely for these reasons. Women who work part-time illustrate this situation. For the most part, these women do not earn high salaries; most earn under $8,000 a year. But they are not working for money. Only 33 percent of all the part-timers we surveyed ranked income as their main motivation. Instead, these are the most likely of all women to be working for "self" reasons. Mitchell S. Fromstein, president of Manpower, Inc.—the world's largest employer of temporary workers and the second largest employer in the United States, placing approximately 200,000 people in temporary jobs in 1979—finds this coincides with his experience. "We do very in-depth interviews with prospective female employees," he says. Such interviews are necessary to quickly match an employee's skills with the available assignments. Fromstein notes that one of the largest and most eager resources for temporary positions is "the midlife mother whose children are in school and who is more interested in getting back into a wider world, in working for personal satisfaction, than in money. Money is, of course, a necessary part of the motivation. But the primary motivation is personal esteem, independence, and a feeling of worthiness. All are psychological rewards rather than fiscal."

Another of women's top work motivators, the desire for an interesting job, often boils down to the simple fact that a large proportion of women find a job more interesting and involving than staying at home. This indicates the rise of outside employment in the hierarchical status of what women can do. Thirty years ago, a woman had to create her own little world in and around the home. There were definite limits on which activities were acceptable and which were not. Now a larger world has opened up, the boundaries have expanded, and awareness of this is acute.

Whether or not a woman finds her job interesting enough to name this interest as a primary motivation is largely related to her attitude. Few women in our survey saw their jobs as boring, lifeless tasks. Most women found something of interest in their jobs, if only the fact that they allowed them to get out of the house and into the mainstream. For women, the perceived mainstream has moved from the home to the work-place. And so the fact that a woman is motivated to work primarily because she finds her job interesting relates back to her self-image in many ways: "I'm not just a housewife, I do interesting things; therefore I am an interesting person."

In stressful economic times, it is especially difficult to isolate working women to whom income is not a factor for at least some measure of survival. But among those with the least financial reason to work are women married to men who earn mega-incomes in or close to the six-figure brackets. I spoke to several such women who were working both full-time and part-time. Interestingly, well-to-do women have been returning to the labor force at a much faster rate than other wives.[34] These women, more than any other group, clarify the nonmonetary motivations for working. Money entered in for these women insofar as they viewed it as a benchmark of capabilities rather than an end in itself. But the main reason they worked was for their own self-esteem. As Marilyn Moats Kennedy observed, "I do not see any of those [upper-class] women who do not know exactly how much money they want to earn and understand exactly what it means in their lives. To this type of woman, getting a job that pays—even though she doesn't need the twenty thousand, doesn't *want* it particularly—to her, it's a confirmation of the acclamation of her worth as a human being, and very important."

"I can't be this little fatted, nurtured, petted calf," said Karla, who typifies the attitude of many such women. Her elegant apartment was rich with gleaming herringbone parquet floors, sueded walls, custom-woven fabrics. One wall was lined with trophies from exclusive clubs (well polished by the maid), another with pictures of Karla and her husband, Bill. Not included was a picture of Karla and Bill that had recently appeared in *Town and Country*. Karla herself was cool, immaculate, blonde, and elegant as her surroundings. In her early thirties, she is the kind of wife that men might once have pampered as a cherished showpiece. But she needs more than this to be happy. Karla pointed out her desk and meticulous files, the command post from which she manages her business of home remodeling, and scrapbooks bulging with pictures of her many successful jobs.

For the first five years of her twelve-year marriage, Karla claims she "majored in what I call the Four F's: Flowers, Food, Frivolity, and Fashion." She divided her time between tennis, country club, and charities. She excelled at all these things, heading various successful fund-raising drives and throwing countless perfect little dinners. Still, in spite of an adoring and supportive husband, she felt that somehow she had been "sold a bill of goods."

"It makes you believe that this is all you're capable of," she explained, reciting a pattern familiar not only to her peer group. "You are well educated, not so that you can get a good job, but so you can make a good marriage. You know— make the product as presentable as possible. So you make the good marriage, you solidify it, you make the baby. And nail down your man to coming home and paying your bills while you float."

She admits that sometimes, after a hard fourteen-hour day on a construction site, this bon-bon scenario has its temptations. "But I know that after about five days of sitting home up to my neck in Vitabath, it wears pretty thin."

Karla and Bill have no children, and after several years of the bubble-bath life she began to feel restless. At first she channeled her energies into volunteer work. Soon she started using her talent for photography and art to take pictures and design invitations for her charity functions. She found herself being praised for this, and she tentatively began to listen to inquiries about the possibility of designing this or that piece for the admirer's business. She decided to get involved in a paying project. Her first work centered around the photography. Then her interest in tennis drew her into the manufacturing area, where for a few years she designed and marketed a line of tennis clothes. When she and her husband bought a stately but run-down apartment, she tackled the remodeling on her own. She did such a spectacular job that friends asked for Karla's help remodeling their homes, and she was able to pyramid her knowledge into a business.

Karla invested a lot of effort to pull her business together. She studied architecture and design, took union electrical and plumbing courses, and became a licensed interior decorator. She visited warehouses, showrooms, and manufacturing facilities all over the country so that she could get better acquainted with her merchandise. She designed a course in kitchen and bathroom remodeling and sold the curriculum to a local school, where she has now been teaching the course for three years of evening classes.

Why has she gone to all this trouble, when, clearly, it wasn't necessary for financial survival, or even to buy a sable coat? "My husband's successes are *his* successes, I have to have my own," is her quick answer.

Karla now earns over $15,000 a year. But, to her, the money is far from the key issue. "It gets me where I want to go physically and mentally," she admits. "But it's a byproduct of my success. I can't eat it, I can't wear it, it looks pretty tacky if I try to sew it together."

When her checks come in, Karla often neglects to cash or deposit them. "At any given time, I probably have six commission checks lying in my desk drawer," she says. "Sometimes I'll just come across one as I'm looking for something else, and it'll remind me that I never cashed it. I'm glad to see the money come in, but I'm not saving for a Chris Craft cruiser or anything. I don't work for financial gain. I just don't think about it. I see the checks more as a measure of myself— a barometer by which I personally measure myself."

Dr. Roy Grinker, Jr., adds, "A woman often projects onto her job something from within herself, which is a need. She has a *need* to see her work as creative, interesting, involving. And very often that relates to the feeling that 'When I was home as a child or an adult with my husband or husband and children, I was made to feel that I was not appreciated, not valuable as a person. What I was doing had no meaning, it was random activity or a lot of routine chores.'" A job offers a woman a new structure for positive reinforcement, a newfound vehicle for pride in herself and for self-confidence. She knows she is valued, because she receives a paycheck that is tangible proof.

"Self" motivations are routes to self-actualization, and they are key reasons why so many women are working today and will continue to do so. And they mean that most working women will be committed to their jobs, even in the face of potentially discouraging circumstances like low pay, which, for men, might be a major obstacle to such tenacity.

When a woman's self-image is so closely tied to her job, she will not easily let it go. She has too much to lose. And increasing numbers of women will join the ranks of the employed to gain the economic benefits of an income and, socially, to maintain status among their peers. These women in turn will provide role models for other women, and for their daughters and other young girls. The whirlpool will continue its forceful pull, which will cause women to drift even farther from their patriarchical moorings.

Who Is Motivated by What?

PRIMARY MOTIVATION*	TOTAL WORKING WOMEN	FULL-TIME	PART-TIME	WHITE-COLLAR	BLUE-COLLAR
Income	46%	50%	33%	45%	56%
Interesting job	24	21	31	25	17
Self-respect	24	22	29	25	20

* Less important motivations include: respect from others; praise for a job well done; authority/power; and companionship.

CHAPTER 2

The Psychological Split

We are in the process of a major change, and the beginnings are already visible in the nature of women themselves. Women who work outside the home are different than those who do not. They think, act, and respond differently. Their self-perceptions are different and they have a different set of priorities.

Already these differences are making themselves felt in divorce, legal issues, political and self-actualization movements, and other impact areas. The result of these differences, combined with the fact that more and more women are working and that this uptrend is fated to continue due to inescapable economic, educational, and social factors, is that a new kind of woman will emerge from the fray.

The psychological impact of the rewards and feedback of employment are great, and this creates the divergence between women who work outside the home and those who do not. Ultimately, this impact will produce the kind of woman who will upset the status quo and accomplish a redistribution of power. Such qualities as aggression, ambition, decisiveness, goal orientation, confidence, and nondomestic directiveness are key to this phenomenon. All of these qualities are significantly influenced by the experience of employment. It is highly likely that it is the work experience, rather than any sexual characteristics, which largely imparts the propensity to assume a power position. Sex is only one variable in a personality; there are many others, and many more important—for instance, relationships with one's parents, the ability to set up reasonable goals, and the solidarity of self-esteem—all of which are enhanced by an employment situation. And self-esteem is regulated by numerous things. For instance, it is customary to think of women as unable to look within themselves to develop self-confidence, because one gets relatively limited self-validation in a domestic role. Raising children, establishing a home and a life-style, and other kinds of validation available to the typical housewife are long-range. On the other hand, the paycheck and other job-related accomplishments offer the kind of validation that is more immediate, more of a pat on the back that permits a woman to say, "Hey, I'm OK."

For instance, our survey reveals that a woman who works is more than *twice* as likely as a woman who is not employed to feel strongly she is aggressive and ambitious. Working women most frequently attribute their aggression and ambition to the fact that they work. A day-care worker commented, "Before, I would never say I was right about something. If someone said I was wrong, I would let it go, even if in my heart I felt I was right. But since I've been working, I don't do that."

A bookkeeper claimed, "I can talk more freely and easier because I'm used to talking to more people, seeing more people. Now I think I'm capable of anything once given a chance."

Women who work do indeed have a larger forum for exercising any latent or incipient ambition. Their jobs also offer them exposure to experiences and role models which validate those ambitions that are not available to housewives. An accounting supervisor explained, "I've been working eight years now, and have five women that work beneath me. It was just a lifetime ambition that I had while I was going to school. When I first started working, I thought that the job was all you were expected to do. That they would just see how you could do the job and give you a better job automatically. And soon I found out as I watched other people advance that that's not the way it is—you have to take the initiative and do it on your own.

"I came in as a payroll clerk and as I became familiar with my work and had time on my hands, I went to my boss and insisted I have other jobs. I said I had accomplished that job and had extra time and would like to broaden my knowledge and learn other things. That's what got me the job I have today. As you get this knowledge and you progress and realize that you've been over this ground before, you're more willing to put your neck on the line and try things. I'm determined I'm going to continue to progress. And other people know it."

Women who do not work outside the home not only feel less ambitious and aggressive, but the ambition and aggression they are aware of is channeled narrowly within the confines of the home environment. The majority of nonworking women who referred to any aggressive or ambitious characteristics did so in terms of home and family, and did not apply the benefits of these characteristics outside this realm. A Virginia housewife, for instance, pointed out that she was assertive about only one thing—her children. "I always manage to get them into the right classes," she said. "I got one into the special education classes he needed. If you're not the one who starts it, it just slides by. You have to make sure your child gets in the right class or somehow he gets overlooked."

A Washington woman summed up the majority opinion of nonworking women: "Around the house I'm assertive. I tell them what I want them to do. But not outside."

Nonworking women were also more likely than working

women to mention the use of sex as a method of exercising assertiveness to gain control of a domestic situation. One woman proudly claimed, "My role in getting my new house was in bugging my husband. That's all I did. Just kept bugging him to please get me a house. I told him I wouldn't have another baby unless we got a larger house. So he bought me a larger house because (ha-ha) he likes kids." Perhaps one reason nonworking women mentioned sex as a power technique more frequently than employed women is that for nonworking women, sex is one of the few power tools available to them, while working women also have control of money and a greater degree of independence generally, which permits them to participate in decision making on a totally different level.

When a women feels more ambitious and aggressive and exercises these characteristics, the consequences are far-reaching. Such a woman is less likely to sit back and flow with the tide of events. Instead, she will take a larger, more active part in shaping those events. When these attitudes are taken beyond the home environment, they become the key to shaping new roles for women. A woman will act instead of merely reacting, pursue instead of being pursued, become the huntress instead of the prey. She will be more likely to become a leader instead of the follower she has traditionally been.

Another major difference between working and nonworking women is that working women are more likely to set goals and to consider their goals ambitious. Goal setting, and the ability to project into the future, is an important skill in changing any status quo.

In general, the working women's goals revealed to us involved accomplishments outside the home that would benefit themselves: A promotion, further education, and a business of their own were among the most frequently mentioned goals. Nonworking women who mentioned goals tended to center their sights on the domestic scene and most frequently expressed goals that would benefit others, not themselves:

• "My goal is to be a good mother. To raise my kids right. To try to bring them up to be good and spend all the time I can with them, so they'll be able to trust me and come to me whenever they need me."
• "I would like to eventually help senior citizens."
• "A family vacation is my goal."
• "A new house."

Significantly, working women are more likely not only to be goal-oriented but to feel strongly that it is important to achieve their goals. They also are more likely to think in terms of specifics, to set timetables, however informal, and to express a deep commitment to their goals. Consider the spontaneous, unsolicited comments of these two women, both of whom mentioned a goal of going back to school for further education:

THE WORKING WOMAN: "I'd like to go back to college and finish. I suppose I would study some ecology, or I might consider business. It's pretty important to me because I've wanted to do this for a long time and haven't lost the idea. So I would say that it's pretty important. I wanted to go back in September, but wasn't able to because I couldn't save enough money. Maybe I'll try for January."

THE NONWORKING WOMAN: "I'm thinking of going back to school. When my youngest child goes to school, I would hope maybe I could take a couple of courses. Maybe not go full-time, but take a couple of courses in things I'm interested in to improve my mind. It's something that I'd like to do, but it's not something that I have to do. If I don't do it, it won't kill me."

If I don't do it, it won't kill me. The pervasive attitudes toward achieving any sort of goal expressed by the vast majority of nonworking women were variations on that theme. The achievement of goals was, on the other hand, very important to women who worked outside the home. Such a degree of goal importance indicates that these outer-directed women are going to be likely to work harder to make their goals happen.

Working women also have a greater degree of self-confidence than nonworking women, according to our survey. And they express this self-confidence in terms of the larger world around them. A teacher commented, "I want to feel important— I want to use my brain, not just my hands. I quit work and I enjoyed being home, but it got to the point where I felt that I wasn't using my brain as much as I could have. I felt unimportant at times. Maybe it wasn't true, but I felt it. So I went back to work. Now I feel good. When I work, I feel better about myself. I think I feel more like a whole person. I have a place in the world."

A factory worker pointed out how her self-confidence had spread to other areas of her life. "Since I started work, I've felt like doing more things. I went to ceramics class. I didn't think I could do that. I did do it. And I found my pieces are better than what they sell in stores! I want to learn to drive next month. When I got married twenty years ago, my husband didn't want me to learn to drive. But I'm going to driving school next month."

A public relations writer explained, "This job is the center of my whole being. It's the thing that is totally stimulating, gives me immediate fulfillment in that I can see whatever I work on take shape. It gives me a sense of status, prestige. I'm doing things I've never done before. I'm meeting new people. I'm going places. I'm feeling much better about myself than I ever have. I'm feeling more confident. I feel like I created myself. If I'm a success, it's because of me."

Nonworking women, when they expressed self-confidence,

usually did so in terms of the home environment. In fact, many commented that the home was the *only* place where they felt self-confident:

• "I am self-confident in certain areas—cooking and sewing, for instance. I will always try new recipes. I will always volunteer to bring a dish someplace because I feel certain it will turn out well."

• "Around strange people, people I don't know and am not familiar with, I'd have to say I'm not confident. But with my own children and husband, I'm more sure of myself."

The domestic boundaries on the confidence of nonworking women are no doubt due to the fact that wife and mother roles are the only ones they know, the only roles they are comfortable and familiar with, thus the only areas in which they can express confidence; the working woman, however, sees herself in a wider variety of roles.

Our survey showed that the positive self-imagery of work even spread to a woman's feelings about her appearance. Working women are more likely to feel they are good-looking than nonworking women. A teacher told this story: "Since I started work I'm more self-confident. For instance, I've always been very much overweight, but this time when I decided to lose some weight I actually did it. I took up jogging. I've lost twenty-three pounds and even my family is surprised. My own sister-in-law didn't know who I was at first when she saw me jogging. I used to think people who jogged were crazy—but now it doesn't bother me what people think."

This kind of positive self-imagery will work in the favor of women, since it will tend to express itself in other positive forms of behavior.

For instance, working women are much more comfortable in areas outside the home than their nonemployed counterparts. Most working women, according to our survey, do not feel that a woman's place is in the home—as opposed to the majority of nonworking women, who feel the opposite. This means that now the majority of all women feel that a woman's place is not in the home. This is a relatively recent development, which shows the strength of the impact of the working-woman phenomenon. In 1967 six out of ten women agreed that a woman's place is in the home. Ten years later, only one in four felt that way.

We found other evidence of the nondomestic focus of the working woman. Almost two-thirds of all working women we surveyed said a career is as important as being a good wife and mother, while two-thirds of all nonworking women felt the opposite.

The nonworking women:

• "I'm content with staying home. The people that I know that work outside the home, their lives are so constantly on the go, they've got to be doing something constantly to be content. Where I can sit home and sew or do something like that and I'm content."

• "My focus is at home because that's where I feel my life should be. I enjoy helping my children with their schoolwork."

• "I don't work, but I think it would make you more outgoing. Like the fact that when you're home you just spend your time communicating with your children, or having your neighbors in for coffee. Whereas if you're working you're with adults all the time, so I think you'd be able to communicate more on that level."

• "I think that everyone can see a difference in children where the mother is at home and the mother is working. I think the children are more understanding and there is a more harmonious relationship within the family where the

mother is at home than where the mother has to leave her
children with baby-sitters and maybe she feels guilt feelings
about leaving them."

• "I think it's my responsibility to raise my child and to see
that she has the things she needs and to bring her up with
the ideals that she's supposed to have. I don't think that's up
to someone else I pay to do that. I think it's my responsibility."

• "Not that I want my children to be totally dependent on
me, but I want them to feel like I'm there. They ask me to
make cookies or make or bring things or drive them here and
I enjoy this. I enjoy being needed and I feel they enjoy saying 'My mom will do this and my mom will help me do that
and she's there to help me.' I just think that's important."

Nonworking women may choose not to work because they
believe this is the way their lives should be, but many expressed a feeling that they did not work in order to please
others—or not displease them:

• "My husband would mind if I worked because I
wouldn't be home to cater to him. In other words, I wouldn't
always be there when he needed me."

• "I don't think my kids would like it if I worked because
they don't like it when I'm not here when they come in.
When I'm not home I get 'Where were you? You're supposed
to be here.' They expect me to participate in activities with
them which I would not be able to do if I worked. Also my
husband prefers that I not work."

• "My eight-year-old daughter likes my being here. I did
think about going back to work a few months ago. There was
a job that I was rather interested in. But she was just definitely against it. So I didn't take it."

Working women, on the other hand, express their broader
and more self-involved focus:

* * *

- "I feel I've got myself to live for plus my family, and I'm not content staying at home."
- "There's not enough to hold my interest at home. I have no interest in spending all my days watching Johnny learn to roll over, or decorating rooms or planning menus."
- "For me, over the years, what I've had to decide is: Is there a tradeoff, or does marriage take away from a career, or can marriage contribute to a career? And what I've determined at this point is I think it could really contribute very much, because I think I'd be more happy personally if I were married, and I think that will do a lot to help my career. I grew up really believing that I wouldn't marry till I was thirty-five, if I ever married, really thinking a marriage would take away from the career, inhibit you, tie you down. It took me a long time to overcome those obstacles, but getting into the working world I observed things and people and realized that wasn't the case. Now I feel marriage will contribute to me personally quite a bit and make me a whole person—a more whole person—and I can bring that to my career. And I view the career as bringing the same kinds of things to the marriage."
- "Without my job, I wouldn't bring anything to the relationship with my husband. I would just be an appendage to him. Any kind of happiness or anything that I can give to my personal life is a result of the stimulation I get from my work life."
- "My work is my life. I'll quit when I'm dead."

Working women, in general, are more concerned about self-fulfillment through nondomestic vehicles than women who are not employed. When they speak of their most prideful accomplishments, they mention their *own* accomplishments, while nonworking women more often refer to the accomplishments of their children as "their" proudest moments.

And working women apply their efforts to themselves, to bettering their own personal situation, as opposed to nonworking women, whose efforts are more concentrated on bettering the situation of their husbands or children. This means that working women will probably tend to push their own interests and attempt to better their own situations to a degree women have not done in the past. Whereas women once dominated in the home, they will now open up this domination and attempt to apply it across the board.

Women will be freer to do so, because those who work prefer smaller families, and fewer children means more time to devote to personal and nondomestic interests. Our survey revealed that the working woman not only prefers a smaller family but, in fact, fewer have children. Only 61 percent of the working women we surveyed had children, compared with 85 percent of the nonworking women.

This is not to say that women who work are less than dedicated mothers—their attitude is simply different. Working women feel, almost unanimously, that it is the quality of time spent with children, not the quantity, that is important. A bank teller said, "The quality of time I spend with the children means time I spend with them is devoted to them. I used to spend more time on housework, less with them. Now what I do in the time I spend with them is important. I play with the boys. We go for walks, to the playground. Or just talk. But that's *all* I'm doing."

Nonworking women are less likely to feel that way, and more likely to emphasize the quantity of time spent with children.

Our survey also showed that working women have less successful marriages. While only 3 percent of the nonworking women were divorced or separated, 15 percent of the workers were divorced or separated. Thus, a woman who works was *five times* as likely to have a disrupted marriage as one who did not work. There is inevitably the "chicken and egg" quandary regarding this kind of statistic, but it is likely that the fact of a woman's employment does aggravate the propensity to divorce. Consider the results of another recent survey, which revealed that working wives are more than twice as likely as housewives to have had affairs by the time they reach their late thirties.[1] Previous studies have also shown that if a woman continues to work, she is less likely to marry and stay married than a woman who does not work.[2] Researchers have found that the longer a wife is employed, the more both partners think about divorce—an increase of one percentage point for each year of her employment.[3] Things get worse as she earns more money. Vassar economist Shirley Johnson calculated that every $1,000 increase in a wife's earnings increases her chance for divorce by 2 percent.[4] This was evidenced by our Pacesetter group, to be discussed in depth in a later chapter. These working women, who earn $20,000-plus, are the most likely of all women to be separated or divorced.

It is impossible to pinpoint exactly the dynamics of the breakup of a relationship to a woman's job, if for no other reason than that individuals are too variable. Were the women who experienced breakups dissatisfied in some way with their relationships, which spurred them to seek outside gratification in a job—or did the women become dissatisfied with the relationship because they were gratified outside the home? And what was the man responding to? We can never know for sure. What we can ascertain, however, is that a woman's entry into the work force disturbs the equilibrium of her relationship with a man. A shift occurs. The woman becomes, as a result of her job, more self-involved. Suddenly she's talking about problems with her own boss instead of discussing her partner's work problems. Economics and chore distribution change, and the woman derives satisfaction from her work—not just from her man. A new balance must be achieved. A woman's old values, symbolized by her husband's role in the home, versus her new values, symbolized by her job, are often set up in conflict, externalizing her ambivalence. Rather than recognize that an internal struggle exists, a woman may choose to pin the blame on the relationship. All of these variables are at work, and cannot be overlooked. Neither can they be easily overcome.

The most common, overwhelming problem of the working women in our survey was lack of time, and most women with romantic or sexual problems cited the time problem as a major cause.

"Exhausted!" moaned one woman. "No time for ourselves together."

"Sex?" jibed another. "I'm too tired to care."

And this particularly pathetic comment: "We see each other less, but it's better this way."

Carried to its logical extreme, the time problem means that single women have less time than ever to found and bond a relationship with a man. Many single women wrote us a variation on the theme of "I have no time to *meet* a man—much less have a relationship." One outcome of this is that still more women will remain single.

Given this lack of time and the implicit pressures, something has to go. Increasingly, it is the relationship.

All in all, the working woman is less family-dependent, less domestic, more aggressive, more self-confident, and more self-centered than her nonworking counterparts. Working women are easing away from the confining domestic focus of the past and into the larger world around them. Their participation in this world is bound to become ever more marked, especially when spurred by their ambition, goal-orientation, and other outer-directed characteristics.

CHAPTER 3

You Are What You Do; You Do What You Are

Using a computer to sort the responses to our survey questionnaire according to attitudes, we identified three overall attitudinal groups for all women. These groups cut across demographic segments, and members of each group can be found in both job and home environments. The significance of these groups lies in their psychological and behavioral characteristics, and in the distribution of working and non-working women among the groups. The type of woman that populates each group, illuminated by in-depth personal interviews, reveals a great deal about who's who in various segments of our society, how they came to be the kinds of people they are, where they are going, and how, in interacting with them, we may all be affected.

The Go-Getters

These are the most active, aggressive women of all, and the largest attitudinal group, comprising 43 percent of all women surveyed. Their major focus is outside the home, and they are the most career-oriented. As such, this group is the most likely to work outside the home.

Members of this group always planned to work and are the most likely of all women to be college-educated. If they do not work outside the home, these women agree that their outside activities take precedence over domestic chores, and they are far more independent than other women. They feel they are as intelligent and capable as men, and if working and married, do not give their husband's job priority over their own.

Women in this group are confident and extroverted. They enjoy being the center of attention and actively seek out the limelight. Unlike other women, who prefer a low profile, Go-Getters dream of being famous.

Go-Getters make decisions quickly and rarely change their mind. They are the most decisive women, and the most likely to set goals.

These are also the most cosmopolitan women, with most living in urban or metropolitan areas.

Of all women, Go-Getters are the most likely to be single, separated, or divorced—working Go-Getters are *80 percent* more likely to be separated or divorced than women in general! Perhaps this is one consequence of their nondomestic, independent nature. They are a young and upcoming group, with most members under thirty-five years old. As such, they will play a significant role in the future.

VERA: ON THE MOVE

At thirty, Vera has been working for seventeen years. Her life has not been easy. She was married at seventeen, and her only child died of sickle-cell anemia when he was eighteen months old. Soon afterward, her husband walked out on her. But she has never stopped striving, seeking, moving. She works eight hours a day selling dehydrated foods—then eight hours a night as a janitor. Vera has her sights set firmly on where she wants to go. She has a trick to help keep herself on track, which she shared with me. She calls it her "Wish Book." In her Wish Book, Vera pastes clippings and pictures of things she would like to have happen in her life: a brochure that symbolizes having her own business, a fur coat, glittering jewelry, a gracious home. On the first page of Vera's Wish Book is a hand-lettered note on ring-binder paper. It is addressed to herself: "If it is to be, it is up to me."

"I take responsibility for my own life," Vera explained. "If it's up to me, then no one's to blame but me. My Wish Book helps me keep an eye on my goals. All of them aren't in the Book, though—I'd also like to be able to send one of my nieces or nephews to college. And I'd like to be an actress. I'd love to do commercials.

"I used to want to be like the movie stars. I'd open up a magazine and look at their pictures for hours, and I'd admire them. But when my little boy had his disease, I had to go to the medical center, and I met a lot of people who were students there. That's when I realized that movie stars are not people I can relate to. That's a dream world, a fantasy. It's better to admire someone I know and can talk to. Like some of the people I met at the medical center. These were the kind of people I would have met if I had gone to college.

"I never went to college, or even finished high school, and I'm sorry for that now, because education opens up a whole new field for almost anyone. And you have to have a high school diploma to do certain things. I don't like to close doors in my life, so now I'm taking high school courses by correspondence. Once I finish them, if I want to go to college someday, I could go.

"There's so *much* that I want. I found out it's easy to get some of the things I want with my own money. And to get

money, you have to have money. That's why I work so much
—not because I'm a workaholic. I found out that what you've
got on your own, no one can take away. So I couldn't survive
without work. I would take work over a man if necessary.

"I was married, but what I wanted from marriage wasn't
there. I wanted something that I can go and do for myself.
All the things I want, I can get for myself. What does a man
have to give me, when I already have these things? Well, I
feel the little part I need a man for—sometimes it doesn't
even function!

"I started working when I was thirteen. I came from a family of seven children. We all had to help. And, coming from
the South, we all would get together and do little odd jobs
and stuff. To me, work is just a part of an everyday routine.

"When I was a little girl, I used to pick up coal after it had
been burned. It was very easy. You just emptied their gar-
bage out in one area of the yard, and you could go through
it there and pick out the coal that could be reused and sell it
to older people that used it to heat irons to iron their clothes.
I'd make maybe fifty cents a week that way.

"Then when I was eighteen I had to go to work and make
real money, because my little boy was sickly. Certain types of
jobs paid more money. I went to work in a chicken factory. I
took the chickens' lungs out with a lung gun. It just sucked
the lungs out, very fast. It was hard, I know that. Why kid
myself? But it was sort of challenging. And it was fun. If I
had a hard day, I could tell myself 'At least I'm not a
chicken.' And if you work with something that doesn't talk
back, you don't have too many problems.

"After I didn't have the baby anymore, or my husband, I
grew up fast. I needed a change. But I try not to regret
things in my life. I joined the Job Corps. I got to take classes
there, it was like a college environment. I wanted to be a
chef. I'd go to school part of the day, then train as a chef
the rest of the time. After growing up in the South, it was

very different for me. There was a lot of things I didn't understand, a lot of different kinds of people. I have a lot of friends now all over the world. Some of them went on to be doctors and lawyers. I thought about going into the army after that, but instead I went to Chicago. The city had a wider reach, more opportunity, more kinds of people. If you want something, it's out there.

"I went to work for a small lamp company. I was a wirer and solderer, I put the cords and lamps together. I worked there for about five years. They worked me hard, but in the end they did a lot of things for me. They gave me goals. I found out that the more enthused you were, the more you would try to do for yourself, the more they would help you. They helped you if you moved for yourself. The lamp company was a very small business, and I was only making $62 a week. I lived in the ghetto, it was crumbling all around me. So I said to my boss, 'I'm in a rut and I've got to get out. My husband is gone and if I don't get out of here it's going to deteriorate around me or I'm going to end up here for the rest of my life. And I didn't come to Chicago to live in the ghetto. I didn't come here just to be a number, an ordinary person, a face in the crowd.' So I volunteered. I said, 'I'll work tonight.'

"And my boss said, 'We don't have a third shift.'

"I said, 'You do now. I need money, so I'll be at work at two; I'll work two till nine. I can clean the place, sweep, do anything. I'll be the third shift. That's that.' And he agreed. The third shift started out just with me. But when I left, there were five people. I developed a whole shift on my own. I couldn't leave and get another job, so I doubled the job I had.

"I got the idea of modeling at the lamp factory. One of the bosses used to have antique cars and he was selling them. So when I went in to work on the day shift, I made the appointments for people to look at the cars. My boss began to take pictures of the cars and he asked if I would stand beside them.

"It would be nice to be a model someday. I'd love it. Right now I have two jobs, and neither of them's modeling. But I'm working on it. I am a janitor from five to one-thirty in the morning, and there are ad agencies in the building where I clean. Some of the people have given me names of places to contact about modeling. And I've done some modeling at restaurants.

"Some of my friends say I should call myself a maintenance engineer. But I don't see the point. I'm a janitor. I come on the floor in my uniform, clean all the surfaces, and I vacuum the floors.

"In the day, I'm a distributor of dehydrated foods. I got into it when I read a book about dehydrated foods and how they would be big in the future. I started by ordering some just for myself, to store. It took so long to come from California. Reading the book, I found out there was a distributor in town. I reached them and I found out how I could become a distributor, too. Every day, I try to spend at least five hours doing this, and weekends I give food tastings, because I'm trying to increase the business. This is going to be something I want to do for life. It will be my own business. My job as a janitor helps me to be able to afford it in the meantime.

"Working in sales, you've got to be aggressive. I'm very aggressive. If I reach a buyer on a Monday, I try to wait two weeks, then I call back exactly two weeks to the day later. The thing of this product is that this is a cash deal. If you want to buy, and I'm trying to close you on an item, it's a little hard. It's not like something you can order now and pay me later. You have to have the money now. So I have to be very aggressive.

"I figure I can't go too wrong. I've got my money invested in food. If I don't sell it, I can always eat it. But I'd like to build up an organization. Recruit other people. I need a person who's like me. Maybe someone in the same slump I was in.

"Right now, the food business is number one. Comes before anything. Men, anything but my mother. I see this as something I can retire with. My work gives me self-esteem. I love it. Because for so long I deprived myself of it.

"I'm not married now, and I never will be again. I wouldn't be where I'm at today if I had been married.

"I had a very passive husband. I guess he didn't realize how aggressive I was. And in a way, I was—I am—very aggressive. I think I put my foot too much in his life, and maybe I didn't have that right. So all the things that happened to me in the marriage, a lot was my fault. I found out, what was wrong with me was, no one loves me more than I love myself.

"I put myself first in everything I do. I'm sorry, but I do. I never did when I was younger. But now I don't say yes when I don't want to. Never. And I don't depend on friends anymore. That's a weak link. You have to depend on yourself. I'm my own friend.

"I don't want children at this point in my life, either. I don't have the patience. That's another thing that's changed in my life.

"I was very upset when my husband left me. I am a woman who hates rejection. But it was the best thing that happened to me. We were too different. A few years ago, my husband came back and asked me to marry him again. I told him he was crazy. I said, 'No thank you.'

"Now I make the decisions about me. Most men are very turned on to me, but then they get very turned off because I am very, very intelligent and *I* make the decisions. If I go to bed with a man, I have decided, before he does. And if I change my mind, the situation changes.

"It scares me sometimes, too, because I'm lonely a lot. But if that's what it takes . . .

"The man I'm with now is a real dog. Always after other women. But I like him because he knows what I'm like. If he doesn't move fast, he won't fit in. He really has to be more of a woman than I am in a sense, because I'm the very aggressive one.

"Right now, my work is my husband. It will be my husband because it will support me if I support it. It can't take from me because I have to give to it; therefore [what I give] comes back to me. It can't comfort me or sleep with me, but it can make sure my surroundings are comfortable for me. Inside I know I have a weak spot—that if I let them, men can destroy me, because it's tempting to depend on them and then be let down. So I built a wall. But this time I built it with water, mortar, and cement. And it's a solid wall. So if a man gets around it or he gets through it, he's meant to be in my life. But force me to let him in? No way."

The Domestics

At the opposite end of the scale, the Domestics place their main focus *inside* the home. They are the most traditional of women, and being a good wife and mother is of primary importance to them. However, this does not mean that all Domestics are nonworking, or that all homemakers are Domestics. Many Domestics work outside the home, usually in part-time jobs if they wish to work and can afford less than a full-time paycheck. But the job is always lower on the priority list than the home and family. Most Domestics, in fact, feel that a full-time job is detrimental to their families' well-being. They feel that domestic activities, like keeping the house clean, are more important than any outside involvements.

What about those women who do not work but are also not

Domestics? Young children, for instance, may keep a Go-Getter woman out of the work force, in which case she will still manage to focus her interests outside the home—perhaps on volunteer work or community projects or further education for herself. The key to a Domestic personality is the focal point of her interests and her self-image in relation to those interests—not whether she works.

Women in the Domestic group have a less positive view of women as a whole. They often feel that men are smarter than women, and they put their husbands' jobs ahead of their own.

These women tend to shun the limelight and also outsiders, and circle their wagons tightly around their family group. This is their world, what makes them happy. Domestics are content with what they are and do, perhaps because they experience the least conflict of all women between what they are and the traditional role of women. They are also unlikely to set personal goals, therefore opening up fewer opportunities to be disappointed. As Dr. Brenda Solomon notes, "If you don't strive for anything, you have no conflict."

DONNA: DOMESTIC

Donna, forty-five years old, is a "career housewife." She and her husband of twenty years have one child, age seventeen. With her home-centered attitudes and activities, Donna personifies the domestic woman.

"I keep a very neat and clean house—most of the time, anyway," she said. "Grocery shopping is done very regularly. The bills are paid very well. And I try to keep as good a check as I can on my teenager. These are the things that are my first concern.

"It seems to have paid off. I enjoy looking at the house. I enjoy the new things that we're able to get. Our daughter is still with us and still in school—one more year to go. I feel I've accomplished what I set out to do.

"I'm pretty content for things to go the way they are. I spend most of my time with our daughter. I feel children need as much guidance and help as any parent can possibly give them—especially nowadays. Being as how we only had one child, I think probably more of the discipline was left up to me. So I can kind of either pat myself on the back or else (*laughs*). Raising my child was the thing I'm most proud of.

"When we were first married, I worked for the Boeing Company, in blueprints, but as soon as I got pregnant, I quit. That's what I wanted to do. Then for a while I was an Avon Lady, but I could do that from home. My husband wouldn't have minded if I worked, if that was what I wanted, but I wanted to raise a family. Now I sometimes think the added income of a job would be nice, but I feel that most women that are working have to let something else go around the house. They don't have as much organization in their homes as a woman who stays home. And I disapprove of that. When you're running all the time, like you are when you work, you can't always get to the house. I don't think anybody has to be immaculate, but a dirty house bothers me. That's one of the reasons that I have tried to stay home.

"Some people feel the need to be involved with other people. Like my sister-in-law, for one, who would prefer to hold any kind of job except housekeeping. She just isn't the type to be confined to her home. We don't have the same feelings about it. You can tell that by walking into her house. She's more of a person that likes to be around a group of people than me. It's your own preference, and I like people fine, but to work outside the home unless I really had to—uh-uh. I would prefer to be at home.

"I suppose women who work outside the home must be happy in their jobs or they wouldn't be doing it. But we have entirely different jobs, them and me, and I'm happy in mine."

COREY: CONTENT

Corey, twenty-five, is married and has two young children, four years old and eighteen months. Between the children, she worked part-time briefly because she found she could not fill her days when her daughter started nursery school. Now she is happy to be home full-time again. She is at peace with herself and her self-image, which is centered around her family.

"I'm content with what I've got and what I do," Corey emphasizes.

"The only time I'm not as comfortable is when I get around people I don't know or that I'm not familiar with. I'm absolutely not a person with a lot of self-confidence. Like when I worked, at first I was always checking myself to be sure I was doing the right thing. I worked mornings, before the baby was born. When my daughter turned three, I got kind of bored when she started nursery school and was gone during the day. I worked in a shoe department. I helped people find things they were looking for, measured their feet, tallied up the day's tickets. It got me to meet people, got me so I wasn't afraid to talk to people. But now with the baby, he needs me for everything he does. He needs his mother to be there with him. To tell you the truth, I would feel guilty if I worked. I don't think the children would really mind that much. I think it's mostly how I feel, that they would miss me. My husband wouldn't like it if I weren't home, either. He likes having me around.

"I'm most proud of my children. Of having a happy marriage. Of just being myself, doing the things I like to do. My kids are happy. They love me and I love them. My husband and I, we're good to each other.

"Maybe someday I'll go back to school, after that maybe get a career. I'd like to go into nursing or maybe be a secretary. Something like that. But I'm not doing anything about it now because I've been concentrating mostly on my family. After all, they're little yet.

"How do I spend my time? I like needlecraft and I like rug work. My husband and I, we go bowling together. In the summertime, the family goes on picnics. And my children love to be read to. My daughter just started kindergarten, and she's just so involved in books, and my son likes to be read to also. And I play with blocks and different shapes, teaching him shapes and stuff like that.

"Getting out of the house is not that important to me. I mean, it's not like we sit home all the time, we go out. We go on the picnics, and to carnivals with the kids. Or maybe we go for a walk in the evening sometimes—which to me is as much fun as going out to a nightclub. Women who work seem to be constantly on the go—going here, going there. Always something. My sister used to work, and when she was working she was just constantly on the go. And now she just had a baby and she's very bored because she doesn't know what to do with herself.

"I'm content with just staying home and playing with the kids."

SERENA: PROFESSIONAL WIFE AND MOTHER

Married for thirty years, Serena has raised her children and feels she is now "semiretired." The wife of a successful businessman, Serena has centered her life around the betterment of her family, and pursued that goal with a calculated, almost professional zeal. The broad scope of her background has led Serena to develop more aggressive attitudes than most Domestics, but her aggression focuses on her husband and children. Now that the children are in their twenties and thirties, she is starting to think in terms of her own personal goals and wants. She is a finely honed Domestic.

"Well, first and foremost I think my two children are my

biggest successes. They were my main job. I consider they were my job because I elected to have children and I elected to raise them on practically a scientific basis. I didn't just let them grow like Topsy. I worked at it every day. I groomed them and taught them and exposed them to travel and interesting things, and I tried to mold them to have good minds to use, and equip them to face the world in a way that I was not equipped.

"My parents equipped me with the social graces and nothing else. I was brought up knowing which fork to use, knowing how to be polite to people, knowing how to ingratiate myself to people, knowing how to entertain, how to be the perfect hostess. I was taught and told by both my father and my mother how to be a good hostess and how to be a good guest. And I trained for my role as a successful man's wife by joining my parents in business entertaining from as early as I can remember. I learned from being exposed to business deals every night at the dinner table and being told how to conduct myself while in the presence of men talking business—how to absorb, how to contribute. I was asked my opinion from an early age, but, aside from helping out at the office, doing clerical work, I did not go into business for myself.

"I was married very young, and I married twice. Both of my husbands were put into my family's businesses. And I helped them. I gave them my knowledge. Why didn't I help myself? Because it wasn't fashionable, it wasn't the trend at the time. Now I'm very, very sorry that I didn't do this for myself. It's my only serious regret—that I didn't pursue it for myself. Instead, I did it for two men.

"I think that if I had pursued it for myself, I would be in the position that my husband is in today. In fact, I think I would be in a better position, because I think I'm more knowledgeable.

"But it never occurred to me to work for my personal benefit. What I did was to help my husband by cultivating relationships with key people he needed for business. My husband's customers, for the most part, did business with him on a friendship basis, because they were friends. I took care of making sure they were friends. I entertained, I ingratiated myself to the customers and their wives and made myself totally necessary. I'm very well qualified in the area of personal relationships, and I used this skill to establish a way of life for my family.

"For the good of my husband's business, I also did volunteer work, which I hated. But I did it because it was essential for good relationships in the city where we lived. My husband hated community work, so I did it for him.

"I felt that it was my position to help my husband, and I considered what he accomplished to be mine also.

"However, I discovered that there are no such partnerships. I found out that when a woman does this for a man, the accomplishments become the man's—in the man's mind and on paper. And the woman gets no credit for this, nor does she have any share in it.

"It's a terrible mistake.

"Having your own money is an equalizer in a relationship with a man. A man tends to use money as a weapon—both to give favors and to withhold favors. Money gives a woman an equal voice.

"Yes, I feel I got no credit. At least not from my husband. I don't feel that it was a blow to my self-esteem because I know I deserved the credit. I was good at what I did. The business people respected me. And I was very good at philanthropic work. I held officers' positions and ran major fund drives for the symphony. At one time, I had three hundred women under me. After seven years, when I quit, they replaced me with two paid men. That was when I started thinking about giving my time away, and I never did again.

"But my husband would never have permitted me to work, at least not in the early years. He had a very negative attitude toward married women who worked. He had very old-fashioned ideas and he felt that a woman's place was in the home. Also, I had young children and I needed to be home.

"I don't think that my children would have reacted negatively if I had actually had an outside job, particularly as long as I was able to care for them. But it would have been impossible for me to work and also care for them as they were accustomed to being cared for. They were accustomed to a great deal of personal care: being taken to lessons and being driven to school and being picked up from school and all such things that required my immediate attention.

"I was always considered to be something of a radical. I still am. I didn't do things in the traditional way. I married a foreigner, I left the country, I learned other languages, I saw and lived in other cultures. I didn't do any of the traditional things other than getting married. Ultimately I did do traditional things. But still I was more aggressive than most other women I knew.

"I have lived in suburbia for many years. I know these women, their problems, the things they consider joys. And I know their limitations. Their joys are the pride in their homes and their families, their children, their environment, and their husbands' positions. They do not feel responsible for their husbands' success. Most of them feel good fortune is smiling on them. They're just along for the ride. It's as though they opened the Cracker Jack box and they got a good prize. I don't feel that way at all. I took an apple out of the barrel and I polished it mightily to get what I wanted.

"While other suburban wives who were my friends sat home while their husbands went out on business entertaining, I would see to it that my children were taken care of and then I would go out with my husband and business-entertain.

"I had many goals throughout what I choose to call my working years. And my work was my home, my children, my husband's business. Those goals have been attained. The goals are now for me personally. I have very specific goals. I want my personal life to be fuller, richer. I now have an active interest in the stock market, and that takes considerable time. I want to do the pleasurable things that I didn't have time to do for many, many years. For instance, I always wanted to enjoy a sport, but I never had time to do it—I had to be available in my home. Now I'm active in the tennis club, and many other things.

"It's true that my ambitions, for years, were not toward myself. I did things for the good of the business, and to get the station in life that I wanted for my children. To establish their life-style, meaning their standards—intellectually, emotionally, physically, and commercially. I wanted all avenues open to them, whether they used them or not.

"I always felt anything would be open to me, and I still feel that way. I could have anything I wanted. But I felt responsible. As I said, I didn't have the children by accident. I wanted children, and I wanted them to be a certain type of human being, with every avenue open to them. And then they could do with that as they wished. And I did accomplish that."

The Malcontents

This group is chock-full of unhappy women. Whatever they do, work or not, they are depressed, insecure, and lack self-confidence to a high degree. Compared to women in general, Malcontents are only one-fourth as likely to feel they are self-confident.

Although they may deny it in casual conversation, and

even to themselves, deep down Malcontents are convinced that they are inferior human beings. Malcontents are 35 percent more likely than most women, for instance, to feel they are not intelligent, and they are less likely than others to feel they are good-looking. The Malcontent feels she has let everyone down by simply being herself, and she feels unwanted and unattractive. Her self-image is constantly at low ebb.

"This kind of personality—which occurs in both men and women—is absolutely based on early childhood experiences," notes Dr. Brenda Solomon. "Sometimes this type of individual is called the 'Injustice Collector.' They always pinpoint the problem on the outside—never on themselves. They were emotionally deprived, but never got beyond the trauma and continue to repeat it. They can't find meaning in what they do."

Women in this group are chiefly characterized by the fact that they are unsatisfied with their situation in life, but simultaneously unwilling to take responsibility for their status. They shirk responsibility for their own decisions, often fearing that commitment to a decision will leave them open to criticism. Malcontents are very indecisive and waver back and forth on issues. They seem to be waiting for someone else to tell them what to do, so that if the decision does not work out they are free to blame everyone but themselves.

Malcontents don't like things the way they are, but they do not seek change, and tend to live on a day-to-day basis. They are only two-thirds as likely as most women to set long-range goals, which shows that they are not likely to actively seek to alter their situation, in spite of what they may claim to the contrary.

Malcontents prefer to react passively to their situation, sitting back, complaining, and feeling dissatisfied. Compared to other women, they are two and a half times as likely to feel that life is passing them by.

CHRISTINE: THE DEEP END

A typical Malcontent is Christine, forty years old, married twenty-two years, with three children aged eighteen, fourteen, and eight. She has never worked, having devoted her life to raising her family. She registers dissatisfaction with her situation—and the feeling that she is at the mercy of her circumstances. However, she does nothing to improve them.

Christine claims she is happy—but her behavior contradicts the statement.

"I didn't want to work when the children were smaller," she sighs. "And now that I've decided that I'd like to go to work, it's kind of hard to get a job at forty with no experience. Actually, about liking to work, it's really yes and no. What I'd like is to work part-time. Probably a secretarial job. I'm definitely capable of running a house and having a job at the same time.

"Inexperience is holding me back. You reach a certain age and you have very little experience and you aren't twenty years old and they don't want to hire you. So you have to keep looking, I suppose, until you can actually find a place where they will take someone like you."

Is Christine doing anything to sharpen her secretarial skills and increase her chances of landing a job? "Not necessarily," she admits. Then, the Malcontent cop-out: "Sometimes I don't really care. I think, if it takes all that to get a job, I'll just stay home and take care of the family."

She continues: "Most of my problems are caused by other people. Around the house, I'm the one who ends up picking up and doing everything. I don't have enough help with the housework. The kids just leave everything for me—drop it wherever. My friends, or acquaintances, they seem to sort of put me down, make catty little remarks. I hate that. I think, 'Why can't we all get along? Why be like that?' It just hurts my feelings and I think, 'What have I done to deserve this?'

"One time I found myself being imposed upon by other mothers. They were trying to get me to baby-sit for them because they thought I was such a good mother they wanted me to take care of theirs, too. Oh, I would do it maybe once, but that was it. Then I found out: They were out running around, having a good time, while I was sitting there with all the work. Not that I really care about things like that. What I really care about is my children and being with them.

"Sometimes I feel paranoid. But then I try to shake that feeling that everybody's out to get me. Basically, I'm a happy person.

"Most of what I do is tied up with my children. I go to their clubs, sponsor their school meetings. Some days if I have nothing to do, though, I get quite bored. I mean if I don't have any activities for the day, plans to do something for the children or with the children.

"I'm not a person who spends a lot of time on herself. I think that women who spend a lot of time on makeup and clothes are selfish. I think they neglect their children.

"I do wish I had more money to spend. If I could wave a magic wand I'd like to be a millionaire. I'd spend it on my children.

"I don't think about the future. I don't like to. I'll wake up some day and find out I'm all alone. I'll probably be one of these people who go off the deep end when all my children leave. Probably just go right off the deep end."

ALLISON: FACADES

On the surface, Allison has had a fortunate and fulfilling life. She has bachelor's and master's degrees, speaks fluent French and German, and lived and worked in Germany for several years, as a ground hostess for a German airline. She returned to the United States to round out her education and change careers. For the next eight years she worked as a legal librarian. Recently she successfully maneuvered another career change, into the financial industry. But her inner life is far less satisfying than the externals would indicate.

Allison is thirty-four, and although she had one serious romance, she has never been married.

Like other Malcontents, Allison is highly indecisive. She refrains from making commitments because she feels that if they did not work out, she would have to blame herself. She cloaks her indecisiveness in the guise of independence.

"I never had any sort of career goals—never any sort of dreams of what I wanted to be—and I still don't," she admits. "I think this was because I had a lack of direction. I was the first in the family to go to college; my mother had quit school when she was fifteen. When you're young, sometimes you don't know what you want to do, and most of the women friends I had were not career-oriented, either. We sort of thought we'd probably get married, so what was the point of really looking into something that would require goals? Although even marriage was not a goal, really. It just seemed like it would happen sometime. Now that I'm thirty-four and still not married, and though I hope to be eventually, I know maybe it won't happen. I have to protect myself for the future, which is one reason why I changed careers. Money is one way of protecting myself. The prospect of being alone and all that still sort of frightens me. Planning for retirement, for illness, for buying a home, property—how do you do all that on your own?

"I have a little facade. I don't like to appear weak in the eyes of others or admit failings or shortcomings except to very, very close people. Other people, acquaintances, generally see me as having control, knowing what I'm doing, independent, having my act together. In reality I'm a little less than that.

"Still, although I like to be noticed, I don't want to be the center of attention. I feel a little embarrassed. When you are in the limelight, you always have to perform. I would never want to be famous. You could not be human. People would expect you to be perfect. I like to be independent. Have choices. Do anything I want.

"I want to be flexible, leave my options open. I don't want to plan my life out. By writing two-year plans or five-year plans, I think I'd eliminate a lot of chance things that may come up and sound better, so I'm not too crazy about being locked into any plan. I guess part of this is a lack of knowing for sure what it is I really want. Plus it's protection from disappointment, keeps you from feeling you haven't advanced to where you want to be and it's too late to change at that point in life. Also, I like variety, different things, different places.

"I really don't know where I'll end up. When I worked as a law librarian, I enjoyed taking care of books. But the career mobility wasn't quite what I wanted then. I would probably have had to get a law degree. Actually, I even started to get one—I had about thirty hours of credit, but I just wasn't interested enough to pursue it for the next five, six, or seven years.

"So after eight years as a law librarian, I got a new job, which I've had less than two months. It took me a while to decide that I wanted to do something different. It's sort of a frightening experience to quit one job and to go into something entirely new. First there's all the basics—new people, new surroundings, new responsibilities. Then there's what will other people say after you go jumping from one job to another. Finally I was realistic enough to decide that I didn't like what I was doing and I wasn't going to suffer for it. And if I didn't like the next job, I could change it, too. I'm not bound by anything specific.

"If I had my choice, I wouldn't work. I would travel all the time. I do not look forward to going to work, but I don't feel terribly negative, either. I'm right in the middle. I feel like it's a ritual. I just accept it as something that I have to do. Sort of a sense of duty. I think it was just sort of drilled into me as a child that you have certain responsibilities and you have to do them, and if you find a particular job too demanding, you still do it, because you should. Actually, I think there's a lot more that I could be doing, if I set my mind to it. I just think I got a little bit of a late start.

"In my last job, there were definite pluses and minuses. For instance, I could tell that I was a lot more qualified than this woman who was the director of my project, even though she had a law degree and was in a position of power. I could tell I knew more than she did, and I thought I had a better feel for people, and it made me feel good to think I was capable of doing things that she wasn't. But there were problems. I was frustrated with the amount of responsibility I had, and the fact that I was not recognized as having it. I was in the middle of the hierarchy on paper, but I really called the shots in a lot of instances, and I was not recognized for that by the director. In many cases, she appropriated my projects and took credit herself. She would even flaunt it. I would always make sure that those people who helped me on a project were recognized, but she never bothered to say who really helped out. That's not something that's easy to live with.

"Stress can get to me. One crisis after another was one of the reasons why I left. I like working with people, but not all day long, and that job was just one crisis and one unfriendly person after another. Also I got impatient with the problems. It bothered me that to get anything done you had to go through the channels—write the memos with all the carbon copies, and things taking six weeks to get an answer. We all have our shortcomings, and I do get impatient. I find all the little intricacies and all the gossip and grapevine trying at work. The coworkers, the secretaries, the bosses, the whole gambit. But I face up to it, and complain about it at home. I just accept it as being part of the work situation.

"There's not enough time in the day. I go home tired from work and I think I should really call my friends and go to the theater or do something constructive and I don't. I just stay home and read or whatever. There are a lot of things to do, but I'm too lazy to do them. And I get bored.

"To be really honest—and I know it's just a cop-out—I can say I'm satisfied, but not happy. I compare myself to other people and then I say: Look at what they have and look at what I have, I should be happy. And when I'm not I feel guilty. So I say: If I'm not happy, but I'm not unhappy, where does that put me? I guess satisfied. I have everything I need: a good job, a nice apartment, I travel when I want, I'm not poor, I'm healthy, I have parents that I'm close to, I have friends. But there seems to be some element where I'm not happy. Where every day I'm not just bright-eyed and bushy-tailed. Maybe that's a fallacy. Maybe that's not what being happy is, I don't know. But I would say I'm not really happy.

"Maybe part of it is being thirty-four. You feel you should have accomplished something by now because the books say you should have or your parents put pressure on you or whatever, and you look back and ask: What have I accomplished? What have I really accomplished? Sometimes that is slightly frustrating.

"I think a lot about what I've done. I'm the type of person who never really regrets what I've done. I've learned from what I've done so far—but I don't really use that to say, well, I did this wrong and I'll do it better this time.

"I feel pretty much that to a point I have choices and make them. But there is a sense of fatalism, too. Things are meant to be a certain way, and so far the evidence is that I have been able to control most of it—but certain circumstances just happen and that brings out the fatalism.

"My mother says, 'You look so unhappy, what's wrong?' Sometimes it's just pointless to discuss it. I don't even know sometimes.

"I just try to determine what constitutes happiness, and I don't know. My mother comes from a more traditional, simpler background. 'Happy' to her means to have a husband and children and a nice home and to be reasonably comfortable. What she needs to be happy is just my father and me. For me, it's more complicated. Supposing I did have a husband and children? I don't think that would make me completely happy, either, but I don't know why. I guess I just don't know what happiness is.

"There were always traditional definitions of the expectations in life: The woman would get married and have children and be a wife and housewife, and that's about the extent of it. Men would have a job and they would have a career, and that would be their means to happiness. But generally, comparing the two, women are supposed to be the happier because men are out there working hard, and how can you be happy busting your butt on your job? So that's a little bit the image that we grew up with: Working is not synonymous with happiness. Working is drudgery, and climbing the career path and all of that isn't really making you happy. So here we are in 1980 sort of caught in the middle. You're led to believe that having a family and getting married is happiness—then you find that a lot of your friends who do that are not happy, they are miserable, and they think *you* are a lot happier than they are. Then you have a job and you do what is thought of as being the male role and everybody says *that's* supposed to be satisfying—you've got your career and you've got your proposal in and you've got your raise and you impress the boss—but I find that only satisfying to a point.

"So what I sort of concluded from all that is: Maybe happiness is totally an illusion. Sometimes in my more pessimistic days I think that life is not meant to be happy. We're meant to be in this world to work and that's all there is to it, and life is not meant to be happy. Life is simply routine. Maybe my expectations are too high, or maybe it's the routine. There's optimism in me that hopes that this is not true. But maybe happiness is only a moment, and it's not a year or five years or fifty years. It's one moment, when you're happy in the morning when the sun shines instead of rain. And that's what I sort of fall back on—little moments of happiness."

Dr. Roy Grinker, Jr., points out that Malcontents like Allison and Christine have chosen a depressive position in life. "They feel discriminated against because they're women, because they're something—not pretty enough, not tall enough, not blonde enough. And the fascinating thing about that kind of woman is when you give them what their heart desires, whether it's a promotion or money or blonde hair, it's just the areas of bitching that shift. They are characterologically unable to stop being angry and complaining. Most of them are women who had those kinds of unpleasant, unhappy childhoods where they constantly strove for something they couldn't get—some kind of success, positive feedback—at any level of life. They complain that life is wrong. But what they're really saying is that people have given them a bum shake and they don't have an optimistic view about people giving them something that they need to make themselves feel good."

What's interesting about the Go-Getters, Domestics, and Malcontents is where they can be found:

WORKING WOMEN		NONWORKING WOMEN	
Go-Getters	57%	Go-Getters	26%
Domestics	25%	Domestics	51%
Malcontents	18%	Malcontents	23%

The proportion of Go-Getters is clearly much larger among working women. While some nonworking women are Go-Getters, the majority remain focused on their homes and families. This implies the dual proposition that the working world attracts the Go-Getter and/or the working world breeds the Go-Getter. The latter has far-reaching and positive implications for women, particularly when combined with the fact that women who work are less likely to be Malcontent than women who are not employed. The five-percentage-point difference in Malcontents between working and nonworking women, for instance, is statistically significant within our study and represents millions of women nationwide.

Dr. Grinker says that this distribution may be the result of the positive reinforcement a job provides. "It's a circular kind of thing," he notes. "You see fewer Malcontents in the working world because they are less optimistic in going ahead and trying to get something for themselves." Also, work provides the vehicle for reinforcement and self-actualization that can move women psychologically to a more positive, aggressive orientation. As Dr. Grinker states it, "The more women try and the more they succeed, the more they continue and do not drop out of the work force. They continue to get either temporary or permanent feedback from the work itself, from the success itself and the particular career they have chosen. And if you're a Go-Getter, the more you go and the more you get, the more you're going to get up and go, because you're not likely to be satisfied with less. You become upwardly mobile, you have a driven kind of quality. You don't stop, you keep aspiring, keep on trying."

Why? Because you are rewarded by your work. "Go-Getters get tremendous gratification from their work," says Dr. Grinker. "Immense gratification."

If women generally become more secure and gratified when working, and if they communicate this to their children and do not undervalue the role of parent, then it is likely that the Malcontent group of women will greatly diminish in the next generations.

If the Go-Getter group parallels the growth of working women as a group in general, they may soon be the dominant type of woman. The traditional woman, of which the Domestic is representative, will quickly be superseded by a woman with the capability and motivation to be a leader.

Not only are Go-Getters more likely to choose to work, but the employment experience changes women into something more independent and aggressive than they were before. Work actively instills Go-Getter characteristics in many women, often with dramatic results.

In the next chapter, you will see how this happens.

CHAPTER 4

Workmutation

Going to work is, for most women, like stepping into a chrysalis. The job enfolds them, spinning a fine web that entangles every aspect of their lives. As Dr. Roy Grinker, Jr., explains it, "A lot of it has to do with positive reinforcement at work. Work helps a woman's self-image, and then she can 'borrow' from the success at work with a feeling that she's more confident. She borrows pride in herself, she borrows confidence, she borrows self-confidence. One spills over to the other, as in any series of endeavors. For instance, take a course in college—getting an A spills over into doing better in other things. Or sports—you learn one sport and suddenly you find yourself trying other sports or doing better in them. It's as if everything gets into gear."

This is the process of workmutation, and the woman who experiences it becomes, in many ways, a mutant of her original self.

The job is the catalyst for workmutation. Through work, women are transformed from their traditional, more dependent, domestically focused role to a newly aggressive, independent, confident, differently focused status. This is not to say that these tendencies never existed before the women went to work. But workmutation brings them closer to the surface, and allows them a wider forum in which to function. In many cases, positive reinforcement in the employment situation provides more fertile ground for self-validation, a broader spectrum of experience and exposure. For instance, one woman commented, "Part of my job is meeting people cold. And it would never have occurred to me that this skill would come in handy elsewhere. But it did, especially when we moved to a new city. I realized I was using the same skills to meet somebody, say, at an open house or community meeting as I was at work. I realized it is the same thing. And as a result I have gotten much more involved here in my new city than I ever really had before we moved."

Workmutation differs with each individual, of course, but from our personal, in-depth interviews, a pattern emerged. The process involves roughly three stages:

1. *Realization.* Due to the social and economic dynamics of paid employment, the woman begins to think differently about her role in life. She finds herself experiencing a new range of activities and relationships outside the home and receives positive feedback from this situation. This initial phase is a honeymoon phase. Whether the woman is a housewife entering the work force or a single woman embarking on a career, the newness is a heady experience. A woman in this stage is often caught up in her new role. She feels she is doing something of value, and her sense of self-worth is increased. As a result, she may begin to rethink her capabilities and question her role within the home.

2. *Ambivalence.* It's hard to integrate a new self-concept without being in conflict about it. As the honeymoon phase wears off and she becomes engrossed in routine tasks, the woman begins an internal weighing and measuring of the gains of the new way of life as opposed to the old—and

she will always encounter tradeoffs. Lifelong conditioning moves in at this point to exert its influence, leaving the woman feeling torn between the traditional female role as she perceives it and the psychological and economic rewards she has gained with employment. This is a crucial turning point, and a difficult one. Many women who reach this stage have problems moving beyond it. As a result, this stage may last for years, or even for a woman's entire life. Not surprisingly, ambivalence is most acute among women with children and older women, who must accommodate a more deeply ingrained set of traditional values.

The degree of ambivalence is largely determined by the rigidity of the values a woman grew up with. One reason why ambivalence is so difficult for some women to shake off is the fact that until fairly recently the working woman, particularly the working mother, was not an accessible role model to many little girls. For these little girls, who grew up to become the women of today, most familiar women were housewives and mothers.

Much depends on how congruent the new life-style is with a woman's value system. If the two are opposed, reconciling them will take longer. Dr. Grinker points out, "If your idea of womanhood was based on growing up and getting married and having babies like Mommy did, then you may never enter the work force, and if you do for whatever reason, you will feel a great deal more ambivalence. You will be going against something that has been profoundly internalized: an identity as a housewife, as a mother—like your own mother. So to go into the work force wholeheartedly you have to really be able to turn your back on the role models that have been set up for you since you were a little girl. To do that you have to be pretty strong, or pretty angry, or pretty determined, or maybe there isn't much at home for you to value—or some combination of these things. I'm not sure that *most* working women don't have some deep internal residual ambivalence." No wonder ambivalence is attitudinal quicksand.

3. *Transformation.* This is the stage at which a woman makes a psychological career commitment. If the rewards of work outweigh her guilt, ambivalence will markedly diminish. Having found work a fulfilling, positive experience, she can no longer accept her old role. So she brings her new role home with her and tries to modify her environment to accept it. At this point the contrast of her roles on the job and at home often causes a woman to rethink her life situation. Depending on how she resolves these thoughts, her entire life may change. In our interviews we found that women often reached this stage long before they realized it—even years before. They clung to the status quo for a period of time, despite inner turmoil, rather than risk the dissatisfactions that could accompany acceptance of a new status. However, those women who anticipated or acknowledged the changes they underwent instead of suppressing them were the most successful at working them through and adapting.

Needless to say, there are many variations on this continuum. For some women, the process jams or halts at one stage or another. Other women skip certain stages or slalom through the full range of the transformation with greater speed than others. All this depends on a combination of numerous complex factors, such as whether the woman has been college-educated, whether her job is white-collar or blue-collar, whether or not she is married and has children, her parental background and upbringing, and the woman's own individual psychological makeup.

But once she has experienced workmutation, a woman is measurably changed. She is no longer malleable material, if she ever was. She becomes a person with objectives, self-confidence, ambition—the will to make changes and the means to make them happen.

An in-depth look at four women's experiences gives insight into the power of workmutation and its significance in shaping new identities for women.

ELENA: GROWING UP

"I grew up after I'd been married twenty years," Elena said matter-of-factly. "That was when I started wanting to make my own decisions and do the things I wanted to do."

Elena's apartment reflects her two lives—past and current. She lives in a small, one-bedroom place, the kind with cockroaches and character, in a brownstone on a busy street. The tiny apartment seems smaller than it is, since it is crammed with pieces from the suburban house Elena left behind. There is a large Mediterranean-style dining room set—but no dining room. A velvet couch. A hutch full of china. Decorator lamps. Then there is the bookcase built of bricks. The studio bed in the corner that serves as her young daughter's "room." Posters form a makeshift art collection, haphazardly taped and tacked to the wall.

Elena, tiny and intense, was banked by her two cats as she sat on the floor for our interview. She had just finished dinner—tuna straight from the can. When I pointed out the contrast between her dinner and her dining room set, she laughed.

For years, Elena had led the predictable life of a suburban housewife: married young, three children. Then, sometime around her fifteenth wedding anniversary, she decided to finish school and get a job. In the process she hurtled through the full continuum of workmutation—and changed her life.

"I married at seventeen because I was in love," Elena commented. "That's where I saw happiness—in the idea of marriage, in caring and being cared for. And when I got married, it was on the basis of dependence. It was like he

was the big parent and I was the child. But when my first
two children grew older, I began to think, 'God, what am I
going to do? Be a checker at the supermarket? Play bridge
every afternoon?' I just started being revolted at my prospects. And I started thinking on my own, about myself.

"I didn't think in terms of a career at first. I just wanted
something to do, something that I was familiar with." Elena
gravitated to the field of psychodrama, a specialized type of
psychotherapy in which patients act out their problems,
fears, and hopes, or experiment in role playing. Elena's
mother had been a psychodramatist, and she remembered
peeking at psychodrama groups from the sidelines as a small
child, fascinated. She called psychodrama her "only experience, only confident place." Elena looked into the qualifications necessary for this career and set about fulfilling them—
a task that involved first completing high school, then entering and graduating from college. It took nine years. When
we spoke, she had had her degree for less than a year.

Elena's husband thought the idea of her schooling and
work was great, and he was supportive—at first. As she became more involved in her outside activities, and started
thinking and doing things on her own, he balked. "We could
have stayed married if I had just been more secretive, more
obedient," she sighed. "He didn't like what he called the
'ideas' I was getting. I'll never forget the look on his face
when I went to a student political rally with the baby
strapped in a pack on my back! I suppose I could have just
gone and done it on my own and not yapped about it at
home, and he might have accepted it. But I couldn't."

As Elena's marriage began to slip away, she found something unexpected to hold on to—self-respect.

"What kept me going was my job. Eight years ago, when I
started working, I had no expectations. But my work became
my lifeline. My job interfered with my marriage, but not in
terms of my husband. It was in terms of me. It gave me all

kinds of thoughts about what I could do on my own. A marvelous sense of freedom."

For three years, Elena worked with one group at one hospital. Suddenly, in one month, she was invited to work with two more hospitals. "This was on my own," she pointed out with pride. "It happened just because they'd heard of my work. That was the catalyst, the turning point.

"I stopped being grateful for being allowed to work and started to respect myself more. When that happened, I left my husband. He never understood that I wanted to be treated like an adult, that I *was* growing up. He just got angry and accused me of becoming a liberated woman! He thought my independence was a problem. So as I grew up, I grew away from him.

"When I first left him and the house in the suburbs, I only moved a block and a half away. Not exactly a runaway wife! For a while I stayed like that, close, in the vicinity. I moved to my city apartment four years ago, after living in the suburbs fifteen years. I moved downtown because—well, I told everyone it was the commuting, but actually, I was just dying out there. Downtown, I still come home and maybe just watch TV with my daughter or sit around, but out in the suburbs I had no choice. Here I can go out if I feel like it. I'm not so trapped.

"My way of life is a million times different than it was, and I admit that it took me a long time to get used to that. The anguish I went through! I was so afraid at first. Afraid to do anything. Afraid of the schools in the city. Afraid of just parking my car. But actually I found out it's more friendly in the city. There's more people to talk to. I like the smells, the sounds, the variety. Grocery shopping isn't the biggest thing in my life anymore. Now I do things I never did before. I take taxis, wear makeup. I'm concerned about clothes and what's new."

Elena feels her new self-confidence has had a positive

effect on her role as a mother. "Before we split up, it used to make me furious that my husband could get up, get dressed, make phone calls, and leave without any kind of conscience, and there I'd be, going through a whole number of apologizing and justifying and worrying. 'Is my car going to work, or will it break down and I won't be able to get home, and the kids will be locked out alone in the dark? Will I get home on time, or will the family think I've abandoned them?' It took me a very long time—up to this year—to be able to leave for work comfortably. But now, sometimes I even leave before my daughter goes to school.

"My two older children were like storybook children. Part of the most together family in the world." Elena felt she had molded herself rigidly into the role of ideal wife and mother, at the cost of much of her own feelings and personality.

"But with my little girl, the only one who lives with me now, things are really different. I feel like it's OK to be myself with her. I swear in front of her, cry in front of her—she knows I'm a person, not just a mother. And she's doing fine."

To Elena, work is synonymous with self-respect. "That's what it really is to me. Each one of my sessions is an hour and a half of respect."

She described the events of the day, gesturing intricately. "Today I worked at the welfare hospital, and we spent the whole time singing. The *walls* were vibrating. Tears came into my eyes because I couldn't believe I was part of it. That they let me be there with them and share that. And that when I work with them, they respect me."

Elena gave another example of an experience that brought her self-respect. "I have a women's group. Last week there was a young woman, and we were acting out how her husband wouldn't give her the checkbook and how she just—gave in. She called him at work and said, 'Can't I please have the checkbook?' And he screamed, 'Absolutely not!' And she just kind of twisted herself up like a little pretzel and said, 'I'm sorry I bothered you.' Well, today, that woman acted out the situation and she said, 'Damn it, I want the checkbook!' It sounds simple, but it's taken her a lifetime to get there. And I was part of it.

"Lots of things about work make me feel good, starting when I walk in the door. At the hospitals, there's a lot of excitement when I come around. Many times I'll see people that I know. Patients are very happy to see me, too. All in all, I feel smarter than I used to. I do my job better now. So I feel more effective, I respect myself more.

"Sometimes the people in my group break down, go berserk, throw things, bump into chairs, slap each other. I've been hit, jumped on, called a bitch. I used to run and scream for an orderly when the furniture began flying. Now I tell the patients to stop it as soon as I see trouble starting, and if they get worse, I tell them to leave."

Elena realizes that the independence she once found so euphoric is also deceptive. "I had always assumed that things would be more free on my own—and they are. But there is also a lot more responsibility. I have no one to fall back on now. Just myself.

"Everything used to revolve around just my husband and simple things like, was he paying enough attention to me, and if I asked him for something, how would he react. That's what my moods depended on. Now my state of mind feels like a yo-yo sometimes. When people ask 'How is your day?' I think in terms of the length of my sessions. Hour and a half to hour and a half, I change. And I still have a lot of questions. I spend a lot of time trying to figure myself out.

"But one thing I'm sure of—I've never been this happy before. People used to ask me 'Are you happy?' And I never knew. Now I know. I am."

Elena is an example of a woman who has run the gamut. Her job offered her the opportunity to grow beyond the four walls of her suburban house—and into a situation that she finds more satisfying. She changed from a dependent child-woman to an independent adult.

It is possible that Elena's relationship with her husband was lacking in some critical areas to begin with and that otherwise it could have withstood the changes she underwent. And it could be argued that she had the desire to be a different kind of person all along. The point is, a job provided the vehicle, the mobility, to foster her own self-confidence to the point where she no longer needed or wanted a life based on her former role. The basis of the marriage contract had been undermined. When the couple could not adapt, the marriage dissolved.

LYNDA: HEAD NAIL

An inscribed pendant around her neck proclaims twenty-four-year-old Lynda "Head Nail." And so she is, as owner and operator of her own nail salon specializing in nail sculpture, a complex manicure technique in which artificial nails are molded and polished to match one's own.

Lynda spends sixty to seventy hours a week running her business, and as a result, is entrenched in the realization stage of workmutation. Already work is impacting on her life.

"I've come a long way," she says, frowning intently, huge, serious eyes dominating her finely boned face. Then she laughs as she gestures around her salon, a softly carpeted cocoon of luxury. "This whole thing is a switch. I'll say it's a switch! What I thought I might do when I was younger was maybe be a dancer, like Juliet Prowse. On stage. In the lights. Or more likely a mother, like my sister is, happily married, with kids living at home.

"The only reason I even started working was because I didn't want to go to school. I mean, I just *hated* school, *hated* it! And I always worked so I could use it as an excuse to ditch school. Any time I could ditch school, I would. But then I didn't like work, either. I worked in an office and I didn't care for it at all."

Lynda at first sought independence and happiness via the traditional route—marriage. "When I was seventeen, I got married. But it didn't work out. We were just kids, it was crazy. When I was eighteen, I was divorced.

"I had a few jobs, but I didn't like them. I was a switchboard operator for a computer place. Then a bagger at a grocery store. I had no goals, nothing.

"I was a spendthrift. I used to spend all my money. I'd blow $400 a week on clothes. Once I went out and bought myself a $17,000 car because I was depressed, which is sick. I decided to pick up the pieces and do what I could with myself.

"Then I went to work at a department store as a cosmetician. That's how I got into this. They asked me if I wanted to learn nail sculpture. And I said sure, I'll be a jack-of-all-trades.

"It only took me two days to learn. The store had me go to a hotel to take a nail sculpture class. The people came in and showed me what to do. It was easy. Within two days, I was working on a job. And I liked it, so I stuck with it. I even thought about opening my own business, but I had no money left. I'd spent it all."

One of Lynda's customers got to know her and offered to back her in her own business. "For a while I did nails during the day, and at night I would come down to my new shop and paint the place. I decorated it myself. My backer helped me, too.

"I've been open a year now, and I think I'm doing great. I could always do better, but I want to take my time. If you take off right away and try to hit the sky, you're going to come down fast! So I just want to take my time.

"I charge three dollars a nail, and people come in every

two weeks or so for a retouch. But I don't feel like I'm selling a product. I feel like I'm selling me. And the work I do is the best.

"I put in a lot of hours—nine to seven, five days a weeκ. And I stay late most nights. On my days off, I get supplies and check up on my two girls who work for me. I'm never home. But that's OK. I love being the boss. I don't think I could work for anybody else ever again.

"What do I like about my job? I look forward to seeing the people that come in. Like there's one lady that's been coming to me for a few years now, and it's fun to see what she's up to. I meet so many different people. And it's interesting to see what's out in the world today. My customers are mostly career ladies. I've got ladies who are presidents of companies. Hookers. The works. And all ages—twenty to sixty. Once I even had a guy who was gay, but he left town."

Lynda sees herself changing as she becomes successful in her work. "I'm saving now, and beginning to appreciate what money can do for you. And it's nice to have a little bit in the bank in case anything was to happen. Now that I'm working for myself I'm slowing down. I only shop for clothes if I'm going someplace special. I spend money, but not like I used to. I've come a long way.

"People I'm close to, they admire me. They think it's great that I can stand on my own two feet—not like a lot of my friends who get helped out by Daddy.

"If I admire anybody, it's Barbra Streisand. Because she's a woman of her own mind, she does what she feels. She's a superstar and she did it all on her own."

Lynda's girlhood ideas of a traditional husband have vanished somewhere along the way. "I don't want to depend on a man to give me anything I can give myself. A man doesn't understand that all I need is love. I don't need him for money, because I can take care of that on my own. I thought for a while that maybe I needed a man with a lot of money, so he doesn't worry about *my* money. But rich men are dull to me. Very dull. I like exciting men. Men who are different. By different, I mean *they* depend on *me*. Maybe that's why a lot of the guys I date have problems. Like I've dated an alcoholic, and even a gangster."

Lynda has no ambivalence about children—she wants them. With or without a husband. She feels her attitude is justified because she can support a child. "By age thirty, I want to have a kid, married or not. Because I would be able to support it. I might work part-time then, because I want to take care of the little one myself. I like to have a man around, I want to be loved. Being married would be nice, but if not, I can take care of things myself.

"But I plan to keep working. Because I've got so much energy, I'd be bored stiff otherwise. You can only spend so much money, only clean the house so often. I'd be lost without my work. I really would."

Lynda has learned to set goals. "I plan for the future. I think about what I'll be doing in five years all the time. I don't live for the day like I used to. I can't, I have responsibilities now. I want to keep going. Maybe have a franchise or two. The sky's the limit. I have no limit on myself. I plan to go as high as I can without getting an ego problem, and still be myself. Whatever that takes, I'm going to do it."

Lynda is still a very young woman, but it's clear that her work—particularly the opportunity to run her own business—has had a tremendous impact. Due to her career, she has developed direction, sense of purpose, leadership skills, and independence. Lynda is still in the realization stage of work-mutation. The throes of ambivalence about childbearing and the child/career conflicts that most women experience in their early thirties or after the actual birth of their children are in the future. But there's no doubt that work has changed the way Lynda views her capabilities and role in life. Already she is a different person for having worked.

SHERRY: ON THE AMBIVALENCE SEESAW

Sherry is forty, and she's spent about half her life torn between a hard-edged desire to make a total commitment to her work and a romantic vision of home and hearth. For periods of time she tried one extreme or the other, devoting herself exclusively to job or home, but invariably she found herself longing for work when she was at home, or home when she was at work. Currently she is trying to do a little of everything so as to span two worlds: work part-time, raise a preschool child, and have a successful marriage. The ambivalence continues, but as she becomes increasingly successful in business, the seesaw is tilting toward the nondomestic side.

Sherry's tailored, manicured looks project competence. She has a pert, Dorothy Hamill kind of image.

"About two weeks ago, I started falling apart," she moaned. "Now I realize that there's been a much greater impact from my splitting working and home life than I've been acknowledging. Suddenly I'm shouting at people. Inside I feel tense. And I'm telling myself, 'Help. Get me out of this. I want to quit. I can't do this anymore.'"

She sighed and picked at her nail polish. "But then I realize that this is a temporary kind of feeling. I *have* stopped work. I *have* quit. I know what happens then. And I can look around at some other women who have done it, just stayed at home, and I know I don't really want to do it. But there are times . . .

"I don't know. I have the continuing debate as to whether I'm going to keep on working part-time or go back to work full-time or quit altogether. And I guess it's not even a debate. I know. I have a very strong sense that I have to go back to work full-time. Not because I want to necessarily; not because I *don't* want to necessarily. I'm not really sure how I feel about it. We're not in a situation of economic need. It's theoretical. I feel it's very important for me to be able to take care of myself, my child, and my husband—if I had to. My husband was just ill for six months, and now it's even less of a theoretical consideration. Suddenly it's become very real."

In college, Sherry adopted the values she saw around her, but not always without question. "In the fifties, by the time you had your college degree in hand, you'd better be wearing an engagement ring or, by God, what was going to happen to you? I never fell for that. But I did fall in love, and that's why I got married right after college. It was kind of ironic because I was the one of my peer group who was not interested in getting married—then I was the first one to get married."

The marriage was brief. After a few years, Sherry found herself divorced. "And then I worked," she said. "By that time I was into my mid-twenties, and I felt I had lost ground, because although I had done some work while I was married, there was no real commitment to a job. I had only done what I call 'unbusy work.' There wasn't much you could do back then in southern California with a degree in liberal arts. So I decided to do something real. I left California and came to the Midwest."

Prospects were not too dazzling there, either. "At first I did what almost everybody my age did, college graduate or not. I went to work as a secretary. I had never really thought beyond that. In my family, even going to college was an unusual situation. And I didn't know what it was I was going to college for, except that it seemed important to have a degree. I knew that the degree was my ticket to somewhere, but I didn't know where. I knew that if you were going to do anything with your life beyond just kind of grub away, you needed that degree. So that was my goal. My only goal. Nowhere in my upbringing or education was there any guidance or role model that suggested that you had to think beyond that." Even this limited experience in goal setting was to prove valuable. Sherry was now able to define a goal—a major step forward.

"I was smart enough to know that you didn't get just any secretarial job. I knew I had some skills with the written word. And having absolutely no information about what the real world was like, I decided I wanted to be in publishing because that was one place I could think of that seemed to require the kind of skills I had."

Thinking about work led Sherry to establish some vague goals. "A lot of women at that time took secretarial jobs and never thought beyond. I was different in that respect. I got my job with a publishing company, but made it clear that I didn't expect to stay a secretary. I really meant it. If I had been there for a year and hadn't moved into a different kind of job, I would have left and looked for something else."

She could have coasted, but didn't. "I worked for the editor of a magazine. He traveled constantly, and to be honest, there was not a lot for me to do except sit behind my desk and look appropriate. Instead of sitting behind that desk and looking appropriate, I went up and down hallways and begged work from people. I learned a few things from that, and more importantly, I made some friends. So later on when the possibility arose of my being given a chance at an editorial job, although there was a lot of skepticism because I had no training or background, there was a lot of goodwill. People remembered how I had done anything, the simplest, dumb kind of work, as long as it was editorial work, because I wanted to learn something. And they were aware that I was someone who really wanted to go somewhere, do something."

Sherry got her chance at an editorial job and moved up through the ranks for ten years. "For a long time work was my life," she remembered. "Not simply for its own sake, not for the glory or anything like that, although I *was* competitive. That was one element. The other part of it was that I wanted to make some money. I had no one to rely on but myself, I was making my own way. I felt, if you're gonna work, you might as well get the most out of it that you can in terms of dough."

At this point, Sherry had entered the realization stage of workmutation. She had begun to think differently about her own capabilities and role in life. Now ambivalence surfaced.

"At the same time my life was being driven in one direction, part of me was saying 'I want to drop out.' My motivations, then and now, are very mixed. On the other hand, I'm a very competitive person. Given a situation, given a track, I want to run as fast as I can. I want to be out ahead. I have that one aspect of my personality. The other part—and this is schizophrenic, almost—is that I want to get away from all that. And there was always a deep, basic drive in me to have a child, too. Maybe that came from my upbringing, which really focused on motherhood."

Sherry remarried about this time. She insists this was not an escape from work, or a way out. "My marriage happened somewhere while I was still on the track. And I stayed on the track for another five years after that. It was still very important to me to be totally self-sustaining and I never thought in terms of stopping work. It took several years, you know, before I would even think about having a child, even though I wanted one. And when I first thought about it, I never thought in terms of 'child equals dropping out.' But somewhere along the line I became ready to drop out, to get off the machine. And the time when I had the child seemed to be the appropriate time to do it.

"I was very happy to be pregnant, although at first it was a shock. I never made a conscious decision to quit work then. But somewhere along the line I felt one should be with one's child. I'm not sure why, but I thought that was really necessary. So after the baby was born I quit."

It didn't take long for the ambivalence to resurface. "At first I didn't miss working. It wasn't an instant sense of loss. It took a while. And it took a couple of stages. Right after I quit, when the baby was an infant, we lived in the city, and I could look out my window and see the world go by and I still felt part of it. The sense of being out of the world came when she was six months old and we moved out of the city. From that time on, I started feeling estranged from myself. I wasn't me anymore. I had lost my sense of identity. I really was lost.

"My reactions really took me by surprise. Because I had never planned to go back to work after my child was born. What I thought was this would be a nice hiatus in life when I would stop being a career woman and start being a wife and mother. On top of that, I've always been able to go through the motions of a job and say, 'Oh, isn't this ridiculous.' And so I thought I really wanted to turn away from that. What I finally came to realize was that I needed the competitive kind of situation that work provides and home does not. At least not a healthy home." Work had made its imprint, and it was indelible.

Sherry continued: "Apparently I need a situation where you can show that you can succeed under stress and in competition. It's gonna make you feel good about yourself. It's got to. It's a measurement." For Sherry, as for so many other women, work provided the tangible proof of success that she could not find elsewhere.

Now the seesaw really began to move. Sherry went back to work but only part-time. "I still felt Mama had to be there when she was needed," she said. She kept her work schedule down to twenty hours a week. And she was lucky enough to find a wonderful baby-sitter, an elderly woman that her daughter loved enough to call "Grandma."

Still, something nagged at Sherry. She found that the part-time situation was not enough. "I was working part-time for an organization where I once was part of the full-time action, and I just looked at the organizational chart and started thinking how my name would have been in a different kind of slot if I'd stayed in the mainstream. I felt like I was losing ground."

When the company offered Sherry a full-time job, she took it. About this time "Grandma" moved away, and Sherry was faced with an excruciating series of disastrous baby-sitters. Finally she placed her daughter in a local day-care center. She visited the center and was convinced of its quality. For a few months, everything seemed fine. Then, another ambivalence attack.

"I started having some real concerns. I mean, obviously I had visited the day-care center and checked it out, and it is a fine center. But still I had this sense that I was abandoning my child. There was this idea of leaving this tiny thing to fend for herself among twenty other children. One day I noticed that her perfect little lady manners were falling down, her speech patterns started changing, she was picking habits up from other kids, and I started thinking, 'Oh, my goodness, what am I doing to my child?' I developed an underlying concern about sending her to the day-care center."

Sherry bargained with her boss, cut her work week back to three killer days, and kept her daughter home with her the other two. She fantasized that they would play together, cut and paste, make potholders, plant a garden—she would be a perfect mother.

But the little girl missed the day-care center. She cried to go back. She had to be dragged home on the three days she attended, always protesting that there was one more thing she wanted to do. "Your plans and your child's plans are not always the same," Sherry commented with a wry smile. "There was just no keeping her home."

Now Sherry works three days a week, and her daughter

spends five days a week at the day-care center. Sherry would, on the one hand, like to quit work, and on the other, she longs to work full-time.

"If you work part-time, I think you still see the home commitments as full-time. I mean, you have two full-time commitments and no part-time commitment. You feel harried, frustrated that you're not doing any of it well. I miss the feedback that I'm performing professionally as competently as I used to when I could devote all my attention to working. I'm not operating at the same level of efficiency, but I think I should be. Even though reason tells me that I can't. I want to be everything, do everything. And if my fingernails don't get manicured, I'm really upset that I haven't found time to do that.

"I still want a better slot on that organizational chart. Isn't that something? For fifteen years I've been sneering at that kind of thing, telling myself I'm above that, but yet it obviously keeps bothering me. So you know, that's telling me something.

"I want to remain competitive, and I feel like I'm not doing enough. The point that I'm trying to determine right now is: How long can I keep doing what I'm doing right now without really losing ground? Right now I feel I can make some phone calls and get a job and pick up right where I left off five years ago. But that's not going to go on forever. The question is: Is it going to be true eight years from now? Seven years from now? Next week? I'm walking a tightrope."

According to our survey, Sherry's attitudes are typical of those women who tend to be most ambivalent: those in their mid-thirties or younger, particularly those with young families. These women feel that they belong outside the home, that they *should* work, but they miss their families when they do and wish they had more time to devote to them. And their ambivalence is proportionate to the amount of time they work: Women who work full-time feel the great-est amount of conflict, while women who do not work outside the home feel the least ambivalence.

Is there an end in sight to this emotional seesaw? Our survey suggests there is—and it is related directly to money and success. Once she earns a higher income, $20,000 and above, a woman is far less likely to feel torn between job and home/family. Regardless of their age, 80 percent of those women in our survey earning $20,000 or more a year felt strongly that they belong on the job, while only a small minority felt they were missing out on time with their hus-bands and families.

This does not surprise Marilyn Moats Kennedy, who sees money as a major issue in women's attitudes. "Women who start their careers, for instance, at $19,000 or $20,000, like engineers or new M.B.A.'s, don't show ambivalence toward the home. To them, the home drops away like the state un-der communism. You find less ambivalence among women who are accountants, lawyers, engineers, doctors. They don't have that back-and-forth act. I think that act is money-related. For instance, a woman making $14,000 feels very differently about her conflicts than a woman making $24,000. And she's going to have far fewer conflicts at $24,000."

Upper-income women can also afford to pay for luxuries that alleviate ambivalence. Kennedy points out that she sees many super-successful women who are in the $70,000 range "propping up the home front" with household help, moves to residences closer to work, and other tactics that free up more time and further ease residual ambivalence. "Every client of mine who got a career step up and is making over $40,000 who lived in the suburbs moved downtown and organized her life around work," says Kennedy.

This all suggests that while many women are experiencing their own kind of job/identity crisis, as they become more successful and feel more comfortable with their roles at work, their inner turmoil will subside. The increased re-inforcements of self-respect, an interesting, involving job, and monetary gain will tilt the balance in favor of work. Our survey showed a direct relationship to increasing commitment toward career and decreasing domestic orientation as a woman becomes more successful. The most successful— and least ambivalent—women showed stronger ambition, a higher divorce rate, and less likelihood to have children.

As one successful (and childless) businesswoman commented, "As I started making more money, I thought less and less about having kids, or ever staying home, or even having an easy job—the kind where you can take a day off and nobody cares. I just got more and more serious about being in business, and I think it's because I became more confident in my abilities. After all, I wasn't sure at first that I'd be good in business, since I'd never done anything like it before. Then *voilà*—I buy a piece of real estate and it's worth a lot more the next year, and I'm managing it and dealing with the tenants, and the whole situation gives me a lot of self-confidence, and just snowballs in that direction."

When ambivalence resolves itself, as with our $20,000-plus group, a woman is free to focus her commitment. And she is choosing a nondomestic focus. With more energy to apply to her job, she will work harder, do better, advance further. This is the role model she will provide for her daughter and other women, who will perpetuate her aggressive characteristics.

KAREN: CHIEF

Karen's surroundings reflect the helter-skelter existence of the working mother: house torn up for a kitchen remodeling she's supervising by phone, work papers spread on tabletops, open umbrella dripping from an after-dinner dash to her daughter's school. She is thirty-five years old, with a husband and an eight-year-old daughter. She's aggressive and ambitious for herself—and only just beginning to realize how much so.

"I pretty much grew up with the notion that the wife stayed home and the husband went to work," said Karen. "But my husband and I got married while we were in college, our junior year, and when we got out of school it was 1969 and Ray was going to business school and I needed a job to keep us afloat. I had determined just one thing, which was that I did not want to become a secretary. I didn't care what I did, but I didn't want to be a secretary. Part of this was that it was 1969, and all that student activist stuff was going on, about not being satisfied with the status quo. And I was very involved with the student movement. So I set my sights higher as a result. That was the beginning of the women's movement and at that point it was still kind of suspect, you weren't sure you wanted to be associated with it, and I identified more with the student movement.

"Basically I went around the university calling up all these people I knew and saying I wanted a job, but not secretarial. And I found a job, working for the school, planning events (at a salary a secretary probably would have thrown up at). Nine months later I got a job in the fund-raising office. I really had no idea what they did there, but I didn't care—it was $150 a month more. I went from $500 to $650 a month. That was dramatic. But I still intended to stop working when Ray graduated. My attitude was, 'Well, alright, I'll just keep on working, but I want everybody to know this is strictly temporary.' I even told my boss that. It turned out that Ray went on to get his Ph.D.; he was in school the first five years we were married!"

Karen interrupted to kiss her daughter goodnight.

"When I got pregnant with Heidi, I was still thinking on a short-term basis: I'll work another year, eighteen months, that sort of thing. But I was beginning to change my notions about it. I knew absolutely no one—well, I think I knew one woman who worked and had a child. There were virtually no role models. So I sought out this one person and I said, 'Tell me about it. Am I doing the right thing? Is it OK? What am I going to do?' And she pointed to her very normal child and I felt better.

"I eased back into work full-time when Heidi was three months old. I got a lot of horrified responses from my friends, and I was positive that something ghastly was going to happen to her, even though I was lucky and had fantastic child-care. I worried about the people taking care of her, I worried that nobody could take care of her as well as I could, I worried about missing the first tooth, the first step, the first smile, the first whatever. I needed support from my husband, and also from other people. The 'other people' was the hard part. There weren't very many. I had a number of friends who couldn't even imagine that I was doing this.

"About this time, Ray got a job, and I actually could have quit. At this point we were making identical salaries. But I had a very interesting job and I liked it. I had been promoted, and I was one of the first people on a new department staff, and I was really pleased that they had the confidence in me to say 'We want you on this new staff, we want you to have a responsible position.' This happened two months before Heidi was born and was one of the main reasons why I was anxious to go back to work."

Karen's success began to outweigh her ambivalence. "I was getting a lot out of my job. For me. I felt like I was really making a contribution. I mean, a whole lot of working for a nonprofit institution is psychic, not financial. Particularly in fund raising, because it's very much behind the scenes. There aren't people wandering around saying 'Wow, gee whiz, you're doing a good job,' not so much as in other jobs. It's the people that made it worthwhile—the opportunity to work with some really fantastic individuals, to be part of that kind of team.

"I pretty much gave up the notion of quitting, or working half-time or whatever. I knew that I was going to keep on working.

"I need the satisfaction outside of just home. I want it. I like knowing people and having relationships with people that have nothing to do with anything else. I wanted—and still want—to be thought of as just me. Ray and I used to joke about that.

"When we were seniors in college, Ray was vice president of the student body, and I was doing a few things but nothing as visible as that. And then when he went on to business school and I started working, he was still very active in other things and so I was always Ray's wife. Then after I'd been working for a couple of years, we went to a party and somebody said to Ray 'Oh, you must be Karen's husband,' and I just about fell down. I was just so entranced. I had an identity! Ray thought it was hysterical, because this was just what we'd joked about—it had happened. But I realized then that I really liked being me and not somebody else's dependent. I think that's what happens with working. You get your own identity, your own set of priorities, your own responsibilities, your own people that you go to lunch with and have relationships with, men and women. You don't have to be just a servant housewife. One of my closest friends is a man I met at work—my mentor, if you will—and I would never have that sort of relationship if I hadn't had that job."

When their daughter Heidi was seven, Karen's husband got an offer for an exciting job that required a cross-country move. The couple discussed the situation, then decided to accept the offer. "I suppose if I'd had an offer like that, something I really wanted, we would have moved for me," Karen commented.

As they planned the move, something happened that startled Karen: "Word got around that we were moving, and the senior vice president of a major university flew out to see *me*, to talk to me about heading their fund-raising office. I was flabbergasted. I mean, it just surprised the hell out of me, and I couldn't believe it!"

Karen accepted the offer. "They made it very difficult to refuse," she said with a smile.

Now Karen had concrete proof of her worth. As a result of this new reinforcement, her self-image changed even more. "Now I know I'm not just bragging. I know I'm very good. I know it because people have told me so. And because of this new job offer from the university."

The feedback she received after the move was significant in showing Karen how much she had changed. "When you're new, and you don't know anyone, it's interesting to see what people think of you. At home and at work. After we'd lived here six months, I got this phone call from somebody I'd met once or twice who said she was chairman of the local antique show and asked if I'd be chairman of one of the committees. And you know, I'd only lived here such a short time, I couldn't imagine it, and she said, 'That's OK, we'll get you a co-chairman who knows all the people. You know how to run the committee.' And I said, 'How do you know that?' And she said, 'Oh, everybody in town knows how capable you are.' And I was just astounded at being able to see me as other people did, at the instant credibility my job gave me. 'Look what she does for a living. Clearly she must know what she's doing.'

"Also, on the job itself: Since we moved, I'm at the top. Now there are other people looking at me the way I used to look at my superiors. I've got some experience. And I'm not low man on the totem pole. I'm moving up the ranks, gaining some expertise, and therefore some confidence in myself and the respect of other people."

This self-confidence has resulted in new kinds of behaviors for Karen.

"Until five years ago, I'm not certain I felt confident enough to really put my foot down and say 'We are going to do it this way.' I always felt it was necessary for me to compare notes with other people about what I was deciding to do. This has some advantages, but on my new job I had no one to compare with. And so I had to be able to say 'We are going to do it this way.'

"For example, I've been spending the past ten days fighting with my boss about something. This is one occasion when I can be aggressive, because I know what I'm talking about—maybe even more than he does. That makes me more determined. Five years ago I would never have done this. I would have done it his way.

"The antique show I worked on was another example. It turned out my co-chairman didn't do anything. Literally. So I waited a while, and after two and a half months I said, 'OK, I've waited long enough.' And I took control and called a meeting and said, 'This is how I think it should be.' Five years ago I would have kept deferring to the other chairman, waiting for her to take the lead, because I was the new kid on the block and she was supposedly the old hand.

"I've become much more goal-oriented in everyday life, too. We're remodeling the kitchen. It's one of a number of things I just decided to get done and did. Now I'm hounding the poor architect to death. I like deciding on an undertaking and then getting it done."

Although Karen admits she hasn't completely resolved her ambivalence about motherhood vs. career, she feels she's on "the upper edge of it," and has it under control. "There are levels of guilt, and there are levels of guilt," she says. "I mean it just depends. If I was really that ambivalent, I would have quit when we moved. Sometimes I feel terrible about not being home with my daughter, and I tell her so. But if something is really that important I take the time off. I don't feel guilty overall. When I'm at home I'm very much at home, but when I'm at the office I cannot even think about home. Of course if the phone rings and it's something to do with home, then I can switch right back to that."

Karen feels she has resolved her ambivalence partly by overcompensation. "I tend to get myself involved in things that have to do with Heidi when I'm not working. I can't go be room mother at school, but I sign up for everything else. I'm team administrator for the soccer team. I worked as a volunteer on a fund-raising project this year. And of course there was the antique show, which wasn't at school, but every other mother she knew was involved in that, so she thought it was nifty that I was, too."

Karen has learned to control her early fears and integrate her career with child-raising, although the excellent childcare she once had has evaporated. Heidi now goes to a neighbor's house every night after school, and when there is a day off from school, she usually stays with neighbors, too. "Heidi is very independent," says Karen. "She has to be. I'm not there answering her every single need. We've been through the whole scenario a trillion times. About how come I can't do such-and-such, or come to school all day long when Mrs. So-and-So is there every day and home at lunch, or whatever. Now Heidi knows that Moms and Dads work, and they are tired when they get home from work.

"Today Heidi came home at 3:30. I wasn't there. She was going to a birthday party. The night before we had laid out all of her clothes; the birthday present was right there by the clothes. She changed her clothes, picked up the present, and went to the party. And I didn't get home till 5:00. But I knew she could handle that. Part of it has to do with me, the other part with her getting older.

"Ray does what he can, we share the chores, but he travels over half the time for his job. Most of the time it's just up to me. Last year something happened that still scares me, but I handled it. The baby-sitter called my office and said Heidi hadn't come home. She was an hour late. She was missing. Someone pulled me out of a meeting and told me my child was missing. Here I was. Half an hour away from home—I can't possibly get there. The baby-sitter was fourteen years old, in tears. What could she do? She had called the school twice already.

"Of course I was panicked inside. It was a day I had felt bad not being home anyway, because it was Heidi's last day at school and she was getting a report card. But I pulled myself together and said, 'Alright, I'm going to find her.' So I got on the telephone. I called my friends, and one asked her daughter, who said maybe Heidi was still at school. I called the school and they denied it. They said she was gone. I said, 'No, I don't believe you. I want someone to prove it to me. I want someone to walk down to that classroom and walk back and tell me she's not there.' So they went to look, and the next voice I heard on the telephone was Heidi. And she was there. Of course, then I was furious and incredibly relieved and anxious all at once. It just shows how you go way up and way down and usually end up in the middle somewhere."

Karen's plans for the future are just emerging, but they are ambitious. She is beginning to think about opening her own business, consulting in her field. "Even if I were sixty-five, I couldn't see myself doing nothing. I will always be active in something, whether or not I get paid for it. I'm trying to decide now whether to go into senior management at the university, to continue what I'm doing, or to get out and form my own business. I never thought about my own business until we had the move. Already I've done a little work on my own: I helped raise money for the church. I think I could do it.

"It's hard to say what I'm proudest of in terms of accomplishments—certainly some work-related thing. Once I developed and staffed a committee from ground zero. I was very pleased about that, especially because I convinced one of the ultimate male chauvinists at the office that I could do it. And I'm proud of the friends that I've made.

"Sometimes I overcommit, it's true. But I can't stand to let things just stay there undone. You know those phrases about chiefs and Indians? I'm definitely a chief. I can't stand to be an Indian."

Karen is an example of a woman who considers herself to be on the "upper end" of ambivalence, but actually she has resolved her ambivalence and entered the transformation stage. This occurred when she moved and made the decision to accept the new job. She defines her future in terms of work, and in terms of non-home activities. Her self-confidence permits her to begin thinking about her own business. She perceives herself as a leader.

Unlike Elena, however, Karen has integrated the changes in her life both at work and at home. Elena clung to the status quo for some time—rebelling at home rather than facing her feelings, then moving out, but not too far away. She had to cut the strings of her environment for growth to occur. Karen, on the other hand, allowed her feelings to surface each step of the way. For her, workmutation was an experience that benefited her family and did not threaten its stability.

The work experience is a growth experience. The extent of this growth, and the process by which change occurs, depend on numerous variables, including the individual, the extent of outside validation, and the congruence of old and new perspectives. Whether or not the changes a woman experiences in workmutation are permanent is difficult to determine. We did not measure this in quantitative terms, but our interviews with women who worked and subsequently left the work force for ten years or more indicate strongly that the psychological changes we have been addressing may be tied to or dependent on the work environment—that if all other elements in her life remain equal but . she once again lacks the validation supplied by the job, a woman may return to her prior, often less aggressive, more domestically centered modes of behavior, or to the behaviors of models she was exposed to as a child. This was also true of men we talked to who left the work force for long periods of time—for example, men in role-reversal marriages.

This suggests that much of the process of workmutation has its foundation in group identification, rather than in any gender attribute or in an autonomous process that is triggered in internal isolation. People follow the pack they run in. This is human nature. One only has to look so far as our social dress codes—to the suits and ties that flood the business world —to see that it is the exceptional banker who wears jogging shoes in the office.

Working women are experiencing a new kind of group identification, and as long as their career snowball remains in motion, so will workmutation. The important point is that for the first time in centuries, women's environment is changing on a sufficiently widespread basis to foster changes in women themselves.

CHAPTER 5

The Pacesetters

The changes women are undergoing as a result of working outside the home are generating the emergence and rapid rise of a uniquely strong, aggressive, independent kind of woman, who constitutes a specific group we call the Pacesetters. The highest-income echelon of the Go-Getters, this is the fastest-growing group of all working women (increasing more than fourteen-fold since 1970),[1] and thus the fastest-growing group of *all* women. These are the women to watch, since they are prototypes of the women of the future, setting the trends of tomorrow. The Pacesetter holds the promise of a dominance and power never before held by American women.

The Pacesetters are working women, specifically those earning $20,000 a year and up. They are the best educated of all women; most are college-educated, and 30 percent hold postgraduate degrees, as opposed to only 6 percent of all working women and 4.5 percent of women in general. Clearly, education is a crucial factor in developing the behaviors and attitudes—and opportunities and role models that create them —typical of the Pacesetter. We found in our survey, for instance, that college-educated women are far more likely to be work- rather than home-oriented, ambitious, and goal-directed, and to have a positive image of women. Pacesetters have picked up these advantages with their degrees.

Pacesetters are the most competitive of all women, and are extremely determined individuals. Pacesetter women are, for instance, 61 percent more likely than women in general to say they play to win. Highly decisive, 59 percent of the Pacesetters say they feel strongly about making their own decisions, compared with 41 percent of all other women. And Pacesetters are twice as likely to feel they make those decisions quickly. Perhaps this is because the Pacesetter is clearly the most self-confident of all women, being less concerned with what others think and more concerned with exercising her own will. In fact, the Pacesetter woman is *two and a half times* as likely as women in general to feel she has a lot of self-confidence.

This self-confidence filters down to the most personal level, where the impact of the positive feedback from a job is strikingly evident. Pacesetter women feel better about themselves than other women. Compared to women in general, they are 73 percent more likely to feel they are good-looking, and two and a half times as likely to feel they are more intelligent than most people (50 percent vs. 19 percent).

Pacesetters are a highly motivated group, too: twice as likely to set long-range goals as other women, and almost twice as likely to feel they have ambitious goals (61 percent vs. 36 percent).

The Pacesetters foretell the shifting focus of women away from the home and into broader areas, where their influence is likely to be more strongly felt by society in general. Pacesetters are two and a half times more likely than women in general to feel strongly that a career is equally as important as being a good wife and mother (54 percent vs. 21 percent). This nondomestic focus is reflected in the day-to-day life of the Pacesetter, who is over *three times* more likely to feel strongly that outside activities take precedence over house-

keeping, far less likely to do the housework herself (39 percent vs. 64 percent), and *twice* as likely to disagree that a
woman's place is in the home! Pacesetters are not the type
to occupy themselves with the volunteer or charity work that
has filled the empty spaces in many women's lives for generations. Only 16 percent of the Pacesetters feel that they definitely should help those less fortunate, compared to 35
percent of women in general. This profile foreshadows a
nontraditional trend: Women will tend to allocate time previously spent with an at-home, family, or charitable focus to
broader areas–specifically, areas that offer this type of woman
a forum for exercising the competence, intelligence, and goal-
orientation that she perceives she possesses. The Pacesetter
woman is, and her heirs will continue to be, a seeker and a
doer, with a desire for measurable purpose. Already these
women are leaders, with most working in professional or
managerial jobs.

This orientation has taken a personal toll, but Pacesetters
are willing to accept the price. Pacesetters are the most likely
of all women to be separated or divorced. A full 25 percent
of this group are separated or divorced, compared with 9
percent of all women in general. Sex seems to be a major
trouble spot, since these women are 58 percent more likely
than all working women to feel their job hurts this intimate
part of their lives. According to Dr. Thomas Murphy, a
therapist, it's a jolting experience for many successful women
to discover that the responses they receive at work are not in
keeping with the responses they get from the men in their
lives. It's stressful to be treated as Ms. Capable at work and
then come home to be Good Old Mom, capable only of sort-
ing laundry. Dr. Murphy cites other conflicts arising from
ambition. For example, a bright, aggressive young legal secretary had a fiancé who was lounging his way through school
part-time, with no goals in mind. Her ambition was so inconsistent with his that it led to a breakup a month before

the marriage. "It's not just a matter of money," points out Dr. Murphy. "It's a matter of being able to feel good about yourself in relation to a man."

Pacesetter women set high standards for themselves and are less than satisfied if a man cannot at least meet, if not surpass, those standards. And men in relationships with Pacesetter women are probably more likely than any others to feel unsettled, competitive, or threatened by the relationship, because Pacesetters are the least traditional of all women, the least likely to fit into comfortable, cookie-cutter roles. As Dr. Roy Grinker, Jr., points out, "It's a terrible kick in the pants for the husbands of these women to realize that they don't have that hold on their wives that they had before —in terms of the wife being dependent on them. Dependent not only for money, but for pride, prestige, position, and self-esteem."

This does not necessarily mean that one cannot combine the goals and life-style of the Pacesetter with the values and roles of marriage, but it does indicate that traditional roles and values must be redefined for the woman of tomorrow and the men she interacts with.

Still, the Pacesetter is a happy woman, contradicting the myth of the "driven woman" who goes home to a life of discontent and raising cats. Pacesetters are, in fact, the most self-satisfied of all women, 55 percent more content with what they are and do than women in general.

It is important to point out that the driving nature of these women does not mean that they want to be like men, or will become like men. In spite of the best efforts of the "dress for success" movement, sexual differences will never disappear.

Although Pacesetters are the most ambitious women, it is interesting to note that our survey reveals that they are not motivated by power to any greater extent than working women in general—which is to say, they are not motivated by power. Instead, they pursue self-actualization and income, although perhaps to a magnified degree. On the other hand, the desire for power was and is a prime motivator for men. This in itself remains a key difference between the sexes. What the Pacesetter seeks is a desire to maximize her own potential as a woman in her own way. Will this hamper women's rise to power? Only if we assume that there are no variables in life, and that only one way is the right way.

The following three women are Pacesetters, and each exhibits this great motivation for self-actualization. Each is, in her own way, an achiever, a striver. None of these women fixates on power. But each has established ambitious goals, achieved professional success, and defined herself in unmistakable terms.

ELLEN: ROLE REVERSAL

In her mid-thirties, moppet-haired and intense, Ellen is a successful manager at a multimillion-dollar pharmaceutical company. Her husband of ten years is the successful manager of their comfortable, river-front home and three children. The couple view themselves as a team, and Ellen, with her powerful ambition, is playing to win.

As she tells it: "I've been a competitor ever since I was a baby, I think. It was born in me. My mother had show business in her blood from three generations, and she was bound and determined that one of us was going to be in show business somehow, by hook or by crook. So she trotted me and my sister around to all the studios and I started working on radio when I was three, so I was used to working and earning a little money from the time I was just a little kid. I was always ambitious. I danced while other kids played.

"But I realized early that to beat out my sister wasn't the be-all and end-all. My sister is a couple of years younger than me, and to this day, just winning and being better than me, the big sister, is all that would be important to her. But to me, beating her out was unimportant after I was about five years old. My sister is only one person. There are two billion people on this earth, and I'm going to tackle them all if I can.

"I think I can do it. Well, actually, I don't know if I can do it, but it gives me something to do to try. If I didn't try, what would I be thinking about in my spare time? It just keeps you busy for the sixty-five years you're here. It's a challenge. If I were running a race with my fourteen-year-old daughter, I'd try and win.

"The idea is to be number one. Although I'm sure I've been number five, twelve, one hundred and sixty. But, to me, being the best—not one of the best—is important. In my opinion, there's no other way, because nobody in America remembers number two. It is the winner, the clear winner, who stands out.

"Once you start a momentum, it's hard to stop. You can make your own life to a certain extent, and I try to do that. For instance, I trained myself to meet new people. Years ago, I used to hate to meet new people. The idea of meeting somebody I had not seen before was almost physically painful. So I decided, well, this can't be. So I trained myself to walk into a room and look right at the new person, and it actually became such a joy to meet and see new people that I'm usually the one that initiates it.

"I never did make it into show business. The closest I got was after college, my first marketing job at Max Factor in Hollywood. I was also a product manager at a cosmetics company and director of new products for a pantyhose company. All this started about ten years ago after my first husband died. After I married Bob, my husband. I was never a success in business until I met Bob. I was just drifting along. He became my role model, someone I could discuss my moves with. When I first left California, Bob and I sat down and reviewed all the pros and cons, what I wanted to do, what I didn't want. And he helped me clarify things in my mind. We made the decision for me to accept my first job, and all my jobs, together. So it's kind of like, it isn't me that's working for a company. When they hire me, they hire five people, our whole family. They get Bob thrown in, no question.

"When I was pregnant with my son, who is eight now, Bob had a nightclub. The club went down the drain, and Bob had to take every penny we had and try to save the business. And I was going to school, hanging loose because I was expecting the baby. And just as I was about to give birth, we literally had not a penny. My uncle came over and left five dollars on the kitchen sink for us. I mean, we were literally starving. Bob said, 'After you have the baby, the first one that gets a job feeds us.' So it just so happened that Bob got the first job and it was this lowly job—when you're hungry, you'll take anything. Anyhow, Bob got a job in this liquor store, and I went in there one day and he was wearing a tag that had his name on it, and I said, 'No, no way, I'll keep looking.' He didn't mind the job, but I did. It hurt me. It was awful. So I got the job at Max Factor and Bob quit and stayed at home with the kids. Actually, we both liked it better because I did not like staying home alone nights while Bob worked at the liquor store, and this gave us a chance to be together.

"So I started work and I was way down the ladder at Max Factor, the lowest of the low. I decided that if I had to spend eight to twelve hours a day in some hole, by God I was going to earn the most bucks per minute I could. And that's what still motivates me.

"I decided to get experience. There's no substitute for experience, not even education—although I am taking graduate courses now. I saw that experience counts. I saw women who had a lot of education and less than two years' experience versus women the same age with much less education and lots of experience, and the ones with the most education were not as sure of themselves. I could see that in myself. When I was just a small little staff assistant, I was more reticent, reluctant to put myself forward. And the higher up I got in business, the more I exercised my will—not only in business but in other situations. On the other side, I'm more tolerant of things now, because I understand more about the kinds of problems people encounter out in the world; I encounter them myself. It works both ways.

"When I was younger, I used to dream of this or that and work toward it, but I didn't learn how to express the goals and work for them until I got into business. Then I learned about putting goals down with timetables and working toward them and figuring out where you were lacking and heavying up in those areas.

"I've got this career path and I change it every six months or once a year, and it's a linear path. It started when I was at Max Factor, and I charted where I wanted to be and then I checked myself against it to see where I am. I had definite goals and I've reached each one. At this moment, I'm just about twice as far ahead as I figured I'd be monetarily. So I know where I am career-wise.

"Personally, my family and I are here together, so what could be better? Our domestic goals have been reached. I think the day I met Bob my domestic goals where reached. And when our baby daughter was born eight months ago, healthy and happy, we got 99.9 percent of what anybody could ever want.

"My goal now is to be free, not dependent on anyone. Things could change in my life—they have before. Change is the order of the universe. Now, if Bob were the breadwinner and something happened to him, there would be insurance and all, but I would have a major problem if I could not take care of myself—besides the fact that all the light would be gone from my life. But if I'm the breadwinner, theoretically the children wouldn't suffer as much because the dollars would still be coming in. I mean, I don't even want to think about it . . . but Bob is older than me; there's a big difference in our ages. So I'm secure because it's me who's the provider.

"What's security? What I hope for is to be free, and I guess that's the same as security. I don't like depending on somebody else's whims. That's my goal for the next twenty years—to have the wherewithal in terms of dollars so that nobody can threaten our roof. So I guess that's what I'm working for, but isn't everybody?

"For this reason, I admire Dolly Parton. Because she is relatively free, she is doing something delightful like making others happy. She's loved, talented, and she's exactly my age. I'd like to travel like she does, with my whole household. When I travel, it's alone. And what I dream about is being able to have Bob and the children with me, because now we can't afford it. So that's what I'd like. To encapsulate my world and take it with me for what I have to do. I guess that's selfish, but it's what I would like.

"I guess I'm not as free as I want. I'll never reach my goal. Because I'll always be dependent emotionally on Bob and the family. It works both ways. We need each other. The important thing is that we're together.

"Still, even though I do spend a lot of time with my children, and with Bob, too, I can plan that part of my life somewhat. I did it when I had the baby, eight months ago. I remember thinking to myself, 'Wouldn't it be interesting if somebody didn't let the actual physical birth interfere with their life?' And then events combined to make that test possible. Our local hospital didn't have the facilities for heavy anesthetic, so I had the baby by totally natural childbirth. So I was able to be up and around right away. And I thought,

'Wouldn't that be something, to see people's faces at work if I went back right away?' Which I did. I had the baby on Monday and was back in the office on Thursday.

"I see no difference between men and women mentally. I am smart. I know my IQ. I mean, you take the brain, you can't tell whether it's a male or female brain.

"How else do I see myself? Somewhat of a wave-maker. More so as time goes on. Recently at the airport this airline jerk grabbed my sample bag with lab samples and glass bottles in it and tried to make me check it through. I told him it contained glass, fragile samples, but he just told me, 'If it breaks, file a claim.' In the past I would have gone along with him, but not now, not me. I went straight to a telephone and called my company travel agent and had him write a complaint letter to the airline president about the irresponsibility and rudeness of the airline employees. I guess part of it is, no one would have cared if I wrote that letter ten years ago so I'd have been less likely to write it, to scream and yell. But now that I'm in a position to make waves, I get results. So I do."

In a stunning example of psychological role reversal, Ellen's husband Bob exhibits the characteristics of the domestically oriented woman, thus conforming to the theory that it is not so much the sex as the formative background and environment of an individual that brings out so-called stereotypical characteristics. Bob comments: "I'm more domestically oriented than Ellen will ever be. I'm family-oriented, had a big family as a child, grew up with brothers and sisters. I cooked in a restaurant during the Depression years because we needed money. So naturally I was really oriented to run a household. It just comes naturally to me. It's not that I was forced to do something I dislike. I happen to enjoy what I do. First, I'm with the children. These children are my life. Without the family I'd die.

"Ellen holds a job, a position, and I feel I'm part of it.

But I don't envy her. In fact sometimes I feel sorry for her. Because I have the children with me, we are together and we have a ball. My goal is for Ellen to be first woman president of the United States. I want her to go as far as she can.

"People are jealous of us," he says. "The women especially. They come over here and wonder how I can keep my home together. I've gone to their homes—they're messy. Women come over here just to see if they can ever find a glass in my kitchen sink, because I'm meticulous. And I always get the children off to school in the morning—I take care of them. And my wife has breakfast in bed every morning, because I feel she's entitled to it. That's the littlest thing I can do for her after what she's done for us. And every morning I take the baby in to her, and she feeds it, and then I give her breakfast in bed. And we have good food on little money. I know the butchers, and I clip coupons."

Ellen concludes, "You know, when I travel there's always some guy next to me who thinks he's sitting next to a housewife on her first trip. I don't say anything, but they sometimes ask. Usually they ask what my husband does. And I say, 'Nothing, he's a housewife.' And they ask how we live. And I tell them I work. And then there it goes. Oh, they make all kinds of comments and it's always 'Gosh, I wish I could do that.'

"I don't believe them one bit."

SUSAN: ENTREPRENEUR

Susan sits forward attentively behind the desk of her small office. Outside the door, a secretary is typing her correspondence. One or two not-too-antique antiques finish off the furnishings. Susan's gaze is direct, eyes never faltering. She seems strong and collected, planning her words carefully and speaking with force.

"I don't go out to compete against other people, but I do decide what I want to do and then I'll climb mountains to do it. One example is opening this law practice. Most of my friends and colleagues think it is completely bizarre to open your own law practice.

"I was with a fairly large firm of about seventy lawyers, and when I gave notice that I was leaving to work in a legal-services center the partner tried to dissuade me. He told me I was their star associate. I thanked him very kindly, but said that eventually I wanted to open my own practice and I felt the legal-services job would give me more general sorts of experiences in law that I would need when I was out on my own. And he carried on for at least forty-five minutes telling me how it was an insane thought to expect to go out on my own, especially for a woman, especially in a big city. And other people at the firm expressed their concern, saying that I didn't know what I was doing, that I didn't really want this, that I wouldn't be able to make it financially. It was a good firm to be associated with—I could see the salaries go up annually. And I knew that if I stayed there for six years I would be a partner, which is very prestigious and financially rewarding. And I considered all that. But having my own business was something I felt was more enjoyable. To me, it was the way to go.

"It's interesting, because I never really had any goals in terms of a career while I was in school. I never even thought about it, quite honestly. I just had a really good time in college, and did superbly well. In my family, it was just assumed you would go to college, and my mother had said it would make sense for me to get a teaching certificate, as she had done, so that's what I did. I did it because I never thought about it, and it didn't hurt me, and I didn't have anything else to do anyway.

"So I took the education courses and graduated in 1969. I taught for one year, then went back to graduate school in

Russia; I thought I would teach languages, I was going to get a Ph.D. But I found the course work uninteresting, so I decided to get out of that field entirely. About then I got married and my husband and I moved to the city, where I got a job with the department of Housing and Urban Development. I was there for two years, and I thought of going to law school, but decided against it because I was afraid I'd be a perpetual student. I decided to wait a few more years to make the final decision. So all the time I was with HUD, I wanted to go to law school. I looked around me, finally, and I asked myself, Do I want to be doing this thirty years from now? and the answer was clearly no. It wasn't challenging enough, it became very repetitive. I tried to think of what I might be doing, and I couldn't think of any jobs that I could have that I would want to be doing thirty years up the road. I decided there was one thing I would like—to be in business for myself—and law seemed like a good way to do that. I had an urge to be self-employed. I think you do better financially and it's more healthy mentally. Then I looked around and noticed that a lot of other women were starting to do things like going back to medical school or law school, and they were really enjoying themselves, so I said, 'Hey, why not me?'

"I had a friend who was a lawyer that I talked to about going to law school, and she said I would love it, especially the courtroom aspect. It helped to have someone like her to bounce the idea off of.

"I chose my law school based on the fact that I eventually wanted to open my own practice. I applied to four law schools and was accepted at all of them, but I picked a school with prestige and connections, one where the vast majority of the graduates stayed around and practiced locally, because that would give me ties with people in other firms, friends that would ship me cases.

"During law school, I kept my job with HUD the first year;

then the next year I clerked for a federal judge. The third year, I started part-time with a law firm that offered me a permanent job after graduation. Now I've had my own law practice for a year and I've been enjoying myself tremendously. And I've already calculated how much I figure I'll make, and it's a heck of a lot more than most people when they first go out on their own—in fact, things are looking rosier than I expected them to, in spite of the expenses of setting up an office.

"For me, my personal life to a large degree *is* being a lawyer and being available to my clients.

"I get up at 5:30 and take the 6:30 train into town, so I get to the office by 8:00. If I have a court call at 9:30 I have plenty of time to get things prepared, or to do work while it's quiet, before the phones start to ring. After my court call, I come back to the office, maybe dictate a few letters, probably see a client for a will or estate planning or an interview for a case. I almost always go out to lunch—I usually meet other lawyers. I do that consciously to make sure they remember me and send me business, because that's how I get most of my referrals. Or I'll meet a lawyer that I'm co-counseling with on a case. I co-counsel with specialists sometimes in order to do the best, most competent job possible. So that will be lunch. Most afternoons I am either at a closing or a meeting. I leave the office by 5:00 and take the 5:30 train home. My husband is usually at meetings two or three nights a week. On nights that he's home we eat out. We only eat at home about one night a week. I also have clients in the neighborhood, so often enough I'll make calls in the evening, or I might take the evening off and have dinner with friends. I try to forget work at night when I can, but I'm having some problems doing it. I find myself worrying about how to handle things. This is not productive, so I'm working on that—I don't want it to turn into craziness. The one time I can forget it is weekends. We have a cottage in the country, and we go up there and play cards and just sit around and relax. It's great. But on Sunday nights, driving back into the city, I find myself thinking about work again.

"I never came anywhere close to deciding to have children. My husband and I never discussed it when we got married. Although I suppose it was in the back of our minds. But then, we were only twenty-two, and at first we were too young. Not having children kind of evolved. Time went by and the time was never right. And then about five years ago we said, 'Let's get serious about this—is it something we're ever going to do or not?' I love kids, but I'm not willing to put in the time. I don't want to do a lousy job with the child, or on the other hand, give up any portion of the professionalism on the job for the kids. Kids are an immense time commitment. Even if you have a baby-sitter, you still have to take care of them from six in the evening till eleven or whatever—and all night for that matter, if the child is sick or something. It just has to take time, and I don't want to commit that piece of time out of my life. I told my husband that I would consider having children if he was willing to take care of them the majority of the time, and he's not interested in that at all. He was very up front about it and didn't expect me to have children. He understands why I wouldn't want to do it, because there's no way in hell that he would do it. I used to think that maybe I would decide not to have kids and then change my mind later, but now I can't imagine it. And I don't think I'll miss anything at all. For me, the die is cast.

"The fact that my career was gaining momentum definitely had something to do with my decision not to have children. As I got more serious about being in business and practicing law, and as I became more confident in my own abilities, saw myself doing things I'd never done before, I thought less and less about having kids or ever staying home, or even having an easy job.

"It certainly gives you more bargaining power in any relationship if you make a good deal of money. In my case, I'm the one that makes almost all the financial decisions. My husband is disinterested in those things. I invest in stocks. I bought silver when silver was down and sold when silver was up. I have bought several pieces of real estate and am in a real estate partnership. I handle all those financial transactions totally. And the fact that I do come out with quite a bit of money does affect my image of myself and what I should be doing.

"I didn't know at first whether I'd be good at business, but then I saw myself buying a piece of real estate and it was worth a lot more the next year, and I saw myself managing it and dealing with the tenants, and it gave me a good deal of self-confidence.

"I work for money, sure, but I want to do a type of work that is satisfying. I wouldn't start doing a type of law that was just run-of-the-mill, unexciting, same type of case, narrow specialty—even if I could make a fortune doing it. One of the reasons for having my own practice was to get both the money and the self-satisfaction together. The profit potential is greater on your own. I'm going to make more on my own than if I had stayed at the law firm and been a partner.

"I guess I'm a very self-oriented type of person. My husband always knew that, fortunately. I am in love with my husband, and we're pals, too, and I want to be with him. But as far as any kind of dependence, no. I could just as easily be on my own. I'm not tied to an institution of marriage in any way. My husband and I have even considered getting divorced for tax reasons.

"When I got married in '69, I remember it aggravated me to change my name and I told people that, but everybody laughed and said, 'Oh, everybody does it, you'll get used to it.' But it really bothered me a lot because I identified very strongly with my own name. So about two years after I got married, when I started hearing people were keeping their maiden names, I changed legally back to my maiden name. I think this probably bothered my husband a little bit, more than he will admit, mainly because his parents hassled him a lot. To this day, his parents refuse to call me anything. As far as they're concerned, I only have a first name. It's ridiculous. It's such an insult, so aggravating every time I see the address on a letter or package from them. Even my own mother refused to call me by my maiden name for a couple of years after I changed back to it. She thought it was improper. Then one day I was visiting her home and a distant cousin walked in and my mother introduced me by my married name. So I walked over and I shook his hand and I said, 'George, it's nice to meet you, my name is actually Susan Ivers, I am married, but I have my own name and my mother doesn't seem to understand that.' And he laughed, and my mother heard all this and was very embarrassed, and since then has acknowledged the fact that my name is Susan Ivers.

"My husband and I both live very career-oriented lives. He is village manager in our suburb and puts in a lot of time at night meetings, so he has no objection when I work later or entertain clients. He wouldn't even know what I was doing necessarily, because of his own work schedule.

"Let's just say, though, that I'm very glad I'm not married to a lawyer. We are in different fields, although to a certain extent they are complementary. He'll ask me certain legal questions from time to time, and I certainly call on him whenever I'm dealing with a city or municipality and have problems, because he has that expertise and can give me good information. We are not competitive. In the past, women used to look for men with big incomes who could support them. Now women like me look for men who are easygoing and who aren't going to make a scene when you make it big."

SALLIE: ALONE

I first met Sallie two years ago. An aggressive corporate manager with a large industrial manufacturing firm, she had been married six years to a quiet lawyer. Superficially, life seemed good for them. They had an adorable house complete with front-porch swing and shady backyard. Her career was taking off, and after a slow start, so was his. But something was off kilter. Sallie's voice had seemed a little too loud, her wisecracks too quick, her language too raw. Two years later, I interviewed Sallie again. She was divorced.

"I suppose that wasn't something that ever crossed my mind before—that you could just get so into a career that you could end up being alone," Sallie stated.

"I didn't want to take after my mother. She was your basic housewife, totally wrapped up with her house and children. She did have a small shop of her own for about two years when I was in high school, but she's been out of touch with the real world for about thirty years. And she simply cannot handle any kind of crisis. Mother is the kind of person who would panic if somebody showed up unexpectedly for dinner.

"Luckily it was somehow expected that I would go to work. After all, nobody wanted that expensive college education to go to waste. I got an M.B.A. in a five-year course. In those five years, I had to grow up and work. My working was totally accepted by my family.

"I married Bryan right after college. Initially he thought of me as a student—nice, young, and available. We had all the traditional expectations. My mother had taught me that husbands were supposed to give you your identity, that you were supposed to get everything you needed from your marriage or else something was wrong. I think those kinds of expectations are unfair, but it took me a long time to realize it. I married Bryan because he was the pinnacle of stability and predictability. He was perfect that way. But after a while he also became on the borderline of boring.

"I got a good job right after I got my M.B.A. I was in a corporate advertising department. Then they moved me to handling the print and broadcast portions of the agricultural equipment advertising for the company, which was one of the biggest in this area. I also worked on merchandising for new-product introductions and any crash projects that might come up. Basically, I acted like an account supervisor, working with products like farm tractors, manure spreaders, cotton pickers—harvesting and cultivating equipment. I loved it. I was twenty-three, just starting a career, and everything was new and marvelous and glowing.

"Meanwhile, my husband spent the first four years of our marriage in law school. He worked very late hours while he was in school. Four nights a week. And I worked till seven most nights. There was almost no time to be spent together just relaxing, conversing, doing anything other than cooking dinner, doing the dishes and laundry, cleaning the house. Life was a checklist. Conversation was reduced to 'This week it's your week to do the laundry.'

"After about four years I was doing well. I had increased my income till I was making over twice as much as when I started, and Bryan was very much aware that this was more than starting lawyers make. He began to get resentful, because he had been going to law school for four years at night and had also gotten an M.B.A. working nights two years before. So he had worked very, very hard for something that he wanted, and it did not seem to him that I had worked as hard for my success. He said that he knew I was capable of doing anything I wanted and all that stuff, but underneath I had the feeling that he thought I was some kind of token woman and had lucked out that way. I was paying the mortgage on the house we bought and he wasn't thrilled about that, either. The house was really my idea, but he went along with it, and then he refused to work on it, pay attention to the lawn or anything.

"Then Bryan had a terrible time finding a job. The market was very, very bad at the time for lawyers and he felt resentful about that—about the fact that he'd spent all his time and money, much more time and money than I had, preparing for a career. And I think he felt helpless that his wife had to support him. Here was a chance for him to do what he wanted to do and he couldn't find a job. After about six months, he was getting demoralized. There were days when he just wouldn't go out of the house or look for a job or do anything. And I began to resent it because he wouldn't get off his ass. I became upset because of being married to somebody who was supposed to be a provider and who was out of work. I also was upset because the fact that I was doing well seemed to be causing him discomfort. I thought the whole situation was unfair. I got much less tolerant of his problems with the role that a wife is supposed to play because, well, there I was working, then taking him to the train on weekends so he could go downtown to the law library, then coming back home and working on the laundry and cleaning. It caused a lot of problems between us.

"Finally Bryan got a good job with a law firm. But I was still making more money. And we didn't see each other too often because he started working till ten o'clock every night. The time factor became a problem. He was never home when I was, and I wasn't happy about it because we couldn't share things. He was totally involved in what he was doing.

"I started to think it was too constraining at home. I was used to making decisions on my own and doing what I wanted at work with a multimillion-dollar budget, and it was very difficult to come home, lose track of that, and become a basic housewife—I felt like a servant! I got used to dealing with men in an atmosphere where I was the only woman, and it was a matter of not taking any shit—not exactly putting men down, but becoming less traditionally 'feminine.' And that made me more independent, a little bit less tolerant, and tougher, too. Throw that image up against the role of housewife, and the two were totally contradictory. At work I was running various groups and responsible for various products, and my boss let me do what I wanted to do. I think it was a matter of the longer I worked, the more independent I became, and the more of an individual I was at work, the more respected for my mechanical knowledge, the more I resented coming home and having to lapse back into the traditional role patterns.

"Also, to be honest, I think being independent caused me to be less tolerant of merely having somebody else around twenty-four hours a day. I sort of wanted him there when I wanted him, and I wanted him to do what I wanted to do. After manipulating people all day at the office, I just wanted Bryan to do things without my having to manipulate him into it. You know—bat my eyelashes and fluff him up and maybe he'll mow the lawn.

"Even after he was doing well with his law firm, I think Bryan felt threatened. One time we were having a cocktail party and everybody from his office was there. I was doing the proper housewife routine, and everything was fine. Then somehow the subject of mechanics and machinery came up—which I know a lot about because of my job—and suddenly I was doing most of the talking. And I looked over and saw Bryan sitting very quietly in the corner.

"There was some talk between Bryan and me about having children, but the time just never seemed quite right. He had an admitted double standard about children. His attitude was, 'Of course we'll have children. I just won't be around.' And I'd say, 'What do you mean you'll work till nine at night while I handle kids? Do I look like a nanny?' If and when I decided to have children, I knew I'd have to be more than a homebody. I also knew that having children would be a big sacrifice. It was taking longer than I had expected to get what I wanted at work, and I was fighting harder. It was a very, very difficult place to be accepted and I was putting a lot of time and effort into that, and to stop and take time out to have children would have meant losing ground. And I knew my relationship with Bryan was having problems, and it seemed that children would have been an unnecessary complication. It didn't start out as a conscious decision, but after about four or five years of working it became conscious. Because after that time I was finally beginning to have credibility at work and I was finally going someplace and that became very important—especially compared to home, which really wasn't much to come back to. I'm very goal-oriented anyway, and that goal aspect became very important. It became more important than having children.

"Bryan and I were not together very much, as I said. So I got into things like upholstery and yoga and took classes at a local park district. I suppose my outside interests increased. But I couldn't get him to take classes or anything. The harder he worked, the fewer his outside interests were. Basically we ended up going out to dinner or to the movies on weekends and that was about it. I think we had very little in common.

"Another problem with the fact that we were so busy and preoccupied was that we became weekend lovers. And that is not exactly my cup of tea—scheduling sex in on weekends. I guess I wanted it more than he did. But then, if I became the aggressor during the week that intimidated Bryan all the more. His response was very direct: 'No.' And it happened more often because I was just becoming more aggressive in general. Bryan wasn't used to the woman being the aggressor. He felt emasculated and alienated by it. He thought a woman should be ready with the slinky nightgown when he was in the mood, or ready with the flannel robe when he wasn't. It became another point of very strong alienation between us.

Although in all fairness, I did not handle the situation very well. We probably should have seen a counselor. We never discussed it. It was a subject that just didn't come up. It wasn't something we felt we could talk about. The attitude was, 'If we ignore it, it will go away, it doesn't exist.' Until it drove me up a wall. What I did was a lot of sewing. Periodically I'd get rejected, and when I got rejected I'd get out of bed and go sew instead. I made a lot of clothes in that period of time.

"I think a big part of what went wrong was that I carried over my aggressive behavior. I became very, very skilled at getting my way at work. There were six product guys I worked with at the office, and I knew just how to make them do what needed to be done. But I couldn't pull that off at home. And if I tried to manipulate Bryan as I did people at work, either he turned off or I couldn't do it.

"Also, if you think that your husband will be the source of everything you need from your marriage, that when you have problems or frustrations he will alleviate the discomforts, you end up with a split personality—independent at work, emotionally dependent at home.

"I do think the independence at work carried over, and I became independent in my life-style. I'm not sure that financial and professional independence has done all that much for marriages. I think it causes acrimony, and also it probably lets you avoid some of the emotional issues instead of working things out. You say, 'OK, fine. I have an alternative. I'm independent. Screw you, I want a divorce.' If you didn't have that option, you might think about it longer.

"I think it was long-term exposure to being able to make my own judgments and do what I wanted that was finally the last straw. I found myself saying, 'I don't need to put up with this because financially I can take care of myself. Or at least be semi-solvent.'

"After the divorce, I changed jobs to make more money so

I could afford to keep the house. The house is important to me. It's about all I have right now. It's important for me to show people that even though my marriage didn't work out, I can still hold my life together.

"One of the repercussions about being completely on your own as I am now is that you're responsible for everything, good and bad. It's not so comfortable to think of being alone forever. You wake up at a point in time when you have to get up and face another week of work and a weekend with all this stuff to do around the house and there's no one to count on but yourself. I've never really been alone before. But I won't fall into what I did before—thinking that a relationship that's frustrating and inconsistent is better than nothing.

"Right now I'm taking refuge in my job. It's the one place where I can handle anything, where I'm sure of my decisions and what's expected of me.

"I used to say that what I wanted from a career was money and power, just like a man. Right now the money is fine, but I'm not as interested in power as I am in understanding the system, becoming acclimated, and mastering a whole new set of goals and job circumstances. Power isn't as important as mastering the learning curve right now. Once I master that, it'll be back to power. I want to be able to head the department in five years, but only if the head of the department has money and power. I don't have a lot of faith in large corporations. I think for a woman to succeed today she needs to start her own business. I think that's the best way to get to the top and learn things and have them the way you want. Part of the reason I made this job change is that it opens up another side of the business to me and will give me a good background for opening a consulting business. I will probably spend two years here and then go in the consulting business and be able to do what I want.

"Which is to write my own ticket."

As Sallie's story and the preceding two interviews indicate, the Pacesetter group is striking evidence of an undercurrent of new attitudes and behaviors among women. This group manifests, to an extreme, critical characteristics already broadly apparent in the Go-Getters.

The Pacesetters are a small segment now, consisting of only 2,305,000 women. But we can expect their rapid growth to continue as more women assume jobs that offer the responsibility, latitude, and income that delineates the Pacesetter group. As this group expands, it will not only be a powerful force in itself, but will provide additional role models for daughters and other women who will strive to emulate its members.

CHAPTER 6

The Catalysts

The Pacesetter group is destined to continue its rapid rise, leaving the Go-Getters in its wake, because of two key factors: education and opportunity. The widening of these gateways is spawning the new women and will continue to do so, in a self-perpetuating cycle, spurred on by the women themselves.

Education

College education is a critical factor for several reasons. First, it seems to prove a basic impetus or tendency to work. The more educated a woman is, the more likely she is to work and to possess drive, ambition, the capacity to set goals, and other characteristics essential to upward mobility and leadership capability. College provides a framework in which to develop skills necessary to these characteristics. A person is not born with such skills, and they are not sexual attributes. According to Sheila R. Coin, a management consultant specializing in leadership-effectiveness training, most leadership skills can be acquired, but "men are trained to present themselves in a certain way, and women have not had that advantage—culturally, by conditioning, or by socialization. That's not to say the necessary behaviors can't be acquired, because any of those behaviors are learned, and anybody can learn them."

College also appears to have a significant psychological impact on women, particularly Pacesetters, as evidenced by the attitudinal differences between women who are college-educated and those who are not. Our survey reveals that college-educated women are less domestically oriented, more self-confident and ambitious, more self-centered, more goal-oriented, and more likely to be found in the more upwardly mobile white-collar professional/technical areas:

	Percent of working women who agree	
	COLLEGE WOMEN	NONCOLLEGE WOMEN
• Outside activities come before keeping the house clean	35%	23%
• A woman's place is *not* in the home	63%	57%
• Men are *not* smarter than women	71%	58%
• My goals in life are quite ambitious	45%	37%
• Those who can should always help those less fortunate	29%	38%
• I don't know what I'll be doing in five years	33%	46%
• In five years I expect to be working	58%	46%
• I have children at home	58%	64%
• I work in a professional/technical job	41%	20%
• I work in a clerical job	34%	40%

Between 1960 and 1977, the number of women in college quadrupled.[1] And now, for the first time in history, the number of women enrolled in college exceeds the number of men.[2] According to the U.S. Census Bureau, there were 5.90 million women enrolled in college in 1979, compared with 5.48 million men. (There were 5.22 million men and 3.87 million women in 1962.) This includes a major increase among women over age thirty-five, who currently outnumber men of the same age in college by almost two to one.[3] Traditionally, this enrollment has been used to predict the future composition of the work force.

College for women is no longer simply a breeding ground for traditional "women's jobs" like teaching. Between 1966 and 1978, the number of women majoring in education dropped from one-third to one-eighth of all women students.[4] Women are now pursuing subjects that offer routes to industrial-based power—business and technology, for instance—to a greater degree than ever before. This is reflected in collegiate enrollment patterns. For instance, in 1975, 12 percent of women graduates of Harvard Business School had technical undergraduate degrees, compared with 32 percent of male graduates. Five years later, the women's percentage had increased to 15 percent. The Harvard Business School, which did not even admit women until 1963, is now 25 percent female.[5] The total number of women business majors quadrupled between 1966 and 1978, and women majoring in engineering increased sixfold.[6] Women are also making significant gains in the sciences, law, and other areas that were traditionally men's terrain.

There is also an upsurge of women in management-oriented education. According to the Department of Health, Education and Welfare, the number of M.B.A. degrees granted annually to women has risen tenfold in the past ten years, and is continuing to grow at a rate of 35 to 45 percent per year. In the early 1970s, women made up about 5 percent of all business school classes. Now that figure approaches 30 percent.[7]

A new and higher level of commitment, assertiveness, and excellence is surfacing among these female students, and is giving them an advantage over their male peers. Sheila R. Coin agrees: "The majority of younger, college-educated women have a new and different perspective towards their professional investment."

A recent article in the American Marketing Association's *Marketing News*, for instance, referred to a "revolution" in the quality of women marketing students, noting that often 70 percent or more of a course's top students are female.[8] Dean Richard Thain, director of placement for the University of Chicago's M.B.S. program, concurs: "I've observed, and many of my colleagues at other institutions have, too, that pound for pound, the women we have in our business schools seem better than the men. The [company] recruiters reinforce this, too. These women are more aggressive, better motivated, more dedicated. They've been self-selective so far—most who come to [graduate] business school tend to be those that are especially aware and well suited for it, whereas all kinds of men apply without being selective about it. So we're getting a greater proportion of women who are Phi Beta Kappas from splendid schools."

In the world of business—and the world of power—the rule has always been survival of the fittest. And women's attitudes, coupled with their natural abilities, are making them more fit. As Dean Thain concludes, "Young women are working hard— harder in many cases, *most* cases—than men. They know they *have* to work harder. The men are blasé; men think they know these things already, they can rely on their early role models—'Dad did it this way, and so will I.' Young women, on the other hand, are aggressively preparing themselves for the future."

Thain recalls several examples of his observations: student– faculty committee meetings, with equal numbers of men and women, that were dominated by the women, who were better prepared and had more pertinent things to say ("They were the better men, so to speak"), while the men "just sort of sat back in a lazy fashion"; an international student meeting in which the women crowded around the speakers, "once again" asking the majority of succinct questions, eager and excited, while the men were "more blasé."

Thain comments, "I suspect the men are worried in a way, because if they look at it in a competitive sense, I think they can see coming head to head against these women in a few more years."

Thain also notes an increase in women participating in pregraduation field internships, and increased activities involving women bonding together to form business-oriented groups that typically invite outside experts to speak on subjects relevant to potential managers. Activities such as these offer women valuable insights into the working world and expose them to role models at an earlier stage than was previously common. In one case at the University of Chicago, the faculty noted with interest that 70 percent of the sales of a book called *The Managers,* described as a prose model of the business world and the functions within it, were made to women.

The management consulting firm Heidrick and Struggles, Inc., went farther, and in its 1979 survey of female executives in America's 1,300 largest companies established a correlation between the degree of career continuity and the amount of education among female executives. Those without college degrees were three times as likely to interrupt their careers as those with degrees.

College degrees will continue to impact on the kind of work a woman does as well as the fact that she is employed. Ambitious, motivated, educated women are going to set their sights high, and will strive to make the most of themselves. While today the bulk of women in the working world hold some form of clerical or service position, the better-educated women of tomorrow will be far less likely than their predecessors to settle for stereotypical, dead-end jobs. A survey

by the National Commission on Working Women, for instance, showed that women with college degrees are far less
likely than those without degrees to have clerical jobs. But
if a college-educated woman does in fact hold a clerical job,
she is the most likely of all working women to be dissatisfied
with her job. Most such women also tend to view clerical
jobs not as a goal but as a means to a better end. "My goal
in life is not to be a secretary," said one young college-
educated secretary. "But it's a chance to get to know the
business, get in the door, then see where I'd like to be in
five years."

As more women become better-educated, they are going to
seek the natural outlets that allow them to best utilize their
training and capacities. Almost certainly this will result in
paid employment and all the attendant psychological and
socioeconomic ramifications. The snowball effect will only
increase.

New Dynamics, New Opportunities

The separation of the sexes into provider and nurturer roles
that locked women into a patriarchal system has traditionally
functioned not only on an overall societal level but also within
the microcosm of the white-collar world. This particular
world has become a significant indicator of any reallocation
of sexual power because it is not only the major growth area
in the labor force, swelling 213 percent in participant numbers since 1960, but also the foundation on which our economic strength is built. The white-collar sector of the work
force is expected to continue to grow at least until the end
of the century and probably far beyond, as we become ever
more cerebral and technological.

Traditionally, men held the power in the white-collar
world, which mirrored the patriarchal attitudes and behaviors

of society in general. This fact is reflected in the clustering of women into female "job ghettos," which are the repository of the housekeeping jobs of industry. For example, one-third of the total female work force is currently glutted in clerical jobs, forming 80 percent of that occupation as of 1979.[9]

The clerical sector is typical of an area that underwent a massive "feminization." In the nineteenth century, office work was male territory, with two or three men forming the core of most offices. Around the turn of the century, organizational growth outmoded the three-man office and spawned the professional functional or departmental manager, resulting in the office structure we know today. This change, plus the technology of the Industrial Revolution, permitted the large-scale influx of office machinery. From 1900 to 1920, bureaucratization and machine technology caused office employment to grow rapidly. The job structure changed. Clerical jobs increased drastically in number—but the opportunities changed, too. Men eased into the more mobile management positions, and women, who were lured to office jobs because they were available to them and because working conditions in offices were a haven from factory and farm, eased behind platoons of newly minted typewriters.

The development of the secretarial role became inextricably tied in with the feminization of the occupation. The most attractive secretarial jobs, for instance, were defined in terms of the secretary's relationship to a particular boss. The fewer bosses she had to work for, and the higher up they were on the hierarchical scale, the more prestigious her job. This led to the development of many facets of the secretarial role beyond the basics of typing, and to a situation in which domestic-type personal services like making coffee, tidying up the conference room, or buying the boss's wife his Christmas present brought out a paternalistic kind of male-female interplay that for many years set the tone for all women's office jobs. These jobs caused women minimal psychological conflict because they were usually a matter of absolute financial necessity, and also because the very nature of the job came to mimic the socially acceptable female role. Women office workers emphasized their femininity rather than their success, most frequently using their jobs as a stepping-stone to marriage. Secretarial schools trained candidates in job skills that included posture, grooming, dress, and conduct. Books and magazines of the time romanticized the clerical role, stressing desirable traits like courtesy, agreeableness, and sympathy. A new heroine emerged in the young white-collar woman whose job set the scene for a romance that would enable her to quit. Eventually, clerical workers became so feminized—and so paternalized—that a man needed only to refer to his "girl" for everyone in the office to know whom he was talking about.

Women have paid dearly for this feminization. Today's clerical wages are the lowest of any white-collar category. A U.S. Department of Labor Study showed that between 1977 and 1978 the percentage of the average secretarial raise was less than half that of other white-collar workers. And although women clericals outrank men in numbers, the few male clericals there are outrank the women in pay, with women earning only 63 cents for every dollar their male counterparts make.[10]

In short, the growth of the clerical field provided new opportunities for women outside the home—but the feminization of the field only served to reinforce the traditional role of women in relation to men. If the Office Revolution showed that women could work in the white-collar world, it also showed them their place.

This and other bottlenecks have kept women, even those with high qualifications, confined to "their" areas of the labor force—trapped in stereotypical occupations with low opportunity. The result was a directly adverse effect on women's ambitions. As Dean Thain put it, "Why would a woman torture herself going every night for three years to an evening M.B.A. program only to remain what she was before—an executive assistant to somebody at best? It just wasn't worth the candle. In banking, for example, it used to be that I didn't know any women who became vice presidents of banks [Thain has helped place more than 4,500 students in the past fifteen years]. They all stopped at this mysterious thing called "executive assistant"—sort of a glorified secretary, really—and many of these women had college degrees from notable undergraduate schools. If a woman didn't have a college degree, she was a stenographer. But now I think one reason our evening school, for instance, has at least as many women as men entering classes is because women in places like these banks are being given a chance; they are scenting the chance to move ahead."

"Women have a sense that change is possible," agrees Ann Ladky, a representative of Women Employed, a thousand-member organization concerned with fair employment policies and career education for clerical and professional women. She elaborates, "The expectations we see are so different from those of women five years ago in terms of what their opportunities are like. Women have a much stronger sense of what they deserve and the opportunities they ought to have. Secretaries, for example, have been successful in organizing committees in their offices. They'll have meetings or group lunches to talk about their problems in the office. We put on a number of career decision-making seminars for secretaries, and women usually will come up and say that they have new ideas on how to present their skills—how to ask for something better, whether it's in or out of secretarial work.

"We also see a huge number of successful women going out on their own. If they can't get into management in companies which trained them, they do not allow themselves to be content with this situation."

She adds, "When you're in a job—as so many women are and traditionally have been—in which your contribution is not valued or ambition not rewarded, it can have an extremely debilitating effect."

In the past, saying that opportunities were increasing for clerical women would have been like proclaiming new hope for the dead. This is no longer the case. Now women in clerical jobs have chances to earn high salaries, gain additional responsibility, and move horizontally and vertically within the organization.

Jim Wildhaber, vice president of the Word Processing Management Association, points out a major change. "Secretaries are no longer paid or evaluated according to whom they work for," he says. "Today's secretaries are evaluated on their own merit, a move away from the Dark Ages approach we used to commonly see." Wildhaber admits that this is still more likely to be true in larger organizations, but stresses that it is the trend. It leads to a new mobility within the field. Today secretaries in a large corporation can move to the top of the salary scale and job classification list in two years if their work merits it. And, Wildhaber notes, at major corporations this can mean a salary of $21,000.

Technological and organizational changes within the word processing field are also creating opportunities where once there was little hope. Movements toward the paperless office, which can mean each person operating an individual keyboard unit with video screen, could virtually eliminate the typing function. Team organization of word processing work has also contributed to new opportunities within the field. This approach removes the paternalistic, one-on-one, "boss-secretary" approach and provides a hierarchy within which advancement can occur. And a growing trend beyond word processing toward *information* processing allows increased cross-communication for those involved and opens access to the data processing area, once a closed province.

The perception of opportunity is psychologically as important as actual presence of opportunity in affecting any individual's mobility in a power structure—regardless of sex. For example, studies among automobile workers in the fifties documented the fact that they had low aspirations or hopes for promotion in response to the fact that realistically there *were* few such opportunities.[11]

A correlation has been observed between motivations and expectations. In her in-depth study of the dynamics of corporate power, *Men and Women of the Corporation,* Rosabeth Moss Kanter suggests that opportunity is a self-rewarding, self-perpetuating commodity, with those in possession of opportunity induced to behave in ways that would generate still further opportunity, and vice versa.[12] Workers with blocked opportunity exhibited lack of job commitment, social isolation, personal stress, ineffectuality as leaders, and a loss of desire for upward mobility.[13] When shut out of opportunity, workers often responded in a defensive manner by building their own alternative reward systems instead of seeking promotion. This involved tactics such as establishing social cliques that put pressure on members to stick with the group ("If I got promoted, I couldn't work with my friends anymore") and denying desire to leave the dead-end situation ("You'd have to be crazy to want the headaches that go with that job!").[14]

One of the reasons why women have been absent from leadership is no doubt linked to this vicious circle, which is not predicated on sex, but which may have contributed to a negative stereotype for women. Men faced with low opportunity exhibit many traits commonly associated with female stereotypes: limiting of ambitions; seeking satisfaction off the job; interrupting of careers; valuing social relationships above other aspects of the job.[15]

The impact of opportunity as it relates to white-collar work is evident in our survey, in which blue-collar respondents had far more negative perceptions of themselves and their role in life and on the job than white-collar women. With the white-collar segment expanding more rapidly, both in numbers and opportunities for women, more and more women will reap the motivating psychological benefits of white-collar employment.

For instance, respondents with blue-collar jobs were more likely to feel they lacked opportunity in general than those in white-collar jobs: 40 percent of the blue-collar women we surveyed said they felt trapped in dead-end jobs, versus only 25 percent of women in white-collar positions. Blue-collar women viewed both themselves and their jobs far more negatively than white-collar women. The blue-collar women are less likely to look forward to going to work. They're significantly less committed to their job: Only 36 percent expect to still be working in five years, as opposed to 55 percent of their white-collar counterparts, and only 39 percent consider their jobs to be long-term careers, versus 59 percent of white-collar women. Blue-collar women are also less likely to feel they are ambitious and to view their jobs as interesting. The impact ripples across the board, since blue-collar women carry their problems home with them; they are more likely to see their jobs as having negative effects on their home life and on personal relationships with the men in their lives.

In the white-collar world, more women than ever before are joining their companies as managers or as participants in management training programs, rather than taking the clerical jobs that trapped them in the past. Heidrick and Struggles, Inc., found that in 1978 two-thirds of the executive women they surveyed reported having begun their association with their employer in clerical jobs. One year later clerical work as an entry path was reported by 57 percent of the women surveyed.[16] The younger women were also less likely to have begun their careers in clerical positions. In 1978 Heidrick and Struggles, Inc., also found that 84 percent of the women surveyed who were fifty years old or older had begun their current career associations in clerical jobs. This was true of 65 percent of women age forty to forty-nine. And of those under forty, only a minority had begun in clerical jobs.[17] This foreshadows upward mobility for women in industry, and a new breed of role models for women in general.

Helen J. McLane, author of *Selecting, Developing, and Retaining Women Executives: A Corporate Strategy for the Eighties,* points out that traditionally it can take an individual twenty-five years to develop into a chief executive officer. Right now, the movement of women into such superpower positions and even the echelons immediately below is slow because, among other reasons, at such levels a talent pool of women simply does not exist. Twenty-five years ago women lacked the opportunity and education to move into the mainstream, which would have permitted them to compete for such positions today.

But twenty-five years from today the situation will be radically different. Already there is proof of the expansion of the female talent pool in the white-collar world. In their 1979 survey of executive women, Heidrick and Struggles, Inc., reports that the proportion of women brought in from the outside to assume officerships is rapidly increasing. In 1978, 90 percent of the women officers they surveyed gained their positions through promotion. One year later this had dropped to 76 percent.[18]

Largely because of this growing pool of qualified women, the U.S. Department of Labor predicts a 21 percent increase in the number of female managers and administrators by 1985.[19]

The result of all this is a synergistic snowball, in which changing attitudes and role models motivate women to seek higher education, which in turn impacts on their attitudes and motivations still further to steer them toward aggressive participation in the white-collar working world. They will enter this world with psychological and behavioral equipment that prepares them to take unique advantage of any available opportunities—or forge new opportunities when necessary through their own initiative to provide self-fulfillment.

On the horizon looms heavier competition for top jobs, as the work-oriented, aggressive Pacesetter group becomes larger and ever more qualified. Men have not had to face the sheer numbers of such competition previously in history. Life-style studies show that in general men are becoming less job-oriented, more personally-oriented and leisure-directed; they are retiring earlier and staying in school longer. Even high-powered executives have been found to show a preference for shorter hours rather than higher pay, and to be seeking more fulfillment from families, hobbies, and outside activities.[20] So far in this century, the average number of hours worked in a week by men dropped from sixty to forty.[21] It is highly conceivable, then, that men seeking top-level positions will be overtaken or bypassed by the Pacesetter women, who could be in a position to gain corporate control within the next twenty-five years.

CHAPTER 7

Like Mother, Like Daughter

INTERVIEWER TO WORKING WOMAN (PART-TIME CLERK/TYP-IST): Has your daughter ever said anything that led you to believe she could be interested in following in your footsteps?

WOMAN: Oh, definitely. She believes in raising her children like I do. That is why she's becoming a pharmacist, hoping that when she gets married and has children she will be able to be home with them and then work on the side if necessary.

INTERVIEWER: How do you feel about this?

WOMAN: I think it's excellent. A wonderful idea.

INTERVIEWER TO WORKING WOMAN (TRUCK DRIVER): Has your daughter ever done anything that might lead you to think she'll do what you do?

WOMAN: Just the truck driving. It's something that looks glamorous to her right now. She likes the CBs, she gets into talking with other truckers once in a while, and she thinks that's really neat. Of course she's only twelve.

INTERVIEWER: Well, how would you feel about it if she actually became a truck driver?

WOMAN: I wouldn't mind—as long as she carried a crowbar in case the truck broke down.

INTERVIEWER TO WORKING WOMAN (AMBITIOUS $20,000-PLUS OFFICE MANAGER): Do you encourage your daughters to share your attitudes about working?

WOMAN: You bet I do. I have one daughter who is eighteen, and she's been working full-time since she was sixteen and graduated early from high school. It was her decision, but I insist that they all be independent. And I make it known that life is not always going to pave their way. They will have to pave their own. I think it's important that they think about a career and pursue a career. My daughters have really always admired me and are very open in their admiration, and they just think that they ought to try the same things. Of course, I point out that they have a lot more opportunity open to them than I did at their age.

INTERVIEWER TO HOUSEWIFE: Do you encourage your daughters to share your attitudes about not working?

WOMAN: No, I don't say anything. I just let them know that some mamas work and some mamas don't. I try not to set any value judgments for them. All I do is encourage them in what they want to do. I'll say, "You can be anything you want."

INTERVIEWER: Have your daughters ever said anything that might make you think they will be like you?

WOMAN: Well, they ask for little babies and play mama a lot. We've got lots of little baby dolls and they like to dress and feed them, that kind of thing. But they've never said they want to be a mama. Right now I don't think I'm influencing my daughters one way or another.

One of the most compelling reasons why women are predestined to work outside the home and to continue to develop accompanying aggressive, independent, tradition-breaking attitudes is the fact that, as young girls, they will identify with and emulate their mothers, who in increasing numbers will join the work force.

Our role models help define our self-images. As young children, we try to mimic—and later, we incorporate—various qualities in individuals we respond to. At first this process is conscious. Later it may or may not be unconscious. As adults, more often than not, our behaviors have moved from conscious to internalized responses of which we may not even be aware.

Women tend to mirror their mothers' basic notions about themselves and their roles as women. As the number of women in the labor force multiplies, they will provide, for the first time, a major group of non-stereotypical maternal role models for their daughters. This will reinforce the growth of the attributes and attitudes of those role models in the next generation of women.

According to Dr. Roy Grinker, Jr., no role model is more significant to a woman than her mother. "There's no question at all," he stresses, "that in all women the first and primary identification is with the mother, the primary role model is the mother, and the primary ideal woman is the mother. Twenty or thirty years or more after childhood, the water has become very muddied because there have been so many other influences on a woman. But the mother is *still* her primary influence."

Many women do not consciously realize that their mothers provided their role models. Indeed, many deny it. One woman remarked, "My mother and I are nothing alike. In fact, we do not get along at all. *We are both so stubborn,* we fight every time we get together."

Another woman, very active and energetic, claimed that

since she worked and her mother never did, her mother obviously was not the person she emulated. She went on to describe her mother's "nonworking" life as a farm wife, which involved chopping cotton, fertilizing fields, making all clothing for the family (starting out by dyeing or bleaching old sheets for fabric), growing, collecting, and canning all vegetables and fruits eaten by the family, and preparing meals for a family of eight.

This pattern of unacknowledged or unconscious similarity occurs again and again, which does not surprise psychiatric experts. Dr. Grinker explains that women are unaware of their mothers' function as a role model "because they probably *need* to be unaware. It's embarrassing and awkward to say to yourself 'Yes, I want to be just like my mother.' That has a kind of dependent, infantile quality. So that in searching for role models and then modeling themselves after them, women—*all* of us—are much more comfortable to have it be on an unconscious level."

But our survey indicates that a woman's decision to work, her attitudes toward work, her choice of a career, and her propensity for success are directly traceable to her mother's influence.

Daughters of working mothers are more likely to work themselves, and to comfortably perceive themselves as working women. A woman whose mother worked is 11 percent more likely to be employed than a daughter of a nonworking mother. And daughters of working mothers are 31 percent more likely to say they always thought they would work outside the home. Among nonworking women, daughters of mothers who worked are the most malcontented of housewives, expressing the greatest dissatisfaction with their situation in life and often planning for a future that includes a job.

"Oh, I'm going to work," said Carla, who is typical of such women. The young mother of two preschoolers, Carla temporarily has sidelined having a job until her children are both in school, but her future career in mental health education is meticulously mapped out. In fact, she had just received her junior college diploma the day before our conversation.

"I'm taking courses now," Carla pointed out proudly. "And in just two more years I'll be able to start the kind of work I want to be doing."

Carla spoke with great eagerness and impatience, claiming bluntly that she was underutilizing her resources and was capable of far more than she is actually doing. She traced her feelings about work to her mother. Because Carla has very strong impressions of her mother's *enjoyment* of work, she herself sees it as something pleasurable. "Mommy worked three days a week at a nursery school, and Saturdays she worked at a local winery, passing out samples to tour groups. I know she enjoyed her work, *really* enjoyed it, because she used to come home and talk about all the fun she had working with her friends. Also, she stayed at those jobs for years. She would never have done that if she hadn't liked it."

Carla's mother encouraged her to share her attitudes. "She encouraged me to be independent, to go for what I wanted," Carla said.

And Carla has done so. Even as a young girl, she busied herself with some kind of work. At first her jobs were simple household chores like folding laundry. By the time she was twelve, she had a steady baby-sitting job. "And then, by the time I was sixteen, I was really independent, and was I a good worker," she laughs. "Because when I was fourteen, I lied about my age and got a job in a hat shop!"

Carla did not need the money at the time she got the job in the hat shop. Imagine the kind of motivation a young girl must have had fifteen years ago to lie about her age in order to have the opportunity to work.

Obviously, she still has that kind of motivation.

Though Carla is devoted to her family, she keeps a firmly directed eye toward the day when she will have a full-time job again. Meanwhile she's being flexible, using her time to the best advantage, as a means to make her end goal so much the better. She's a woman with plans, objectives, and places to go.

"I'm the only woman in my family who's gone to college," Carla states. "My mother never did, although she wanted to and still talks about it." Because of her young family, it has taken Carla six tough, determined years to find the time to get her junior college diploma. But she has done it. And she is moving steadily, if slowly, toward her dream job. She told me, "If it takes me ten years, I'll get my college degree—and that job in mental health."

We can speculate that the daughters of today's large group of working mothers will also harbor this strong tendency to join the work force, and to be less than satisfied if they do not have jobs. The trend is already emerging, and our survey shows that younger women are more likely to have had working mothers.

The mother's job provides a young girl with a career to idealize, and often she grows up to choose work herself—not unusually in a related field. Lea, for instance, a college-educated secretary aged twenty-five, mentioned that her mother had worked as a bank teller and a secretary to the clerk of the local county courthouse. She described her mother as "an aggressive, fast-paced, efficient person who likes to get things done and keep busy," and she added, "I think that since my mother worked all her life, the idea was kind of built in. I've got two sisters, and that's been built into all our minds. Both of them work: One is a secretary and one works at the bank—the same bank where my mother worked while we were growing up.

"When we were all younger, my mother would take us to the bank, and she'd introduce us to her coworkers and some of the upper-level managers, and that was how we'd spend a whole day. We'd go in and talk to everybody, and she'd show us the books she kept and her typing and the offices; then we'd go shopping together afterward. It was really fun. I liked what my mom did because it was something I could see myself doing.

"I don't really feel like I want to be a secretary all my life, though. I want something more of a career goal to work toward. Right now, I'm checking into a school where I could go part-time to take courses toward paralegal work. I doubt if I would ever reach law school, but this would be like a stepping-stone, to check it out and see how I like it and go from there.

"Whatever I do, I work hard. I'm like my mother that way. I wouldn't feel deserving of the paycheck otherwise, and I wouldn't be fulfilling my mind. I think I'll be working most of my life. Otherwise I'd be bored stiff with nothing to do."

The mother-daughter connection also holds strong in the area of career choice. Blue-collar mothers tend to raise blue-collar daughters, and daughters of white-collar mothers cluster heavily in white-collar jobs. (See the table "Like Mother, Like Daughter" on page 156.) Of working women whose mothers worked, 54 percent of blue-collar women have mothers who worked in blue-collar jobs, while only 37 percent of white-collar women have mothers in blue-collar jobs. Conversely, 62 percent of white-collar women have white-collar mothers, in contrast to 46 percent of blue-collar women.

This is important because it indicates that increasing numbers of women will seek white-collar jobs. Since the bulk of working women hold white-collar jobs, and since this is not just the most rapid growth area in the labor force but also the one that imparts the most positive psychological benefits to women, we can expect to see a mushrooming of women in white-collar fields and a synergy of the positive reinforcement that this kind of employment can provide.

The mothers' employment also seems to have had a strong

influence on working daughters' levels of job commitment. Daughters of working mothers are more likely to have long-term commitments to their jobs than daughters of their non-working counterparts: More than half (52 percent) of all the women surveyed who were planning long-term careers had mothers who worked. On the other hand, working daughters of nonworking mothers appear to be the least comfortable with the notion of having a career: Two-thirds of those who planned to quit within the next five years had nonworking mothers. This suggests that daughters of today's working mothers are more likely not only to seek a career but to stick with it.

Working mothers bestow a legacy of independence, self-confidence, and nondomestic orientation upon their daughters, who are 26 percent more likely to feel they are independent than are daughters of nonemployed women. They are 67 percent more likely to feel they have a lot of self-confidence. And they are more likely to feel that a woman's place is not in the home. Not surprisingly, a working mother is the most apt of all women to produce a Go-Getter daughter: Women whose mothers worked are 23 percent more likely to be Go-Getters than daughters of nonworking women.

Rachel, who holds two jobs, is a typical ambitious working woman who incorporates her mother's highly positive career attitudes. Although there were five children in the family and most of the women in the community did not work, Rachel's mother had a job. "When I was a kid in the forties and fifties she was very active," Rachel recalls. "She was very energetic, very involved. She's got an alert mind and she's really an admirable woman. At seventy, my mother is still working full-time, and she's on the local school board, too."

Rachel has always admired her mother's independence.

"Not just financial independence," she points out. "Independence of another person. She's very close to my father, but she's not dependent on him."

Through her mother, Rachel sensed the rewards of work. "Mother loved being with people," she says. "She loved doing something besides talking baby talk and changing diapers. She couldn't have been enthusiastic about her job if she didn't enjoy what she was doing."

Rachel's mother also projected the image of a job as an element of self-esteem, and Rachel remembers this with pride. "She always talked about the progress she made on the job, and she received very regular raises and commendations. She worked in the office of a lumber mill as an invoicing clerk, and while she was there she also learned how to run the switchboard and did all kinds of odds and ends. Actually, she was a pretty indispensable part of the staff."

Rachel admits that her mother had a strong effect on her own career path. "I started taking different courses in high school with the one thought that I would eventually work. And, of course, I started working right after high school, and my goals have always been very similar to my mother's. I wanted to achieve and wanted to make the most of myself as well as my time. That is a direct result from her. I've never been content to stay home and change diapers, either."

Although Rachel admits she felt certain twinges of resentment when her mother was busy or preoccupied with her work, far more significant were the good feelings her mother instilled in her about herself: "She instilled this in all of us— that we were the most mentally gifted people. But when we fell short of a goal, she never criticized. Instead, she was very positive about it, because we had tried."

Through her own career, Rachel feels that she is living up to her mother's philosophy. "I think that Mother's influence produced a refusal to be satisfied with having nothing—and if you were dissatisfied, you could go out and do something

about it. In order to change things, you had to get off your
lazy duff and do something." Rachel herself has ambitious
financial goals, and she is "doing something" about it, working two jobs—as an office manager for the Department of
Labor and as a part-time secretary.

"I'm so much like my mother, it used to distress me when I
was younger," she admits. "I could see characteristics coming
out that were so much like her, and at that time I did not
want to be like her! I was afraid I would have to compete
and I would not measure up."

The conflict ended after Rachel and her mother actually
worked together, jointly opening a telephone answering and
secretarial service. "Working together every day, we formed
a very unique and very close working relationship," Rachel
says. "At the end of the year, my husband was transferred
and we had to dissolve the business. My mother made a re-
mark then that has always stuck with me. She said to me, 'Of
all the people I know, you're the one person I like working
with best.'

"Then I knew I didn't have to compete with her anymore.
I was an equal."

A woman's managerial tendencies, like her propensity to
work, are closely tied to her mother's work situation. Our
survey revealed that working women whose mothers worked
have greater expectations, ambitions, and confidence in their
abilities as managers than women whose mothers were
housewives. A woman whose mother worked outside the
home was 22 percent more likely to feel she would make a
good supervisor. And she was 43 percent more likely to feel
she had room to advance on the job.

There is a popular theory that successful managerial
women, having been raised by traditional, nonworking mothers, are more likely to have followed the role model provided by their working fathers. Our survey, however, revealed
that in fact the opposite is true. Of the "managerial" women

earning $20,000 or more a year who were included in our survey, only 14 percent chose male role models. The majority who named role models chose female ones, usually the mother. Managerial women are indeed most strongly influenced by their mothers, as indicated by the fact that 61 percent of the managerial women in our survey had working mothers, compared with only 47 percent of all working women in general. The father, whether he worked or not, did not impact on these women's career choices or attitudes at all. One key to a woman's propensity toward managerial capacities appears to be the kind of career followed by the mother. (See the table "Like Mother, Like Daughter" on page 156.) Thirty-two percent of the managerial women in our survey had mothers who worked in *professional/technical* occupations—as opposed to only 19 percent of the nonmanagerial women surveyed.

Commenting on this fact, Dr. Grinker points out that role modeling has again come into play. "These particular women probably saw their mothers getting a lot of gratification from their jobs," he says. "They saw their mothers not just working, but enjoying their jobs. Having such positive identificatory figures probably led to these women developing better attitudes about themselves as working women, which, in turn, could make them more likely to succeed on the job." He adds, "If a mother is positive about her working, "the daughter will identify with the mother as a positive person who works and also as a person who enjoys her work and has a positive attitude about the working world. Just as a woman who is happy with her femininity tends to produce a more feminine daughter, a woman who is happy with her work tends to produce a daughter who values work."

How a woman reacts toward her daughter is also important in the formulation of the daughter's attitudes about work. "So much is determined not by work opportunities or by a woman's relationship with her husband, but by her own relationship to her role model—her mother's attitude about her. Is her attitude that a woman is good only for bearing babies? Does she see herself only as a housewife? And how does she see her daughter's ultimate aspirations when the daughter is a little girl, growing up?" Today's mothers are more likely to see those aspirations as reaching beyond the hearth and home. We found that 51 percent of all nonworking women said they want their daughters to work outside the home, and working women are even more supportive of this idea, with 61 percent agreeing that they would like their daughters to work.

"Self-fulfillment is a double-edeged issue," warns Dr. Grinker. "One edge is the very beneficial emancipated role of women, and their search to achieve their greatest personal potential. But the other is a kind of narcissistic quality which says that self-fulfillment is the most important thing in the world and the devil may care in regard to others—in this case, the child's needs. That's the kind of attitude which leaves the child not only deprived of the mother but aware that she isn't cared as much about by the mothering figure as the mother cares about herself. And that could cause resentment that then would lead such a child to grow up to hate the notion of a working mother—or even a working woman."

Sometimes a mother's eager involvement with her work can backfire. For example, if a mother feels very positive about work but the daughter feels neglected or unloved, possibly because the mother is too busy with her job to give adequate time or attention to the child, the daughter will pick up ambivalent cues about herself. As Dr. Grinker explains it, "The child may feel that work is good but being a wife and having children is bad. Or, if she takes it to the next step, she might think, 'Mother works *because I* am bad.'" When this happens, the daughter reacts with a very negative identification toward the working world. If she marries and has children, she often has the notion that she would never work and subject the children to the psychological trauma she herself experienced. In such a case, the fact that her mother might actually have enjoyed working is not enough to overcome the daughter's own ambivalence.

Sharon, for instance, chooses not to work outside the home, mainly because she resented her mother's career. Sharon worked for about six years, before the birth of her children, as a teacher. When the children were born, she retired—permanently. This is quite the opposite of the course taken by her own mother, who could not resist the lure of a career. "She felt she needed work," Sharon explained. "Every couple of years she'd stay home—but then she'd get another job. She hated housework, found no joy in it. She just had no outlet when she was home."

Sharon's mother never finished high school. She worked in a factory and at an automobile plant. Eventually, she trained as a beautician and became licensed by the state to run her own shop. Sharon remembers her mother's excitement in finding a job she liked. "The only thing she wanted was to be a beautician. That was her goal, and she trained for it and succeeded at it. It was fulfilling to her, you could see that. Because when she wasn't working she became very depressed, and when she went to work you could see the difference. Her whole being was completely different. You knew that she was doing something she felt was useful, and she was being successful."

But her mother's enthusiasm toward work produced the opposite feelings in Sharon. Unspoken but definitely felt was the question, "If my mother only cared about being a beautician—where did I fit in?"

Sharon's feelings emerged when she was young. She remembers specifically how much she hated doing the housework that her mother did not have time for. "I resented it," she admits. "Other girls my age would just have little chores, like doing the dishes. But since my mother worked, my sister and I had to clean the whole house! And when my mother said 'Clean the house,' she meant *clean* it! Not that I was a child slave or anything . . . but I did miss out on having fun with my friends sometimes." Sharon also vividly recalls that her mother was usually too busy to drive her to the activities in town or to after-school events.

The highlight of Sharon's childhood was one year her mother did not work. "She quit for a year when I was in sixth grade, and I loved it," Sharon remembers. "That was fantastic because she was home, and when I walked home from school she would always be there. That was my time to be with her by myself."

Sharon enjoyed her own teaching job until she herself had children. Then her childhood reactions to her mother's career surfaced, and she quit work. "If someone likes to work and can handle a job and a family, fine. My feeling is that I can't," she says. "I decided that I would not work, at least until my children are all in school—and then possibly only part-time. Not that I want my children to be totally dependent on me, but I want them to feel that I'm there."

Sharon likes being on call to make cookies or attend PTA teas. "I enjoy being needed, and I feel they enjoy saying 'My mom will do this, my mom is there to help me.' I just think that's important." The morning of our conversation, Sharon had dashed off to her son's school on half an hour's notice to watch him receive an award. "Now, if I was working I would have missed that award," she said. "I can always go back to work. But I couldn't see him get that award again." When feelings like these outweigh positive feelings toward work, a woman will usually choose to stay at home, if she can afford to do so financially.

Much of what happens to women in the future depends on how today's working mothers interact with their daughters. If this research can be used as a model, these daughters will probably view work in a positive light and become more dynamic, independent, career-oriented individuals as a result. Other recent studies of daughters of working mothers also confirm that these daughters exhibit an expanded image of their potential and increased self-esteem, perceiving women's roles as less traditionally restricted and a job as less threatening to marriage. They have also been found to have greater self-esteem than daughters of housewives; greater respect for women; and higher aspirations for education, career, and achievement in general.[1] But even if for some reason there is a backlash, and some women do not move into the work force because of negative identifications with the role model of the working woman, economic necessity will probably push them into jobs, where they will experience workmutation and absorb new attitudes and behaviors—and their daughters, in turn, will become the beneficiaries and keep the whole process in motion.

Daughters of women who work outside the home are going

Like Mother, Like Daughter

BLUE-COLLAR WOMEN
    with working mothers
	WHITE-COLLAR WOMEN
	    with working mothers

54% of them have	62% of them have
BLUE-COLLAR MOTHERS	WHITE-COLLAR MOTHERS

$20,000+ WOMEN (MANAGERIAL)
    with working mothers
	UNDER-$20,000 WOMEN
	    with working mothers

32% of them have	19% of them have
PROFESSIONAL/ TECHNICAL MOTHERS	PROFESSIONAL/ TECHNICAL MOTHERS

to pick up on the fact that these women are goal-oriented, and the daughters are going to become similarly goal-oriented from childhood. In the future they will become far more capable of running an enterprise, because they will be more likely to have the necessary abilities. For example, they are likely to become more leadership-oriented and feel more comfortable with mathematics and other areas women have traditionally shied away from—all of which will lead us to a generation of women in the future that is highly capable of solving its problems.

The Death of the Saint

The daughters of domestically oriented, family-focused women may grow up loved, but they also grow up at a disadvantage to the daughters of women with a wider focus, which is the automatic fringe benefit of a job outside the home.

In our interviews, we discovered that adult daughters seemed strongly polarized in their view of their mothers, with their perceptions involving two extremes. That is not to say that the mothers were in reality like this; but this is the way they *appeared* to their daughters.

One type of mother seemed almost too good to be true. We call her "The Saint," because she seemed virtually flawless in the eyes of her daughter. "One of God's own angels," "Everything you would want a mother to be," "Anything in the neighborhood, and she was the first to help," were typical descriptions. Adjectives frequently used to describe The Saint were "unselfish," "caring," "loving," and "warm."

Saint mothers appeared to be basically outer-directed, driven not so much by their own needs as by the needs of others. Their own real wants and desires—and personalities —were hidden from their daughters, who tended to perceive their mothers as one-dimensional and self-sacrificing. Consistently, these mothers were viewed by their daughters as perfect human beings, which is not surprising, since the daughter of a Saint found herself at the center of her mother's universe. Time after time, these daughters chorused a single, glowing accolade: "She was always there when I came home from school." They rarely mentioned what their mothers did while they were *at* school, or after they left the house to play in the afternoon. Saint mothers simply appeared like magical genies with milk and cookies to await the bidding of their daughters' pleasure.

Saints almost never worked outside the home and their interests were limited. Daughters rarely mentioned the existence of any hobbies, friends, sports, or other activities that did not directly relate to providing for the family's immediate needs.

Adrian, thirty-five, is the typical daughter of a Saint. A homemaker, she is extremely satisfied with her role in life as a wife and mother of an eight-year-old girl. On her survey questionnaire, Adrian wrote that the person she most admired was her mother because she respected her values and hoped she could be as giving and loving a person.

When we talked, Adrian recalled happily that her mother was "home all the time" when she was growing up. "My mother was a very loving, very caring, all-around good person," she said. "She was always there for everything I needed. She's very understanding, and I respect her in all ways." Adrian went on to point out that her mother liked sewing and was involved in church work, but that her main activity was caring for the family. Her mother did not work, did not drive, and rarely left the farm where the family lived, which was fine with Adrian. "I liked her being there when I came home, instead of coming home to an empty house."

Adrian recognizes that she wants to be like her mother. "I think that just comes natural," she says. "Little boys want to be like their fathers, little girls want to be like their mothers. I think my mother did not work because she had my well-being in mind. And I am concerned with *my* family. I put their well-being and their happiness first. I think that's a good thing to pass down from generation to generation."

Adrian went on to say that she actually felt guilty the few times she had to leave her daughter with a baby-sitter. "I think it's my responsibility to raise my child," she said. "And to see that she has the things she needs and to bring her up with the ideals she's supposed to have. I don't think I should pay someone else to do that. So I just don't leave my little girl with baby-sitters anymore."

Adrian claims she would never work unless family finances forced her to. At one point this past year, she was tempted briefly to think about going to work when she heard that an extremely interesting job was available. But her daughter—and, I'm sure, deep down, Adrian herself—was "just definitely against it," so she dropped the idea.

While Saints are self-sacrificing, Supermoms are self-fulfilled. This type of mother is inner-directed, allowing her own needs to be expressed and recognized rather than sublimating them within the needs of her husband and children. Whether they worked or not, the Supermoms in our survey were highly multidimensional women. They had interests in a wide variety of things, and appeared to be extremely active. Nonworking Supermoms were usually jugglers of volunteer work, hobbies, the PTA, classes, political work, and a myriad of other activities that took them outside the home. Other Supermoms held jobs that were usually perceived as a source of enjoyment. Daughters of Supermoms had vivid memories of their mothers' many and varied interests and activities. One commented, "My mother is a compulsive doer. I thought it was neat. I mean, she could do more than anybody else's mom in the neighborhood."

Unlike the personalities of the more one-dimensional

THE TWO BASIC TYPES OF MOTHERS AS PERCEIVED BY DAUGHTERS

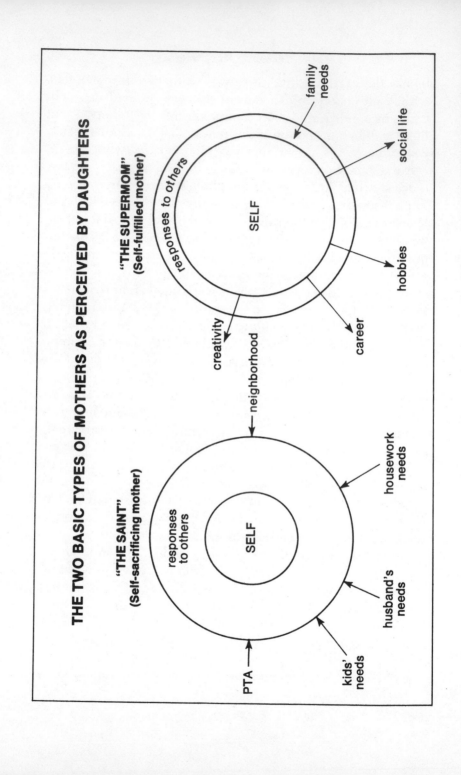

"THE SAINT"
(Self-sacrificing mother)

responses to others

SELF

PTA

kids' needs

husband's needs

housework needs

"THE SUPERMOM"
(Self-fulfilled mother)

responses to others

SELF

neighborhood

creativity

career

hobbies

family needs

social life

Saints, the real personalities of Supermoms, with all their complexities, were apparent to their daughters. As a result, their flaws as well as their merits surfaced. Daughters admired the directness and involvement of such mothers; however, Supermoms ran the risk of being perceived as selfish or overly self-indulgent.

Because their mothers were so involved with activities outside the home, daughters of Supermoms benefited from a wider range of exposure than daughters of the domestically oriented Saints. The households of Supermoms often involved daughters in a rich variety of social, cultural, and intellectual experiences. These daughters, as a result, felt better prepared to handle opportunities and problems when they arose later in life. They simply felt more comfortable in more situations.

Helen, the thirty-four-year-old executive daughter of a nonworking Supermom, bears this out. "My mother is very active," she said. "My mother has more energy than I will ever have in my entire life. She doesn't know how to relax. I mean, if she were here right now she'd be scrubbing the floor, picking up the kitchen, doing needlepoint, doing something else." Helen ran down a partial list of her mother's activities. "When I was younger, she would make skirts for my sister and me, or knit scarves. She took flower-arranging courses, she took photography, she took a course in upholstering furniture, she went back to college. . . ." Helen actually ran out of breath just describing her mother.

The importance of all this is not only that Helen remembers wanting to be like her mother, but that she feels she became what she is today as a result of the many influences her mother exposed her to. "I took French in high school, and my mother encouraged me to speak foreign languages at home," she said. After her first year in college, Helen went to Switzerland to improve her French—and her mother went along. Helen told me, "Europe was important to her, and she dragged me there when I was nineteen. That was my first taste of Europe."

From that taste evolved Helen's career. She went on to earn her M.B.A. (her mother went on to become a high school French teacher!) and got her first job in the Swiss office of an international firm. She returned to the United States for several years, then became the first female assistant general manager of another company's Belgian office.

Helen credits her mother's influence for much of this. "Because of my mother, I learned to speak French. Because of her, I went to Europe the first time. And being familiar with living in Europe and also speaking French were two important reasons why I was picked for International."

More importantly, Helen sees the vistas her Supermom opened up for her as paving the way for her predisposition to accept and take advantage of such opportunities. "A lot of people are offered International," she claims. "Take my husband, for example. Before we were married, we worked for the same company and he was offered the same job I was. But he had never been to Europe before and he spoke no foreign languages, so he felt uncomfortable and turned it down. You have a tendency to shy away when something is unknown. But because of my mother, I felt comfortable with it, and I was more likely to accept a job like that."

A daughter's perception of her mother results in many parallel characteristics in her own behavior and self-image, which influence her predisposition toward and preparedness for a job situation. Daughters of Saints tend to be nonworking, or if they do happen to work for whatever reasons, to be highly uncomfortable and dissatisfied. The role model with which they identify simply lacks the dimension for them to operate with ease beyond its relatively limited confines. Kindness, warmth, generosity, unselfishness, and a loving nature—all the qualities idealized by daughters of Saints—are highly admirable. But unless they are balanced by other characteristics, they are not traits which, when emulated, sketch the image of a career-oriented woman.

At the other end of the spectrum, Supermoms offer their daughters models for traits such as organization, stick-to-it-iveness, self-motivation, efficiency, and independence, which coexist with a measure of family life and warmth. In emulating such qualities, these daughters find themselves better prepared to enter a work environment, and more at ease with the job of combining work and family. Daughters of Supermoms are likely to grow up to be active, involved people, like their mothers. They are the most likely women of all to be independent and aggressive, to work, and to say that they always expected they would grow up to be working women. They are better prepared than the daughters of Saints to handle a multitude of roles—wife, mother, worker—and are better equipped psychologically to take advantage of a variety of options and opportunities.

As increasing numbers of women join the work force and assimilate the inevitable nondomestic, outer-oriented forces that come with a paycheck, Saint mothers will become an endangered species. They will be replaced by a generation of Supermoms. By the next generation, we can anticipate that the majority of daughters will be raised by Supermoms, who will in turn pass down their attitudinal heritage.

CHAPTER 8

Moving Toward Matriarchy

Although the distance is lessening, there's no denying that women have a way to go before they attain real equality with men, much less superiority. The facts make this glaringly apparent. Women are still vastly underrepresented in positions of authority. Despite the numbers of women flooding the work-place, as of spring 1980 only 6 percent of all women were white-collar managers—5 percent middle managers, a mere one percent upper managers—representing only 23 percent of the total management pool.[1] Among blue-collar workers, the picture is about the same, with women comprising only 6 percent of the more highly paid skilled craft workers;[2] women are traditionally excluded from apprenticeship programs that lead to the higher-paying, skilled jobs. Overall, women earn only 59 cents for every dollar men make.[3] And while 52 percent of all women over age sixteen are working outside the home, the remaining 48 percent are not gaining the psychological and fiscal rewards of paid employment. Women in government are still a small minority, and 80 percent of all women in the work force are clustered in "women's ghetto" jobs that pay less and offer less upward mobility than other job classifications. In the field of education, the same trend prevails. One study revealed, for instance, that women hold half the graduate degrees in art history but only one-fourth of the faculty positions, and although 70 percent of the undergraduates majoring in English are women, only 7 percent of English professors are women.[4] Women comprise only 10 percent of the nation's doctors and 12 percent of the lawyers.[5] Parallels exist in virtually every occupational category. At home, women are still at the service of their families to a greater degree than men. Seventy percent of the working women in our survey said they did most of the housework themselves, for instance. Other studies have shown that less than 60 percent of all husbands help around the house—and then only about eleven hours a week—while housewives put in fifty-two or more hours a week of housework, and working women twenty-six hours.[6] The discrepancies could fill another book.

But women are gaining ever-increasing status in our productivity-obsessed capitalistic society, establishing the foothold to move ahead. Their psychological makeup, combined with the speed of their transformation, gives them the incentive, capacity, and momentum to surpass their male peers. The massiveness and swiftness of recent attitudinal shifts underscores this compelling momentum. Women under age twenty-five are 47 percent more likely to be career-oriented than women over age forty-five, while women over forty-five are twice as likely as the younger group to be home-oriented.

The Pacesetter women of today, not the domestic housewives of yesterday, are the indicators of where women are heading in the future. We can see that this trend is broadening, since the Go-Getters, who exemplify in a less extreme way the attitudinal and behavioral tendencies that characterize the Pacesetters, are already the largest attitudinal group among women, comprising 43 percent of all women and 57 percent of working women. These women are unlike any large psychographic female group to date, not only in their characteristics, but, equally important, in their widespread social acceptability and high status, which will allow them to grow and expand as a group, rather than be snuffed out by society as minority and so-called extremist groups have been in the past.

Society somehow always manages to justify and popularize what is necessary for survival. And if it is necessary that women work, then that work will be granted a positive status. The recent reinforcement and glamorization of women's work and independence is reflected in current media, with movies like *Norma Rae, An Unmarried Woman,* and *My Brilliant Career,* which depict women placing more emphasis on independence and career than on home and family. In *Kramer vs. Kramer,* we were able to identify sympathetically with the idea of a father raising his child and deemphasizing his career, while the mother jettisoned her family life to further her own self-development through a career. *Savvy* magazine, for and about the managerial woman, has experienced the fastest growth of any woman's magazine in history. Advertising, books, and television shows are also following suit, lionizing the self-sufficient woman. All of these things are popular indications that the Pacesetter type of woman has achieved status in our society. She is the heroine of today; movie stars like Jill Clayburgh, Marlo Thomas, Jane Fonda, and Barbra Streisand are popular not only because they are talented but because they fit our image of this kind of woman, on and often off the screen. This is a nourishing environment for the Pacesetters, and they will thrive, multiply, and strengthen. They are the power base that will allow women the maneuverability and status to gain equality. Given the aggressive nature of the Pacesetter, she is fated to keep striving for superiority.

The Zigzag Line: Breakthrough vs. Backlash

It will not be an unopposed struggle, nor will it be a speedy one. And it will happen as a result of the women themselves, not as a result of legislation or external pressures, although these are necessary components that will legitimize the phenomenon. Like any group in power, men will be naturally reluctant to give up control, and will fight to maintain it. This will result in many levels of backlash, as has been evident in the resistance to the Equal Rights Amendment. As Dr. Arlene Kaplan Daniels, professor of sociology at Northwestern University, points out, "This is a social movement, and once it gets going, people begin to see what the consequences will be if it keeps going on. It would mean a drastic reorganization of society. So they want to stop it wherever they can, right here, right now. In their mind, the issue and the consequences of the issue are the same. And people are afraid of the consequences. They see abortion on demand as a threat—and they are quite right—to one of the threads holding the family together in a certain way. They see sex education in the schools, teaching evolution, the mixing of the races—all sorts of things like that—as threats. So they think, 'Keep those women in the hole, or keep them at a disadvantage.' Why? Because it maintains the status quo."

For instance, one survey of how managers and labor leaders viewed potential changes that could alter their work life revealed that the managers viewed such changes negatively and perceived them as harboring the potential to undermine their prerogatives.[7] For those in power, the status quo is simply less risky. This attitude is unlikely to change, given human nature.

Backlash is not exclusively reserved for men. Women who do not work outside the home, particularly those who never have done so, also may feel they have much to gain by pre-serving the status quo. Marilyn Moats Kennedy observes, "If you want to get slugged and flattened, go to a party and say to another woman, 'What do you do?' If she turns out to be someone who does not work outside the home, she's going to be very defensive. And then when she asks you, and you turn out not to be someone who is a homemaker, she's going to be even more defensive. It really is a barrier between women, because they're not getting the same strokes from society for staying home and taking care of the children that they did in the old days. It used to be that women who stayed home and took care of their children were very proud of that. Now they're the most defensive group." Their defenses are evident in highly vocal women's antiprogressive movements. No one wants to lose status—including the housewife. And one way to preserve your status is to inhibit someone else's: The "total woman," for instance, implies that any other kind of woman is incomplete. The length and strength of the back-lash against women's achievement of power will depend largely on whether the public response is fearful and threat-ened or positive and supportive.

The line charting women's accession to power will be un-avoidably uneven, with retreats and defeats, backlash and backsliding for every step gained along the way. It cannot be stated that matriarchy will prevail at a particular predeter-mined time, since its advent depends on the meshing of circumstances and attitudes. Economic conditions, social pat-terns, women's and men's responses, childbirth rates, child-care distribution, educational trends, and the responsiveness of our systems all will be significant factors. The power of the pull of any element in this mix, at any given time, will shape the movement toward matriarchy.

Preludes to Power

We have already discussed how one significant predicator of power is the perception of opportunity; women must scent that there are real chances for them to move into power positions before they will even let themselves desire such positions. As more women see other women in power, they are more likely to perceive it as achievable for themselves and to be motivated to achieve it.

Equally important is how well women understand the concept of power and its attendant vocabulary. Women have been held back because they have been distanced from power not only by the circumstances set up by society and bureaucracy, but also because they have lacked the skills to cope with power, and even because they have chosen to avoid it.

This is changing, albeit slowly. Marilyn Moats Kennedy, who has supplied career counseling to more than 7,000 women, has observed that women are not yet completely comfortable with power. "They really do not like to lead. They are not comfortable with command, have had very little experience with it." Our survey indicates that power is currently a negligible motivator for women—even Pacesetters—who are driven mainly by reasons of income and self-satisfaction. This may be a real situation, or a distortion brought on by the fact that women have not been socialized to be comfortable with an overt expression of a desire for power, to perceive power as an acceptable goal for themselves. Income and self-satisfaction in themselves are leading women into an understanding of the dynamics of power, but, notes Kennedy, "for women to get power, they have to want it."

What will make them want it? "As women realize that income is a direct result of power, they'll be motivated by power," she says. "They'll become interested in organizational politics."

Women are already acknowledging the importance of one of the more important accessories to power: informal network systems. Traditionally, women have been basically isolationist and self-centered about their success, pulling in the ladder without extending a hand to other women. In general, this has slowed their acquisition of power, because by isolating themselves women have inadvertently cut themselves off from role models, potential allies, mentors, information, and the giving and taking of favors that is part of power negotiation. Women's networks have opened up these possibilities on a wider scale than was previously available. One woman commented, "If you can't get what you want or need to know on your job, you can find someone in a competitive environment who will help you."

Kennedy has seen this happening. "Women are learning to cooperate," she says. "Although it's not easy, because they haven't wanted to cooperate with each other. But things are changing, because they realize that the women below them in an organization can punish them if they don't cooperate. I see that all the time—they set you up for failure, they cut you out of the information networks, they spread rumors about you. They can do it, and a lot of women higher up realize that this can happen, that they can be victims of other women if they don't offer cooperation."

Other women offer the point of view that now that women have opportunities, are moving up in the various hierarchies, and have some power to make things happen, it is worthwhile to cooperate and exchange information; as one banker put it, "You never know when another woman's going to be in a position to help you."

Perhaps one reason why women are only recently utilizing networking systems successfully is because, until recently, they simply lacked some of the key prerequisites of participating in a network, which Dr. Arlene Kaplan Daniels defines as "a high level of energy, a big array of available resources, a model of the free marketplace, and an appraisal system which lets you see that others will help you if you help them." As more of these elements become increasingly available to women, they will become more successful at helping each other, and more prone to do so.

Another skill that is key to achievement of power is the art of negotiation. Kennedy comments, "Women have some elementary skills learned by the fact that all people who are powerless learn to negotiate to some extent. But negotiating is the skill that I see that women must acquire—that's where it's at for women in the future. Women will use negotiating skills to try to get economic power, via better salaries and more money. One reason they'll be interested in power is because there will be things like this that they want to change."

Kennedy sees women consolidating groups of issues for negotiating purposes, instead of pursuing one interest area singlemindedly, as they have tended to do in the past. "They'll try to get five things together and say, 'If you'll support this, we all will do X.' "

To be comfortable with power, however, one must also be comfortable with risk and failure—something women are only just beginning to achieve. As one successful executive said, "You reach a point in management where the only way you can become successful is by making it the central purpose of your life. It has to become the most important thing. So when you become a really top manager you are not really managing the business; for the most part, that business is managing you. It's got you by the balls, so to speak. Because unless you make it the most important thing in your life, you are going to fail, and for most of us who are so achievement-oriented, failure is out of the question. And as a result, you're not going to become so achievement-oriented, so much so that success is your whole focus. Because, then, if you fail at that, having given up family, home, hobbies, and other things to do so, what have you got? It's not worth the pain."

For women, success and power are traditionally won at the price of sacrificing elements of life that are perceived as more "normal." While men are brought up to have a more one-dimensional, success-oriented focus, women are reared to cherish the home above all else, and it has been ingrained in them from an early age that to be a "good" person, one must succeed primarily as a wife, mother, and homemaker. This notion has been inherent in our feminine role models. A woman who had just left a company in which she was highly successful in order to accommodate her husband's career said to me, "You know, I went X far in my career and I thought I went pretty far pretty fast. I became a vice president and my next job would have been general manager of an office. And when you get up there, you can find you're all by yourself, and there you are, and you're successful, and I must say I was a little bit disappointed in the rewards that it brings. Once in a while you feel good, but there are other things that are better and needed."

To this woman, "better" meant doing things that made her more accessible to her marriage. This may have been necessary and good for the relationship. But the point is, she changed jobs and sacrificed her seniority—her husband did not. It is likely that he would not have felt "better" had he given up his job for the sake of the relationship. This woman recognizes the dichotomy: "Men are brought up to do one thing and have clear direction, whereas there are so many other things pulling at women—the motherhood thing, and the love and the home and all those feelings men often don't have because they are not brought up with them." To sacrifice any of those things is, to many women, a failure to be feared. Better to be less than a major success outside the home and leave yourself time and energy to pull all the strings at once, and if no one thing is a dazzling success, at least no one can accuse you of failure in any area.

Fear of failure can result in two things: The woman may hold back from realizing her fullest potential, consciously or unconsciously, or she may attempt to "have it all," to be a superwoman. Right now our society is big on superwomen. The pressure is on to not miss a beat at home or at work. Women who try to span all roles to perfection may not so much be superachievers as failure-fearers. As marketing psychologist Dr. Sid Levy observes, "They're afraid to drop a stitch."

Leadership-effectiveness-training consultant Sheila Coin concurs that a great many women desire nothing less than perfection. "It's a terrible demand to make on yourself," she says. "I think a lot of it comes out of a self-consciousness that if you don't do it one hundred percent and get A-plus perfect results, you're going to elicit the castigation, the vindictiveness of your male counterparts in the organization—so God forbid you should make a mistake! That whole posture makes women less likely to be risk takers than men because they have such a fear of failure and such a fear of judgment."

Coin adds, "A woman must develop a sense of personal ability, personal self-worth, trust herself, allow herself to make mistakes."

For women to achieve power, they must not fear being human. The Pacesetter woman, with her greater self-confidence, is in the best position of all women to be able to accomplish this.

The Means for Matriarchy

Achieving power is inevitable as long as certain elements remain interactive in our socioeconomic composition. These are the four basic factors that will insure not only women's eventual equality, but an upheaval in the balance of power between the sexes.

1. *The powerful Whirlpool Effect of economic and social forces is pulling increasing numbers of women into the work force—and keeping them there.* This phenomenon has been described in an earlier chapter, but since it is such a significant factor it bears some further elaboration from the perspective of its impact on the future.

Although 48 percent of the women over age sixteen currently do not work, this is a deceptive figure. The percentage of men in the same age range who are not employed is 20 percent, which leaves a difference of only 28 percentage points between the sexes in employment participation. Meanwhile, women have been entering the labor force at a much faster rate than men. In the last decade 13 million women joined the labor force—compared to 9 million men,[8] which indicates that women have the momentum to catch up with and numerically surpass men in the power forum that is the fulcrum of our society. Of course, many more women than men still work part-time, and thus women's work commitment in general remains less, but the nature of the Whirlpool Effect insures that increasing numbers of women will continue to enter the work force with greater commitment, thus increasingly narrowing the gap between men and women in this area. The fact that more women than men are currently enrolled in college indicates that this trend will continue.

2. *Women's leadership style will be increasingly more effective and appropriate than men's in dealing with and solving the complex issues and problems facing our future.* In a society of increasingly complex problems and opportunities, effective leadership is desperately needed, and whether that need is fulfilled by men or by women, solutions will be welcomed. Does either sex have an advantage in coming up with the answers? Recent studies suggest that women do.

There are many variations on leadership styles, but two overall categories or modes of thinking, which reflect different values or life orientations, can be identified as critical to dealing with today's problems. These are termed alpha and beta.

The alpha leadership style is pervasive and historical in our society. Highly competitive, it is characterized by analytical, rational, quantitative thinking and relies on hierarchical relationships, like the corporation. Alpha-style leadership is detail-oriented and task-oriented. It focuses narrowly —on individual achievement, for instance, or the details of a particular task. In the alpha system, once a goal is set it's full speed ahead, damn the torpedoes. Values encountered along the way become incidental to reaching that all-important goal. Change—perceived as a potential threat to reaching the goal—is considered chaotic and disruptive, and something to be avoided at all cost. The strength of the alpha approach is its ability to look at the short run—for instance, immediate technical issues. Problems are characteristically not anticipated, but dealt with after they develop. The alpha style is appropriate when speed is of the essence, but in dealing with long-term issues, problems may occur, since reevaluation does not enter into the process. Because of this, end goals may become confused, over time, with instrumental values, like profit and power. This is how corporations have come to build nuclear power plants that may endanger human life, to pollute our waterways, and to destroy our natural resources seemingly without considering the consequences; it is because the end value—say, betterment of human life, even if only for those connected with the corporation—has become confused with the *means* to that end, i.e., profit.

On the other hand, the beta style of leadership focuses on long-range issues, values, and goals, and the ramifications of each increment of a process. Beta-style leadership has a group rather than individual orientation. Support relationships assume great importance. Growth, learning, and quality-of-life issues are also stressed, in contrast to the alpha style. The importance of self-actualization that surfaced as a primary motivator for women in our survey reflects these beta concerns.

Beta leadership incorporates many criteria for decisions, including intuition. It is an integrative, more multidimensional, subtle style, which is good for adapting to change. The reevaluative nature of beta style makes it especially flexible, as does its perception of change as a natural evolution of life. And its long-range perspective permits planning and an examination of different value choices, another plus when adaptability is called for.

Alpha and beta styles have been defined and studied extensively by SRI International (formerly Stanford Research Institute) as part of an effort to develop and encourage new leadership and overcome problems that have led to a growing concern about the quality of American leadership in general.

Lynn Rosener, an analyst at SRI International, points out that the alpha style is currently dominant in every institution in our country except the family, where we incorporate the beta style. She also makes the point that in our culture the alpha style is perceived as more masculine, the beta as more feminine, and that, in fact, there is some behavioral foundation for this.

"These two styles are heavily associated with American sexual expectations," says Rosener. "And in fact the work that we did brought in different studies that supported this. Women tend to be more comfortable with, in a sense more tuned in to, the characteristics associated with the beta style. So this perception is in fact founded on some actual group behavioral differences—critical behavioral differences —between men and women."

Rosener stresses that these are socialized, or cultural, not biological differences. "But our contention is," she adds, "that it doesn't matter why the differences are there—there *is* a difference between men and women. It really has nothing to do with sex—just sex in America, the sexual expectations that have developed."

As an example, she cites Japanese management techniques, which have been highly successful in the era since World War II. Japan, an island, has evolved its leadership techniques to maximize the country's limited resources. "Japanese management and Japanese political leaders exhibit beta style, and it is respected and used quite frequently," she notes. "In Japan [beta] traits are valued among men, but in the United States they're perceived by most men as being ineffective."

Instead, the beta style has become common methodology among American women, evolving out of women's roles in the family. "Women in general have had emphasis on nurturance and concern for people's growth and well-being, both emotionally and physically, as their primary role," says Rosener. "And women's role in the past has been to provide and assure the satisfaction of emotional requirements. Effective communication, making emotionally based value judgments, juggling several different roles concurrently, are all skills that women over the years have been socialized to cope with.

"Survival equips men to see their role as a producer, a provider of materialistic goods, and to be a specialist in this. This distinction was once based on necessity, but as this is no longer valid, it is being shed. But those basic survival skills that have been developed by women during centuries of experience are the ones that are best suited for the beta style, which is concerned with long-run growth—whether it's the growth of your child or health in a family, or whether the style is applied to the growth of the corporate life or the economy, or whatever."

The specialization of labor has resulted in men focusing their attention even more narrowly toward one role—the job. And so we have seen the rise of the "corporate man." Beta style, on the other hand, by means of involvement with children and family, utilizes integration of a lot of different things—being a wife, mother, housekeeper, cook, nurse, worker, etc.—the kinds of things that have involved coping with critical value judgments. This distinction in style gives women an advantage in dealing with the kinds of problems we are facing today as a society, at a time when we have fewer options than when our country was young and bursting with resources; when the issues are more complex; when we can no longer afford to say "Damn the torpedoes" because they might blow us off the map.

"I think it's becoming increasingly clear to men and women that we need some new ways of dealing with our most basic problems," says Rosener, citing her organization's clients as examples. "They know that they don't have all the answers. That there are some things that aren't explained by the basic finance and accounting skills they've been working off of for a long time. Our clients' interest is an indication that there is an awareness out there at high levels of management." Rosener suggests, further, that part of the current paralysis in leadership and lack of corporate credibility has been brought about by the dominance of the alpha style, which is leading us in the direction of an authoritarian, homogeneous society. Continuation of the alpha style in isolation could produce solutions that are inappropriate to our problems.

In the past, we charged ahead, with less concern about the options, or consequences, without weighing and integrating values, without reevaluation, because we were facing a less complex situation armed with more resources. This is no longer the case. Now we must face issues such as: Which is more important—taking the profit or polluting the environment? Lack of continual assessment of values and goals can cause further problems. Without the methodologies of the beta style, we risk isolating ourselves, when in fact we all must interact with our environment.

Rosener further notes that studies involving leadership skills have shown women's to be superior at dealing with problems involving creative solutions. She cites an example: "Two groups—one all men and the other all women—were given a survival problem to solve. The men immediately established a hierarchy: Someone assumed leadership and then relationships were set up underneath him. And then they attacked the problem very systematically. The women, on the other hand, worked in a very participative style. And when it came right down to it, their style sometimes took a little longer to reach a conclusion. But because they had some experience with testing which solution was better, they were more successful. In terms of solutions, the women's groups tended to rank much more highly than the men's did. The point of all this was that when dealing with problems that require creative solutions, or critical solutions where different value judgments had to get involved, the style that the women used—which was a beta style—was more effective."

Although the issues are different, our society is coping with problems that require the kinds of skills which were successful for the participants in this study.

Ideally, leadership should involve both alpha and beta skills, using each when appropriate. And women are likely to have the edge in adapting to both styles. "It is much easier to go from the beta style to learning the alpha style," is Rosener's opinion. "A person who has worked predominantly in the alpha style requires a radical internal shift to try and deal with the beta style. What's more, the integrative beta style is learned through socialization, while the alpha style involves more of a *technique*.

"Women get inputs from both alpha and beta, whereas men get a little beta through the family, but it is generally ascribed to 'Mom and her craziness.' There aren't a lot of social cues that teach men to be aware of how to act with the beta style, while even though women are socialized in the beta, they go to school in the alpha, they see it on TV, they read it in the newspapers."

Women will not only adapt to the existing alpha-style structures, but will bring beta thinking to them. If it is effective, the beta style will give them a unique advantage in the power structure.

This kind of "beta power" is necessary to bring about change. "The next twenty years are really going to demand those skills," emphasizes Rosener. "But I think it's going to be easier for women than for the men, because some of the problems that are going to be hitting on all of us as individuals are going to require a way of thinking, a beta style, that is going to be easier for women to handle. It comes to the ability to integrate all sorts of things, and juggle several roles and make value judgments and tradeoffs and decisions that all have to happen at once. Women, right now, are more comfortable with that. And it's a really difficult thing to learn. So, in that sense, it's going to be very hard on men. But, hopefully, in the end we'll all learn from each other."

3. *A new breed of women are coming to the fore. Forged from the work experience, they are radically different from their traditional predecessors.* It is highly likely that this trend will not only continue but intensify dramatically. There is already evidence that the woman of the future will exhibit the characteristics we now see emerging to a far greater degree. Our survey reveals that younger working women are significantly less home-oriented and more work-

oriented. For example, 50 percent of the women under twenty-five always thought they'd work, compared with only 37 percent of those aged thirty-five to fifty. Sixty-five percent of women under twenty-five disagree that a woman's place is in the home, versus 52 percent of women age thirty-five to fifty. Women under twenty-five are 52 percent more likely than women over thirty-five to feel a career is as important as being a good wife and mother. And half of the younger women feel their goals in life are quite ambitious, compared to 35 percent of the women age thirty-five to fifty. Add to this the fact that there is recent evidence that women become less passive, more active, more aggressive and dominant as they age.[9] Then imagine what today's young women might be like in thirty years.

In many ways, the new breed of working women is already more aggressive than men. They are more likely to seek divorce than men.[10] They display an increasing propensity to hold two jobs—with the percentage of women doing so doubling from 16 percent to 30 percent since 1969, while the number of men with two jobs remained the same—and their motives are more ambitious. One economist with the Bureau of Labor Statistics noted further that women's motives for holding two jobs tend to be professional—gaining of experience, planning a career move, or as a step toward self-employment while men's motives tend to be economic, involving family expenses.[11]

Women also seem to be beating men to many of the new jobs created by the expansion of industry. From 1968 to 1978 some 18 million additional jobs were created in new or expanded industries. Eleven million women found work in these jobs—compared to 7 million men.[12] And in 1980 women were hired for 60 percent of the 2.4 million new jobs.[13] Part of this was due to the expansion of the service sector of the economy, but another aspect signifies the result of women's new industrial aggressiveness, especially

considering the fact that much of this period was recession-
ary and that in the past women have been traditionally
forced to relinquish jobs to men in times of recession.

Motivational changes are also working in favor of women
in the power structure. There is a trend toward women actively seeking money, power, and prestige, while men are
becoming increasingly motivated by humanitarian goals.
This does not imply a waning of women's more integrative
approach; rather, it adds to the variety of values they are
incorporating in their management style. But this is a reversal of the traditional skew. Men, for instance, seem to be
hopping off the money treadmill. A national survey conducted for *Playboy* by Louis Harris and Associates involving
1,990 men age eighteen to forty-nine indicated that men
named money as a low-ranking value, while family life and
health were top priorities.[14]

Industrial psychologist and personnel director Kay Riegler
has analyzed psychological tests given to approximately
1,000 men and women nationwide, and she concludes, "Ten
years ago the men who were most suited for the business
world were motivated by money and status. Women back
then were less motivated by status and prestige and were
more interested in humanitarian goals. Today it appears that
men are more likely to develop their social/humanitarian
side, while women have become more oriented toward
money and status. Women are learning at a young age that
having these goals in business is OK. For example, recently
I spoke at a Girl Scouts Career Day to children in seventh
grade and younger. There is also much more of a business
orientation in academia for women, which encourages them
toward business goals and careers."

Women's motivation to manage is not only increasing, it
may be surpassing men's. Linda Keller Brown, Ph.D., director of the Cross-National Project on Women as Corporate

Managers at the Center for the Social Sciences at Columbia University, notes, "Some studies suggest that the male motivation to manage is declining." Citing a 1980 study of male and female managers which concludes that women managers are significantly more highly motivated and challenged by their jobs and that they aspire to higher levels than their male counterparts, Brown feels that women's motivation may give them an edge. "Women entering the work force are buying the extreme version of the work ethic," she comments, "while men in the work force for a long time are disillusioned with the greedy occupation of management. Women may be one of the few groups left to whom management may be able to sell the compulsive-work ethic."

Evidence of women's increasing motivation to manage, says Brown, can be seen in the fact that they have become more professionally mobile than men. *Business Week* reported that today's women managers are moving more readily than men. "When the company says 'You'll get a better title if you move,' they move," the article noted, referring to women as "the new Horatio Algers."[15]

Perhaps a more subtle—and, because of the sheer numbers of women involved, even more critical—trend involves the clerical work force, where the bulk of working women have traditionally settled, to become trapped in low-opportunity, low-paying jobs. Although the sheer numbers of younger women flooding into the job market caused a growth in the clerical segment between 1968 and 1977, the distribution of younger women nonetheless began to shift away from clerical work toward professional, technical, and managerial jobs.[16]

Those women who are entering the clerical work force are doing so on a different basis than in the past, usually with company approval. Secretaries, for instance, have always controlled crucial aspects of business communications, and they are beginning to utilize their power and expertise to benefit their careers. For the first time, there are signs that secretaries are joining forces and forming organizational pressure groups and power blocs. At corporations like Borg-Warner, secretaries and women in nonmanagement positions meet regularly for seminars on career planning, assertiveness training, and other business skills. These meetings are not only approved by the company, they are sponsored by it. There is also a growing, if embryonic, trend toward unionization of female office workers. The Working Women–National Association of Office Workers is one organization that has been formed to accomplish such a goal. In Chicago, clerical workers at the University of Chicago last year voted to unionize and are represented by the Teamsters and General Service Employees unions. Regardless of whether or not women in clerical positions do eventually unionize, the point is that these moves indicate that clerical women—and their employers—are looking at their jobs in a new and different way that leads to increased strength and upward career mobility for these women. They are tending to view their positions as stepping-stones to other kinds of jobs. Marilyn Moats Kennedy has perceived a new thirst and drive for power among female clerical workers, who, she feels, not only control word processing, but are moving beyond and into data processing, setting the stage for women's control of virtually all communications aspects of business. "There are a couple of areas women are moving into where they're going to have enormous power," notes Kennedy. "One is word processing, which could very well absorb data processing. If they absorb data processing, women will control the information flow in an organization. That's real, hands-on power. When these women talk to management, management listens because they can show you the bottom line—how it costs $5.65 for a secretary to type one letter and they can give it to you for 30 cents in as many variations as you want. That's the bottom line.

"You look at the woman who's a supervisor of word processing, and she's absolutely so ambitious, she can't keep her hands off the power structure. She's reporting to top management, talking to the chairman of the board; she controls huge amounts of money and big numbers of people. Those women understand numbers, and maybe you'll find them suggesting that the data processing people don't manage very well—why don't they take over data processing and organize it too?

"Meanwhile, the men in data processing are saying 'Oh, word processing—it's just typing.' But, you know, those men are going to be reporting to that lady before they ever figure out what's happening. They'll be standing around wondering what the hell hit them when their new boss moves into her corner office. Computers are getting cheaper every day, while word processing equipment is getting more expensive, because it does more things. Word processing will suck up data processing like an amoeba. I myself have seen companies where they are on the verge of taking over right now. Women will control that power base through people and money, big-budget allocations. Just the equipment they control will be a hard investment. And nobody will say 'Mary can fix one of these machines with a hairpin.' Mary will not be wearing hairpins or fixing machines. She'll have somebody to do that for her."

Mary and the new women like her will not only make strides themselves, they will provide the role models for others. As Kennedy says, "They are the superstars of tomorrow. They will be to the next generation of women what movie stars were to the previous generation." Male children will learn from their example that women are capable of more than a domestic existence and that men and women share a great many psychological attributes. The boys will also see that supporting a wife and children need not be a fate cast in concrete, especially when a woman can be self-supporting. Thus the new women will open up cross-sexual flexibilities that were formerly closed out for both men and women, and their children, in turn, will pass them to the following generation.

4. *The failure of our social institutions to adapt to the needs of the new women will ultimately lead to the women themselves short-circuiting those institutions.* In establishing relationships of equality in their private lives, Pacesetters and Go-Getters will provide models for others and ultimately generate pressure for change in our public structures. Ideally, this would result in simultaneous, reciprocal adaptation of personal and social change. Realistically, however, this will probably never be the case, if only because of the varied viewpoints legitimately represented in this country and the elements of backlash that will inevitably retard such multidimensional equalization. Meanwhile, women's dissatisfaction with the immobility of traditionally oriented institutions is on the rise.

It is naive to assume that the institutions and organizations currently so firmly entrenched—the ones that led to women's secondary status in the first place—will magically accommodate the changing nature and role of women. Nevertheless, when institutions and systems do not adapt quickly enough to stave off their own obsolescence, the price will be their very existence, because women are not going to back off and cease working, and the attitudes and behaviors we see emerging will only intensify in the future. If necessary, women will sacrifice the status quo for their economic and psychological survival.

One has only to look at the day-care—or lack of day-care—available to see that one arrangement that could help maintain a semblance of balance between the old and the new is responding sluggishly at best. Although there are more than 6 million mothers of children under age six working outside the home, there is little social recognition of or support for the dilemma of the working mother. The United States, as of 1980, had only 1.6 million licensed day-care openings for children—fewer than in 1945. Meanwhile, almost every industrialized country except America has a national day-care program. By the next decade, it is projected that 14 million working mothers will have young children. Relief is nowhere in sight. But notice that women are not responding to this problem by staying home. They are simply having fewer children or no children, or having their children later.

In spite of the fact that ambitious working women do tend to have fewer children, most still feel that having and rearing a child of their own is desirable and important. And biologically there is still no way around it: Women will have to conceive and bear their children themselves—at least until the technologies of in-vitro fertilization and surrogate motherhood mature. The vast majority of the women we surveyed and interviewed, including the Pacesetters, did not want to exclude children from their lives entirely—they simply wanted to make having and caring for them more convenient, more under their control, and they wanted to have more options available.

Although day-care is widely underdeveloped, it offers a realistic alternative to exclusive maternal care. If there was no available means perceived for economically caring for children, the women we interviewed simply tended to put off childbearing that much longer and invest that much more in their careers, feeling, as one woman said, "I can always have children, but I can't always walk into a vice presidency." This strategy works nicely until such women reach an age when they can't "always" have children—their thirties. They push the childbearing clock to the limit, and are often forced to make a "now or never" decision. Such pressures are both unfair and intense. It may be easy to justify not having children when you have ten or fifteen good child-bearing years ahead of you. But what happens when the years are used up? You may be forced to face the music and accept the fact that a choice is at hand. And, more and more frequently, that choice is dictated by economics. Many women I spoke with justified their decision not to have children by saying that they were "not the maternal type." More realistically, the likelihood is that they had no options. It is often unfeasible for a woman to quit her job to raise a child; and unless a working woman has a high income of her own added to her husband's income, it is likewise unfeasible for her to hire private day-care. Women are going to be increasingly frustrated as motherhood, which they have grown up feeling is their natural right and destiny, becomes a luxury fast drifting out of reach, and as being a mother and pursuing nondomestic goals becomes an either-or proposition.

Parallel problems, indicative of the widespread lack of workable support structures for working women, exist in household maintenance, transportation, and other areas where these women's problems are viewed as personal, not social. A pressure-cooker atmosphere is building.

Social institutions like the male-female relationship are equally slow to change, and are feeling the sharp edge of women's dissatisfaction. Men are clearly not picking up the slack that is necessary in a positive relationship with a working wife. The working wife of today doesn't have one job, she has two: in her home and at her place of employment. Seventy-four percent of the working wives in our survey responded that they did most of the housework themselves. These women are victims of the Double-Day syndrome—working a domestic shift along with the job shift.[17] A recent United Nations study confirmed that a major effect of the working women's revolution has been to "put a disproportionate share of the workload on women."[18] Another study estimated that when both partners work full-time, wives average sixty-six to seventy-five hours of work, including home and employment—eight hours more than their husbands.[19] Child-care also still falls to the woman. A survey by the National Commission on Working Women revealed that when the child of a married woman is sick, four out of five times it is the woman rather than her husband who stays home with the child. And 80 percent of all married women said that if a problem arose at home, they were expected to stay home and handle it. Building in flexibilities at work is a possible answer, but it has not been a solution in Sweden, where paternity leave is a commonplace job benefit but is used by only a small percentage of men.

Nor do two incomes ease the problem by allowing women to hire household help. In most cases the wife's income provides day-to-day living essentials, without which the family standard of living would suffer. Studies have shown that for the average middle- or upper-income household with a working wife, the household would drop to the next lower income class without the wife's paycheck.[20] A 1976 survey showed that only 3 percent of couples earning $25,000 or more had live-in help, and only one-third had any help at all.[21]

While some men accommodate the needs of their working wives, most are not readily willing to make changes. A 1970 study of college men in their senior year indicated that only 7 percent were willing to significantly modify their own career and domestic roles to assist their future wives' careers.[22] Most felt their wives' work would be secondary to their own and expected the women to stay home with young children, when that time came. These young men are the husbands of today, and many of them are no doubt now wrestling with the actuality of a working wife. Given these kinds of expectations, it is not surprising that husbands are chafing under the bridle of their wives' career aspirations.

Men married to working women have, in fact, reported less marital satisfaction and lower mental and physical well-being than husbands of nonworking women.[23]

Women do not react by pulling out of the work force. Instead, they endure a jam-packed existence and suffer the ambivalence of home/job conflicts. Having tasted the benefits of the job, Pacesetter and Go-Getter women shun the home scene for the escape valve of career success. To achieve this end, women are sacrificing the one thing that could help keep the status quo afloat—time. In our survey, women wrote again and again of the problem of lack of time. It is estimated in another study that women who work full-time do so at a sacrifice of at least fourteen hours a week —hours that were previously applied to working on a relationship with a husband, running a household, counseling a child, eating, sleeping, doing chores, and enjoying leisure.[24] Most working women feel they have little time for anything but the essentials. This is the price of their paycheck, but they are willing to pay it. What are the consequences of all the things that will go unsaid, undone, unprepared, unfathomed? We can never know for sure.

But the result of such inflexibilities on all sides is that many aspects of society are out of synch with the realities and needs of employed women today. These women have found one solution: invalidate the system that caused the pressure. Get around it, rework it, ignore it, break it. When the pressure cooker explodes, women take the traditional social structures with them. As one woman said with a frown, "So you've got ring around the collar? Go wash your neck."

If our social institutions continue to resist adaptation, or adapt too slowly, trends indicate that such women will simply abandon them or challenge them in such a way that the systems will no longer be necessary or workable, which will in turn cause a drastic reorganization of our traditional

way of life. The fact that already one-fourth of the Pacesetter group is divorced or separated illustrates this phenomenon as it impacts on marriage. Of course, men and
women marry or live together for numerous reasons: love,
sex, family, companionship, and emotional and financial security, to name a few. These all interact in complex ways
with the psychological composition of each couple. The self-
validation provided by job and money are too important to
women for them to discard or disregard these things in
favor of a man's expectations or a life-style they perceive as
less rewarding.

Whatever the cause—whether the marital structure fails
to fit a woman's needs or she fails the needs of the marriage—
the end result will be the same: We will see women altering
or abandoning the system rather than sacrificing to maintain
it. It's happening right now, on a fragmented basis, in numerous aspects of everyday life. For example, a woman may
postpone childbearing for the sake of furthering her career
(this is happening so frequently that from 1975 to 1978
there was a 37 percent increase in the number of women age
thirty to thirty-four having their first child, and a 22 percent
increase in women age thirty-five to thirty-nine doing so).[25]
An ambitious woman who finds herself trapped in a dead-
end job refuses to accept this as her fate; instead, she leaves
for better opportunities. If that fails, she may found her
own business and simply skip the corporate hierarchy completely.

Married women are refusing to put their husbands'
careers ahead of their own. Only 32 percent of the women
in our survey felt their husband's job was more important
than theirs, and in a survey by the National Commission on
Working Women only 3 percent of the women respondents
stated that they would not take a job because their husband
was opposed.[26] One woman who accepted a job that was 500
miles away from the city where her husband of five years

lives and works crystallized the attitude: "I feel I've worked too hard for what I want to do. I can't deny myself that. I had offers in his city, but it wasn't what I wanted to do. This job is exactly what I want." Meanwhile, the system is only slowly adapting to such changes. A survey by Merrill Lynch Relocation Management, Inc., found that only 30 percent of the corporations questioned provided job-finding help for the spouses of transferring executives.[27]

Other trends evidence women's impatience with or avoidance of the way of life they embraced for so long. Fast-food sales are booming, and women are cooking less than ever; Americans now spend 40 cents of every food dollar eating out; one in four people skip breakfast—who has time to prepare it or eat it? Stores are staying open evenings to cater to the working woman, who is finding new shopping alternatives: The mail order business grew 27 percent in 1979, an increase experts attribute largely to the increase of working women, who no longer have time to linger in stores.[28] Volunteer work, once a staple of the feminine image, is no longer viable for most working women. According to our survey, 35 percent of all working women feel they should definitely help those who are less fortunate, but for Pacesetter women, this drops dramatically to 16 percent. Heidrick and Struggles, Inc., has reported that about 42 percent of the women officers in its 1979 survey are involved in no civic or charitable undertakings whatsoever.[29] Observing these trends, Marilyn Moats Kennedy notes, "Women seem to not be very compromising at this point. They seem to be saying, 'It's my time now and I just can't compromise. I'm just not going to do it.' "

The Feminine Edge

An explosive combination of social and demographic factors will also work in favor of women, allowing them to exercise more of their newly created options and offering increased opportunities to assume leadership roles.

Women's increasing numerical superiority, combined with their increasingly higher level of education, is likely to lead to a change in social consciousness and political representation. Attitudes are changing already. For instance, after the 1980 election the chairperson of the National Women's Political Caucus commented that not only were the largest number of women in history elected to Congress, but for the first time ever, being a woman was not an issue. In 1950, women outnumbered men for the first time in history. The Census Bureau projects that women in the United States could outnumber men by 7.2 million in the year 2000. This would have immense political ramifications and would result in increased power for women, as women of voting age would outnumber men by 9 million.[30] While there were 17 women in Congress in 1980, compared with 11 in 1970, there could well be 250 female members in Congress at the turn of the century.[31] And perhaps a female president.

In any case, women will become more involved in politics as they gain more time to do so. A woman who must shoehorn political activities into a double-duty work and domestic schedule will not find much time or energy for political activities. However, as we have seen, women are becoming increasingly less domestic, devoting more time to outside activities.

The likelihood of political involvement swells as women become increasingly at ease with public exposure. As Kennedy points out, "The reason there haven't been many women interested in politics is that they haven't liked exposing themselves to a public failure, which is what it is when you don't get elected. [But] women are going to get more interested in politics. The ones who are really into power, as opposed to power and money, will turn to politics, because politics is the theater for power. Once women have tasted power at the corporate level, or find that they do like to lead, they're going to want it at the public level. There will be a tremendous explosion of women running for office when this happens."

Why have women had a near-invisible political profile? One study involving the sexual division of labor in politics sheds some light on the issue. Diane Rothbard Margolis noted that while women actually worked more hours than men in political activities, it was the men who usually were chosen for important positions. She charged this largely to the fact that the women gained self-esteem from task completion, while men measured their performance according to their involvement in decision making. Also, women tended to work in seclusion, avoiding the limelight and staying in the organizational trenches, while men sought center stage and the aura of authority.[32] This goes back to basic attitudes, which, as evidenced by the Go-Getter and Pacesetter women, are now changing. Rather than shun the limelight, for instance, Pacesetters, unlike nonworking women, actively seek it. And our survey also shows that younger women are far more likely to be comfortable in the glare of the public spotlight than their elders. We found that 43 percent of women age thirty-five to fifty claimed they had no desire for fame—compared with only 26 percent of women under age twenty-five. The attitudinal changes are already evidenced by the increasing numbers of women in politics and are likely to have a ripple effect on the nature of women's day-to-day political involvement and rise to authority within party structures, especially as these younger women mature and gain experience.

The acceptability of the female leader, once established at the industrial level, will also pave the way in a similar manner for mass acceptability of women as authority figures and power brokers. The political arena will then become an easier conquest for women. Easier, perhaps, than they suspect: Consider the case of Margaret Thatcher, who in 1970 predicted that within her lifetime no woman would ever reach a high cabinet post in Great Britain. Nine years later, she became prime minister.

As the number of women in the labor force continues to increase, the ratio of female to male workers will also grow accordingly, giving women more footholds for power. Already this ratio has surged from 58 per 100 in 1970 to 69 per 100 in 1978,[33] and it is likely to increase to the point where employed women outnumber employed men. This is especially probable not only because of female population growth but also because the number of years women spend in the labor force has risen sharply since 1950, while the number of years men spend working has been on the decline. Meanwhile, women's life expectancy is also increasing, as men's declines proportionately, with women gaining an average of about 14 years, to reach age 76.8, compared to men's gain of only 8.5 years, to reach age 69.2, since the turn of the century. Today women at age 20 are expected to live 14 percent longer than men.[34] This leaves women with more years to be active in the work force than men, a substantial advantage in the increasingly active and productive later years. Widespread female employment and resulting physical trauma will not equalize male and female life spans, as is often assumed. In fact, a recent California study states that despite the fact that women incur more high-risk factors than men (such as smoking and physical inactivity), women live longer, not because men's jobs are more hazardous, but because women are biologically superior.[35]

One interesting response to the social changes caused by

women's flow into the work force is the prediction that it will go away. For years, the economy was cited as the bugaboo that would pull the rug out from under women; according to the "last hired, first fired" theory, a good recession would force them back home. The 1980 recession proved this to be a fallacy, as the unemployment rate among men climbed nearly three percentage points, compared to an increase of slightly more than one percentage point for women, and the jobless rate for men actually topped that of women for the first time since the end of World War II.[36] Another favored fantasy is that women will be flogged back home by feelings of guilt. But, as our survey reveals, most women do not feel guilty about the time they spend on the job, and most working mothers feel that their children receive adequate care.

One prediction seems particularly unlikely: that we will lure women back to the home by offering new systems of housewife compensation. Who will devise such systems? Can we realistically expect it from the same lawmakers who deny the homemaker Social Security benefits and disallow the deduction of child-care expenses from income taxes? It is possible that those who predict a return to the old values are those who grew up with them and have a more nostalgic perspective and a heavier investment in the status quo. For instance, one recent generational study of mothers and children in their late teens revealed that the offspring were more likely to favor the mother's getting out of the house than the mother herself.[37]

Certainly it is far more comfortable to envision a retrenching of our traditional ways and values than to anticipate their disintegration. But this upheaval is more than a possibility—the momentum is accelerating. The rise of the new woman will lead to a chaotic, transitional era in which outmoded socioeconomic structures are forced to either change or collapse, and from which a new foundation will emerge.

We have seen how women are becoming increasingly impatient with compromise. It could be said that they are sprinting—equipping themselves for mental, psychological, and physical change through education, training, and job experience—and this trend is intensifying and broadening Meanwhile, women's opportunities are increasing and their life span is lengthening. Men, in comparison, are running in place. And as long as women are making most of the adjustments, men have little motivation to change. This attitude only compounds the pressure and intensifies the cracks in the status quo.

As stereotypes ease, each sex will explore gender attributes that were previously inhibited. Men will be able to develop more humanistic, domestic, artistic qualities, while women's emphasis will shift to independence, competitiveness, and power. The new variation on "feminine wiles" has unlimited potential.

As they equip themselves for a changing life-style, women are giving themselves the edge. They are less in need of those things that traditionally could be provided only by men, from financial support to basic validation as human beings. Men's dependence on women is more complex, because mothers are female. Psychologist Porter Bennett notes, "There is a certain deep expectation—a woman is going to put food in our mouth, hand us clean clothes, and kiss it where it hurts—that really goes deep because that's what good mothers do." The mother is and always will be the primary dependency figure for both men and women. For men, the nurturing figure has continued as the homemaker. And so men still maintain their dependence on women for certain basic nurturing needs: domestic services and ego support. It is difficult for men to equip themselves to satisfy most of the psychological needs traditionally supplied by women, except through massive social changes that they have been reluctant to support. And, of course, they will always need women to bear children.

If the traditional institutions continue to crumble under pressure, who will make the most sacrifices to keep them afloat? Those who are in the neediest position—the men. Less psychologically prepared than women to live in a changed world, men will be forced to compromise if they want certain things: For example, the privilege of being fathers, the luxury of female companions or wives, the financial relief of the income that an employed woman can provide. As these things are increasingly no longer men's rights to possess but women's rights to bestow, the balance of power will shift—subtly at first, but with inevitable and increasing momentum.

A Turbulent Transition

In the total historical scheme, the changes we see happening are occurring with phenomenal speed. But the evolution toward matriarchy will seem subtle.

The next phase—which we are entering even now—will be a transition period. This will be a time of uncertainty and insecurity, characterized by conflict and competition between men and women.

Already we see this competitiveness surfacing in sexual harassment, and other put-downs that are typical tactics of a person who is threatened or insecure. As women gain more power and are in a stronger position, competitiveness will become more overt and acute, especially in the near future, as the baby-boom generation serves up an overabundance of qualified candidates of both sexes to compete for choice positions, and working women simultaneously continue to flood the job market. Men will find themselves faced with a group of women who are not only capable on the job but are also highly competitive, play-to-win types in little awe of the male power mystique, with a network of their own to rival the Good Old Boy system. Hostility is inevitable as women jockey for—and win—jobs once earmarked exclusively for men. (Note that articles and books on how to maneuver for organizational power have flooded the market since women's movement into the work force became widely evident, about six years ago.)

This competitive situation will be heightened as women move into management in greater numbers, because men, entrenched in the alpha-style management process, will feel hostile toward women's beta-style management techniques. Lynn Rosener of SRI International makes the point: "As women enter into high levels of business, if they promote a new kind of management style, they're going to be seen as a threat. They're going to be seen as using certain skills which up to this point our society has considered tantamount to witchcraft, and referred to in a way that implies they are not rational, they are mysterious. And I think that frightens people. When you use something that somebody can't see or understand, it creates a threat. It's going to take very careful work on the part of women who are using this style to integrate it into corporate leadership."

As women begin to integrate their management styles into the corporate environment, we will see two things happening. First, sparks will fly as feelings of conflict, hostility, and fear run rampant through organizations. Women already are noticing this trend and facing it as a serious problem. To avoid stress, they will couch their beta-style skills in alpha terms, much as we see them donning pin-stripe suits, or they will acquire the necessary alpha skills. These skills are technique-oriented, and they are being learned and adopted by women who want to succeed in the existing mainstream. This will give women the necessary entrée within the existing systems, which will in turn increase the head-to-head competition as women and men vie for the same management positions.

This competitiveness will carry over into personal relationships, generating more undercurrents of hostility between men and women. Greater numbers of domestic disagreements will be precipitated by work-related conflicts and jealousies. Whereas twenty years ago women hung admiringly on men's words as they described their discussions with the boss, the new woman will take the measure of how she herself would have handled the situation, and will be more prone to comparison, criticism, or advice that may be interpreted as criticism.

Women will ask more of their men, looking for the same drive and aggressiveness they exhibit themselves. In fact, just keeping pace may not be enough for a man. He may also find it necessary to offer credible, enthusiastic support for the woman's career and her goals, or she may well feel that he is undermining her potential and decide to send him packing. If the man is unable to keep up, the relationship will fall apart due to lack of respect on the woman's part or resentment and jealousy on the man's. For this reason, it is unlikely that role-reversal situations will work out on a widespread basis in the foreseeable future. When and if co-parenting becomes the norm, there will be fewer stereotypes and sexual role barriers, which would in turn make role reversals more acceptable, but even then, economics will make them unlikely; for financial survival, both partners will probably have to work.

Due to the combined effects of the woman's time squeeze, job commitment, and self-involvement, sex may diminish in frequency and also in emotional meaning during the transition period. This trend, too, is already on the horizon, with Pacesetters and women under twenty-five reporting that sex is one of the areas most impacted by their jobs—and the impact is negative.

The social issue of power will be played out on a smaller scale within each relationship. Without a clear-cut indicator like income to determine the balance of power in a marriage or domestic arrangement, a wider variety of issues will provide opportunities to establish power, and this, too, will intensify conflict.

As all these conflicts become more widespread, popular vehicles will spring up to handle them. While the past decade, the "me" generation, dealt with personal development, the transition to matriarchy will probably spawn methodologies for dealing with career and personal conflicts. For example, we may see a proliferation of company-sponsored seminars and retreats to help employees and their mates deal with this volatile situation. Negotiating as a personal skill will be taught on a more formal and widespread basis, perhaps beginning in high school or sooner.

Relationships between men and women will become more demanding and require greater cooperation to survive—an element that will be in short supply. In the immediate future, as overcommitted women and bewildered men struggle with outmoded values, role imagery, and institutions, we can expect increased tension between the sexes. As a result, women probably face a mammoth backlash against their new independence, such as the highly vocal criticism of the proposed Equal Rights Amendment. This eventually will be overcome by sheer numbers as women move into positions of influence in all segments of society, driven, in spite of the backlash, by their own strong desire for self-fulfillment and the overriding need for economic self-sufficiency.

This transitional period will most likely continue until certain social functions change. Equal parenting and child-care is the key to a shift in the balance of power. Women working outside the home, redistribution of domestic responsibility within the family, the advent of external child-care systems that provide both men and women staff members as role models—all are necessary if a generation of children is to be brought up free of the confining and negative aspects of sexual stereotypes.

It is likely that the phenomenon of the working woman will precipitate, of necessity, these kinds of changes. But first, women must let them happen. The most immediate step toward a change in our patriarchal society must be for women to outgrow their superwoman complex. As long as they attempt to "do it all," they will do it at their own expense, and they will suffer in the social hierarchy. They must accept the fact that to share responsibility, to narrow one's responsibilities, to be less than perfect jugglers, is human and real and not a negative thing. This is beginning to happen, and when the realization spreads, it will open the door not only to men's sharing of traditionally female territory like child-care and domestic services, but also to the maximization of each woman's natural potential.

CHAPTER 9

The Coming Matriarchy

In the coming matriarchy, women will have the power advantage, but will not brandish it like a big stick with cleats. Most likely, in fact, men as well as women will have a wider range of sanctioned opportunities than they do today, for this will be a society of nearly limitless options, with a broadened status quo. There will be no preprogrammed, single, "right" way to raise a family, fill a job, fall in love, live a life.

Rather than a sex based role reversal, we will see role diversification. Some women, if they can afford it, may choose to stay home with their children. So will some men. The point is, sex will not be the dividing line for opportunity. Society will be far more complex than a simple flip-flop of roles. When one sex is no longer the "provider" and the other not exclusively tied to the home and child-care, all possibilities open up.

There is obviously no way to foresee the future. But we can consider some of the more viable options, and make predictions based not on speculation but on real trends already in motion. We are heading in a certain direction, and we had better be prepared.

Good-bye, Goody Two-Shoes

Once upon a stereotype, the ideal woman was supposed to be *selfless*, considering the needs of others—particularly her husband and family—before her own. As the Pacesetter type of woman moves into prominence, the so-called selfless woman will be eclipsed by a new image of womanhood.

This change is already evident in the Pacesetters, who are more than twice as self-confident as women in general, and are quite comfortable promoting themselves and striving for their own gain. They are also highly unlikely to help someone less fortunate, and put their job on an equal footing with their home and family.

The Matriarchal Woman will be far more self-oriented than the average woman of today. In this sense, "self" is not confined to the superficial aspects of beauty and body. "Self" will mean a woman's capability of appreciating and investing in her own needs, not necessarily at the expense of others. This trend can be detected on the horizon, with a recent rash of women's magazines that stress self-development, not fashion and beauty, and popular "self-help" movements directed toward this end. The Matriarchal Woman will ask herself first and foremost, "What's in it for *me?*" The new measurement for a woman's status will become not her competence as a wife and mother, but how much she can accomplish for herself. The value system women have been brought up with for centuries will be razed. Previously emphasized attributes such as niceness, sweetness, gentility, and motherliness, all of which are other-directed, will be broadened to include attributes like competence, intelligence, achievement, and strength, all of which are self-directed. If the traditional woman can be diagrammed as

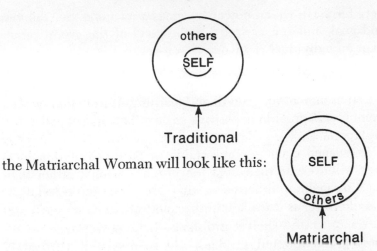

the Matriarchal Woman will look like this:

Volunteer work will not be considered fulfilling by Matriarchal Women because the rewards will not compare favorably with those of paid employment, and they will have little time after ministering to themselves and their families to minister to others. As one Pacesetter woman expressed it, "Volunteer work? To me, those women are time-wasters. And I happen to feel my time is very, very valuable." Another jibed, "You won't catch me making cookies for any bake sale. If anybody's going to eat the cookies, it's going to be me."

This does not mean that women of the future will no longer be willing to invest in others. They will, instead, consider that their most precious investment is themselves.

Beta Power

Under the current system of alpha management, power in itself is an end goal. This kind of power is highly individualistic and involves personal gain at the expense of others—taking someone else's self-respect and giving it to yourself. When women look at power, however, they tend to do so in beta terms, in which power becomes a means rather than an end goal, and is exercised for the good of the group rather than an individual. To women, self-respect is a more appropriate goal than power. This perspective involves a sensitivity to those who are not in power, and fosters a more fertile environment for growth and learning. Within this system, women will provide a positive rather than negative leadership force.

As women become comfortable in positions of influence, they will exercise their beta power more openly, rather than masking it in alpha terms, as they are prone to do today. If it is effective, as it is likely to be due to the long-range, complex nature of society's problems, beta power will be respected and adopted, gradually, by men as well. Ultimately we could see a balanced integration of both alpha and beta power, with each style being utilized by each sex when it is most appropriate.

Beta power will add a diversity of approaches and solutions, a new perspective on life.

Although beta power is a more people-oriented approach, it does not imply the end of the profit motive. Profit will remain an important measure of certain functions in an organization, but it will no longer have first priority. Instead, beta power will bring a greater recognition of the quality of life, and the improvement of this quality will become a more important goal, with profit as one means to that end. Flexible schedules, job sharing, permanent part-time work, and other work strategies will come into prominence and widespread use as human life takes precedence over profit.

The rise of beta power, with its implied emphasis on the long-term perspective, will lead to a new kind of decision making, in which things are not decreed but evolve incrementally. Since conditions rarely remain static over long periods of time, a reevaluative approach will become necessary.

The process will also become more integrative, since long-term decisions involve a wider variety of criteria.

One result of the reevaluative, integrative approach will be a change in the hierarchical structure as we know it, involving a shift to the decentralization of authority. As our business affairs become increasingly complex, it becomes more unlikely that a lone individual or chief executive officer can be all-knowing, so input will be necessary on a more frequent basis from a wider variety of sources. We could see an evolution to management by committees of advisors or managers, rather than by one person. The role of each individual manager would be stronger than today because he or she would be responsible for evaluating decisions and their effects on employees more frequently than the current alpha system permits.

Women would be members of these management committees. Their beta style would motivate them to seek positions in which they could exercise influence for the good of the group, rather than power as a visible show or end in itself. They might or might not be chief executive officers, but, then, the point is that an all-consuming position would be less desirable than it is today—not only because it would hold less power, but because it would take time away from human needs, like leisure and self-development.

The end result would be a less autocratic kind of organizational structure, and one which is more in tune with human needs.

Domestic Derailment

The Matriarchal Woman's major interests will not be domestic, a trend that is foreshadowed by today's Pacesetters. These women are not going to see home and family as the ultimate achievement. In the future, women who follow the trends of the Pacesetters will work outside the home. It is likely that, considering the psychology of the Pacesetters and the economic circumstances of our inflationary trajectory, virtually all women will be employed for part if not all of their adult lives within the next twenty-five years. The woman who does not work will be the oddity, perhaps part of a very small minority of mothers of very young children, older retired women, women of limited interests, or wives of extremely wealthy men who have no psychological desire for outside work.

As a result, there will be a greater number of women—and men—living alone or together outside of marriage. We see this tendency already among the Pacesetters, 43 percent of whom are unmarried. Many of the women of the future, who will be economically independent as a result of work, will choose to never marry, since their financial need will be less pressing and their first concern will be to pursue their ambitions via a career, not to capture a man. Also, women's jobs will provide much of the self-validation that previously was available to women only through their husbands and families. As they find the monetary and psychological rewards of work more appealing, women will not find it necessary to marry to receive a source of self-confidence. This can be seen already among the Pacesetters, who, although they are the most likely women to be divorced, are also the most self-confident women.

Establishing a good relationship will be more important to Matriarchal Women than achieving marriage. Those who do choose to marry will probably marry later than the women of today, after having given themselves time to make a mark in their career. Women of the future will mirror the attitudes of this Pacesetter bride, marrying for the first time in her late twenties: "I grew up really believing that I wouldn't marry until I was thirty-five—if I ever married. I really thought that there was no way a working woman can be married, that it would take away from the career and that it would inhibit you, tie you down, all kinds of negative things. And it took me a long time to overcome those obstacles. For me, making a decision to get married was very difficult. Over the years, what I really had to decide was: Is there a tradeoff? Does marriage take away from a career or can marriage contribute to a career? What I've finally decided, after observing other women at work who are married, is that it will contribute to me personally and help make me a whole person—a more whole person."

How does she define "more whole"? "More to give to my career."

Inevitably accompanying the decline in marriage and the fact that women in general will have less interest in child-raising and more in their careers will be a continued decline in the birthrate. If the United States continues to drag its feet in providing affordable, quality day-care, women will not choose to stay at home to raise their children; they will simply choose to forego children altogether or have fewer of them. Already, the number of white women in their mid-twenties who are expected to remain childless has tripled to 30 percent. It is projected that 20 percent of nonwhite women in this age group will choose to be childless. Women who do have children may drop out of the work force temporarily, but peer pressure and their own sense of motivation will carry them back to their jobs as soon as feasibly possible —not unlike the Pacesetter mother, Ellen, who had her baby on Monday and was back in the office on Thursday.

Motherhood as an ideal will lose its dominant status and will no longer be the proudest role a woman can fill. It will, instead, become one of many roles available. Future ideals will be based on what a woman can accomplish for herself, not what she can accomplish for others. The farther and more successfully she can carry herself, the more status she will maintain. This status will also become more realistic than it is today, when women have finally overcome the image of the housewife obsessed with battling waxy yellow buildup only to face the equally irritating image of the super-woman who brings home the bacon, fries it up in the pan, then waltzes off swathed in perfume and chiffon. Lacking role models, working women today are struggling to accomplish everything at once and do it all well, and many feel guilty if they cannot. Significantly, the Pacesetters do not feel guilty. If they must leave their children to go to work— so be it. They are more likely to recognize the imperfection of reality and settle for the rewards where they can find them. Likewise, the next generation will see by observing their working mothers and role models that it is impossible to be perfect in all ways, so they will not feel as obsessed with perfection as today's women. Their expectations will be more realistic. They will be able to focus their attention more narrowly, without feeling guilt. Of course, this means that something must go. It will be the trappings of domesticity.

The Motherhood Makeover

As the Matriarchal Woman evolves, motherhood as we know it will undergo a major transformation, a change that in turn will have dramatic behavioral and psychological effects on men, women, and their children. As already fore-shadowed by the Pacesetters, the Matriarchal Woman will be less likely than traditional women to have children, not because she does not want or care for them, but because they will not fit easily into her ambitious, work-oriented scheme. It is probable, though, that Matriarchal Women will continue to desire motherhood, because, given a positive childhood experience, these women will identify positively with the maternal image. If such a woman has children, it will be as late in life as physically possible to permit herself more time to establish her own career and reach her personal goals. If science and social custom have made surrogate motherhood and test-tube babies possible and acceptable, these may be the routes to motherhood chosen by many women, who will not care to be sidelined or inconvenienced by pregnancy. In any case, motherhood will take on a new definition, and will no longer be synonymous with round-the-clock personal service to a child or children.

Biological motherhood and parenting will probably become separate functions, with the parenting role being split and assumed by a combination of father, mother, and parental surrogates of both sexes, like day-care personnel. All are capable of nurturing instincts, and such a cooperative effort would be essential in a society in which mothers cannot or will not devote their exclusive attention to child-care. This does not mean that mothers will not love their children, but that caretaking and love are not necessarily synonymous.

The most significant result of such co-parenting would be a realignment of sexual images and roles. Under our traditional parenting system, in which the mother carries the bulk of the child-rearing responsibility and the father is perceived as relatively distant or unavailable on a day-to-day domestic basis, women and men perpetuate their own roles in the gender hierarchy. In a complex, multilayered psychological process, both boys and girls grow up with an unconscious image of the mother as an omnipotent and consequently somewhat fearful figure. This image evokes hostility from both sexes, but more from males, who must undergo a greater separation process in the evolution to their eventual identification with the male gender. Girls, in separating their own identities from those of their mothers, do not have to focus on a different gender, and so retain less ambivalence and hostility toward the female image.[1]

Child-care which is almost exclusively maternal results in excess psychological baggage that reinforces the patriarchal society. Males, on one hand, grow up to be both attracted to and dependent on women; on the other hand, they may unconsciously fear the concept of feminine control as established in the mother relationship and, as a result, consider women a threat. Boys' early primary dependence on their mothers surfaces later, in a need to assert independence outside the maternal relationship, in order to better facilitate identification with the male gender model, the father. In adulthood, devaluing women is one way in which men may strive to assert superiority in an unconscious effort to emancipate themselves from their mothers and identify with the male image provided by their fathers. The father's relative absence from the day-to-day operations of the home results in a boy's idealization of the masculine role, since there is no role model for masculinity that is easily accessible. The mother's overaccessibility, on the other hand, often leads to a man's resentment and dread of women, and ultimately to devaluation of the feminine gender.[2]

Females also undergo a psychological shift of self-image away from the maternal figure, but it is an easier task for them because of their sex and our social expectations. For women, the overavailability of the mother and lack of access to the father found in the traditional nuclear household result in a perpetuation of the traditional maternal role. However, women also can be socially impeded by the dominant presence of a larger-than-life mother as the source of almost everything. For instance, adult women who were reared in an environment in which the mother controlled the situation, no other female figures were actively present, and the father was either not present or ineffectual have been found to have problems experiencing themselves as autonomous adults, separate from their children.[3]

Young children grasp what they can. When the mother is present too much and the father is present too little, they tend to formulate perceptions via the most readily available means—cultural stereotypes. If society sees men as authoritarian and dominant, and women as maternal and passive, children will mimic these views.

One result of a society in which child-care is a sexually shared responsibility would be a decline in sexual stereotyping, with both men and women perceived as sharing role attributes. There would also be less resentment of women by men, since boys would be less likely to view their mothers as omnipotent and so have less cause to develop immature fears to carry into adulthood.

Of course, a biological mother will, by force of nature, infant bonding, and the maternal relationship, remain a primary influence, but the scope of that influence would be subject to change. While the mother would still be in a position to shape her children's perceptions of the adult world, if parenting was shared or cooperative, children's perceptions would be significantly different. More important than pure gender would be the subtle interplay between the parents, or the nature and quality of the child-care institution.

Day-Care Revisited

As women gain money and power, more of their needs will be met by society, if only because they will be in a position to get what they want. Child-care has the potential to be handled in a social manner, rather than as the one-on-one situation we see today.

Women will choose not to have children, or to have fewer children, if bearing and raising them continues to impede their work outside the home. We already see this trend in the Go-Getters and Pacesetters. By having fewer children, women will be freed to establish a social, economic, and political power base from which they can more effectively create, lobby for, legislate, or otherwise establish child-care institutions. During this transitional period, a severe decline in the birthrate is likely. This decline will ease proportionately to the availability of child-care facilities, although we will probably never again see a trend toward large families as long as most women work outside the home.

With a matriarchal society would come at last the perception of affordable, quality child-care as a social necessity, not a private luxury. As a result, there would be an influx of a wide variety of day-care situations, ranging from in-home cooperatives shared by groups of parents to on-the-job, employer-provided facilities to government-sponsored programs. Children of all ages could be cared for, including infants, who might have their own separate and specially staffed facilities. The increasing interest in and demand for quality day-care would also expand careers in the field for both men and women, who would be trained and educated for the work. The child-care worker would in turn gain higher social status and salaries than at present and so attract a richer pool of candidates. This kind of child-care would have a very positive impact on women in the work force, since it would reduce the job/child ambivalence that is so prevalent today. With freedom from worry and guilt about the mechanics of who would care for the children while both partners worked, the commitment of both men and women to their children and their job would be strengthened, and the benefits would be multidimensional.

What would be the effect on the children? This is a question of great significance, but there is no answer that is either simple or certain, because there are too many variables. However, we can make some tentative speculation, based on current experience.

The overwhelming consensus of research to date is that most children of working mothers develop normally and without undue hostilities. However, there is still some disagreement and uncertainty among the experts as to the exact effects of nonexclusive mothering.

As Dr. Roy Grinker, Jr., explains, "The returns are not in yet, because this is a sociological and psychological study that has to be a prospective one. But the *early* returns suggest that working mothers by and large do not have children with more problems than nonworking mothers. That kids adapt well to day nurseries. That kids adapt well to nurses and baby-sitters. That these kids so far don't seem to have any significant number of psychiatric difficulties, more than any others. It may be too soon to tell, however, because the day-care movement is less than ten years old."

Although employed mothers spend about half as much time with their children as housewives do, there is as yet no evidence to suggest that this harms children, given the substitution of *quality* child-care. The effects of day-care seem to be linked to a complex spectrum of variables, including the sex of the child, the husband's presence or attitude, the quality and consistency of the caretaker or facility, the hours worked by the mother, and the family income.

Arlene Cohn, director of the Wesley Day-Care Center in Glenview, Illinois, a superior institution with the crucial element of a highly stable staff, points out, "I see no effect of the mother's working or not working on the children we care for, who are over age two and a half. The child's situation is related to the kind of child-care, and most importantly, what's happening at home." Cohn feels that group day-care can be a positive experience, causing children to become more socially advanced and independent. "You'll hear a child say to another child, 'You're really making me very angry, you know.' This is the kind of thing that comes much later— or never—with children who are not in a situation where they are constantly encouraged to express their feelings in a constructive way. They become very independent and responsible."

Cohn has found that most children at her facility are very well adjusted, once they get over the initial separation from the mother. "Even then," she notes, "it's in many ways more difficult for the parent than for the child. But when mothers work, I find that they tend to compensate and spend a lot of time with their children—quality time, when they are free —and do a lot more for their children than the mother who is always at home.

"However," she cautions, "I can't make any judgments about what is better for a child, since there are basic things that none of us really know."

Still, research is unanimous that high-quality child-care by mother surrogates does not harm children under most circumstances, and that an unbroken maternal presence is not necessary for a child's healthy emotional development. There is no evidence that the mother-child relationship becomes impaired when the mother is not always available. Children, even infants, have been found capable of forming multiple attachments, to both their mothers and other caregivers, and studies confirm that bonds and attachments can be formed between parent and child even if they spend only a short time together each day.[4]

Much will depend, as it does today, on the quality of child-care. If women continue to work and to exhibit Pacesetter attitudes, and if all other variables remain the same as they are today—extreme lack of sufficient high-quality day-care, and parenting with little male participation—will the next generation of children suffer, not because they are not loved, but because their mothers will be so heavily burdened? Our research comparing daughters of working mothers and daughters of nonworking mothers offers some clues. Adult daughters of working mothers did not seem to suffer psychologically, although they were in fact more likely to feel their childhoods were unstable than daughters of nonworking women. However, this may be *perceived,* not real, instability, involving comparison with the stereotypical mother who is always at home with milk and cookies. If you see this image often enough, on television and in books, you may come to believe it is the only "stable" way.

The impact of the working mother on her children seems to be attitudinal. Most studies report positive effects: Compared with daughters of nonworking mothers, daughters of working mothers hold fewer sexual stereotypes about themselves and their roles and exhibit higher career aspirations, while sons are more likely to accept dual work roles in their own future families.[5] Daughters of employed mothers also exhibit better education performance and have higher educational aspirations than daughters of nonworking mothers.[6] And, as our survey confirms, daughters of working mothers are more likely than those of nonworking mothers to feel that they are ambitious and independent, and to say that they always thought they'd be working women. On the other hand, sons of working mothers, especially in middle-class families, were found to be more negatively influenced, with lower grades or intelligence scores than sons of nonworking middle-class mothers.[7] This may suggest that the women's work revolution will make sons more accepting of an expanded role for women, but less personally achievement-oriented, while providing role models and inciting premature skill formation that spurs daughters on to greater ambition and achievement. This would in turn reinforce the development of the Matriarchal Woman.

New Sexual Dynamics

Since marriage will no longer be a woman's primary source of status and economic support, women who choose to marry will do so for healthier motives. There may be a revival of romantic love as an ideal, as women gain the luxury of marrying purely for this reason.

As male-female relationships change, marriage may actually increase in popularity as the ultimate expression of love and commitment. Whereas today we are seeing an increase in the divorce rate, the coming matriarchy may bring about a decrease in both marriage and divorce, with marriages predicated on terms that better fit the new roles of both men and women. When earning power does not determine control in a marriage, individual skills, sensitivity, creativity, and resourcefulness will become the key to sexual dynamics. Women will be more likely to choose their partners with a discriminating eye toward the total man, thus increasing chances for a successful relationship. In cases where a relationship or marriage does not work out, however, there will be less reluctance to end it. The Matriarchal Woman who finds that her relationship with a man is undermining her sense of self-esteem will not consider it necessary to cling to the relationship for the traditional reasons, and she will have the self-sufficiency to stand on her own.

Shared finances will become a thing of the past, due to women's desire to protect their hard-earned interest. Written contracts will become a way of life for couples living together whether they're married or not. Even the minority of women who do not work outside the home are likely to require contracts, by placing dollar values on their contributions. And men will do the same.

As women control their childbearing more carefully, men will no longer be able to take it for granted that fatherhood is their natural right. A society of self-supporting women will be able to evaluate a man's appropriateness as a father on terms that will include more emphasis on the father as an emotional rather than financial provider. Men who do not appear to fit this criterion simply will not be chosen by women as fathers for their children. This will be a powerful motivator for men to change their traditional behavior patterns. As parenting also changes to allow men and women to share elements now confined to one sex or the other, more men will be able to provide the emotional environment that will become the standard.

As for sex, the Matriarchal Woman will not be a passive partner, nor will she be forced to trade it for financial support. Her sex life will probably reflect her aggressiveness. One study of professional women indicated that they are more sexually adventurous than more traditional wives,[8] and this trend will be continued by the Matriarchal Woman. As one Pacesetter woman commented, "I never knew how sexual I was until about the last three years. I always thought I was cute, maybe because I was *supposed* to be cute. Well, I ain't so cute. There's a playfulness about me in bed that is really shocking." What's shocking to today's woman will become standard for the Matriarchal Woman and her partner.

Due to the woman's lack of time and energy, and preoccupation with her career, it is likely that sex will diminish in frequency and emotion for both men and women. Fantasy sex may increase, however, as individuals dream of what is not realistically the case. When emotional attachments are formed, however, the courtship will become more romantic and protracted since it will be founded on real love, rather than a tradeoff of caretaking needs. And so after making an emotional commitment to each other, couples in the coming matriarchy are likely to be sexually monogamous, with the sexual commitment lasting as long as the emotional one. This is not to say it will last a lifetime, but divorce will probably be less common in the coming matriarchy than it is today, because the social institutions and sexual dynamics will have evolved to the point where there will be less friction in the crucial area of expectations. The fact that a woman works, for instance, is less likely to cripple a relationship when both members of the couple have been raised by two working parents in a co-parenting situation.

Family Redefined

The concept of family as we have come to know it will be revised. Dr. Domeena C. Renshaw, professor of psychiatry at Loyola University, points out that "one description of the family is 'a group of persons of common ancestry,' a definition that must now be questioned due to social changes. There are many family styles: extended family; nuclear family; single-parent families; homosexual families; communal families; and many, many combined or step families—remarriages with children from at least two, sometimes three or four, previous unions post-divorce. The traditional two-parent American nuclear family used to be a working natural father and a full-time natural mother at home with the children. However, 1978 statistics show that this family style now comprises only 7 percent of U.S. families. Working wives and the high divorce rate have changed society's family pattern considerably."

In the coming matriarchy, families will be thought of as sets of diverse individuals rather than homogeneous social clusters, and the definition of "family" will broaden to include many kinds of living arrangements, as is happening now without widespread social recognition. We may see the advent of the rotational family, in which there is no single, stable cast of characters for a lifetime, but rather a series of individuals—male and female—who will be added to or phased out of a continually reconstituted family unit as the needs, interests, and emotional commitments of the couple, individual, or group dictate. The first five years of a woman's adult life may be spent living with male and female roommates; the next five with a male mate; the next five with a husband and a child; the next five alone with a child; the next three with two female friends, and so on. This pattern is already emerging, but when it occurs on a large scale, we will see the rotational family replace the nuclear family as the status quo.

New Lifestyles

As women move out of the domestic forum and into the work-place, life-styles will change.

To better accommodate women's needs, cluster living will flourish, in which unrelated individuals live in professionally managed complexes, not communes, and share support services formerly provided by women. In this way everyone, male and female, will have a "wife," if they can afford the services. Landscaping, maintenance, cleaning, decorating, housekeeping, shopping, chauffeuring, delivery, laundry, receiving deliveries, a restaurant, and child-care are all typical services that will be provided by the cluster for its residents. Low-upkeep materials will be emphasized in construction, furnishing, and decorating.

Since the unmarried state will be prevalent, residences for single people, including those with children, may become common. Like the cluster residences, these could offer appropriate support services. They would also provide a ready-made social environment for the residents.

Industries and technologies will be built up around the woman who has left the home for the job. Consider video-catalog shopping, which displays merchandise and relevant details on a television-like viewing screen and lets shoppers place their on-line orders by punching in merchandise, credit, and delivery codes. Imagine local delivery/errand centers: places that would receive your deliveries, pick up your dry cleaning, and let the plumber into your house—all for a monthly service charge. Envision grocery stores in office buildings, stocked with products for convenience eating and cleaning. And think about domestic cleaning services that would be a tax-deductible expense to both employed men and women.

Leisure will take on new emphasis, as beta tendencies stress fulfilling human needs. Since time will be precious, at-home leisure will be especially important, and home entertainment will flourish. Much of this leisure activity may be educationally oriented: art appreciation or home remodeling courses on video disc or cassette, for instance.

More flexible work schedules will permit people to enjoy their leisure more, and the letup of emphasis on profit and productivity as ends in themselves will open the door for new life-styles in which leisure has a social value as great as work does today. People will plan for leisure, not just happen on it, perhaps factoring it into careers—planning, say, four years of work followed by six months of leisure. As men and women alike learn the value of leisure, we may well see an end to the workaholic syndrome and a richer enjoyment of life.

As for food, who will cook it? Most likely, someone else. In the last fifteen years there was a 40 percent per capita decline in the number of at-home dishes consumed per household.[9] This slide will continue, as busy working women seek refuge from time-consuming kitchen chores. Both men and women will no doubt do some cooking, but with an increasing demand for convenience. And eating out will continue to be a trend. An enormous variety of semi-fast-food restaurants may develop, specializing in catering to an almost infinite number of segments in a multifaceted market. There will be fast pasta restaurants and fast family restaurants and fast but tastefully decorated "theme" restaurants, plus an increase of restaurants that offer mini-meals conveniently located to workplaces. Also, a wider variety of carry-out and home-delivery food facilities will be available, and catering of home entertaining will become much more widespread.

The big suburban home will become a dinosaur on the market, as women streamline their life-styles. Whereas in the past families have sought the broad lawns of suburbia, there will be fewer families as such and fewer children per couple to play on the lawn, and priorities will shift to emphasize convenience rather than marigolds and trees. Everyone will want to live as close to work and centralized services as possible, as time becomes as precious as money. The biggest status symbol in town may be the ten-minute commute, and residential neighborhoods may coexist with industrial ones for the sake of convenience.

The patterns of personal relationships in the coming matriarchy will be far less predictable than they are today. Women's careers and outside interests will expose them to a broad range of social structures and class elements. Whereas traditional women have chosen their companions from a limited environment, employment will expose women to a wider scope of society. It is possible that the social structures and values of a woman's place of employment will supersede those of her home as the work-place assumes a larger social role than it does today. The Matriarchal Woman will be open to more social crossover, which will result in less homogeneous and predictable relationships. One Go-Getter explained, "It used to be that even if you met certain people you wouldn't have anything to do with that kind of person, because they weren't like you, maybe you thought they were beneath you—which is B.S.! My ex-husband taught me not to be such a snob. He'd work easel teardown, which was a tough, backbreaking kind of labor. After our divorce, I became a semipro volleyball referee. And what I found on that job was a lot of men who were day laborers, and a lot of them were younger, a lot were intelligent, and just like anyplace, a lot were stupid. But you can't judge a man by the color of his shirt. I have a wonderful relationship with one of these men, a construction worker. I am not confined to where I live or what I was brought up with."

Tomorrow Today

You may have felt, as you read this chapter, that it didn't seem all that futuristic or improbable. The seeds of the coming matriarchy are germinating now, and they're visible, if you look for them. We all know young women who are planning careers, women who are postponing parenthood, women who are independent, who are running their lives and their families with competence. Perhaps we know women who are running companies. These may seem like small changes because we have become familiar with them, in the way a parent observes the growth of a child. Our close vantage point has allowed change to creep up on us in a most disarming way.

We are living every day with the elements that will turn our world upside-down.

We are those elements.

CHAPTER 10

Prologue, Epilogue

JULIA AT EIGHTY-FIVE

She is blind now, but she is still proud, still the perfect hostess. In her small room in a residence for the elderly, she serves tea and cookies. And she remembers.

"I was born and reared in northwest Missouri on a farm that my grandfather started in 1830. My father and his mother lived there through the Civil War.

"My father was a competent, well-educated, intelligent man. My mother was a darling, but she was not so well educated. She was a dear, sweet person; my father called her his little sweetie woman. I come from a big family—six children—but there are only my sister and myself left, and the next generation. The rest are all dead.

"It was lovely growing up on the farm—we just had a grand time. It wasn't hard work, none of us worked. My father ran the farm like a business and had hired men; my mother had help in the house.

"I went to a one-room schoolhouse where all the grades were taught in one room. When I got to high school, I went the first two years in another town, and when the third year came up, my father thought the school wasn't good enough and sent me to a girls' boarding school in Columbia, where the University of Missouri is.

"I decided I wanted to be educated in economics, and that's when I had the idea that I wanted to be—not a teacher, never—a secretary, a very high-powered secretary.

"I went to the University of Missouri for a semester. One of the best-known economists in the country was there at that time and I heard him lecture and I wanted to know more about it, but they discouraged me. I went to the economics department and they wouldn't let me in. 'Why, you're a young girl. You don't know anything about economics,' is what they said.

"I felt infuriated.

"So I came home and said to my father, 'I'm sick of going to Missouri—I want to go to the University of Chicago.' I had gotten that idea from two young women who had come to my sorority house to visit someone, and they had been to the University of Chicago, and they said to me, 'If you want to go to the School of Business at the University of Chicago, you can, because they do educate women as well as men.'

"I had the grades to get in. So I came up to Chicago and stayed with a married woman living there, so my mother wouldn't be scared for my life.

"This is a very romantic part of my life. I went to the School of Business to talk to them and said I wanted to see the dean and was told, Sorry, the dean wasn't there that day, but I could see the assistant dean. I said, 'I don't want to see any assistant dean—I want to see the dean!' Finally I agreed to see the assistant dean, which was how I met my husband. He was the assistant dean.

"I met him a time or two in the hall afterward and he always had this lovely southern bow and he would say, 'How are you, Miss Gately?' And I thought he was the nicest man I ever knew. It wasn't long after that when he asked for a date, and that was that. Around the time of World War I, we were engaged.

"I was graduated from the University of Chicago in 1919. A few days later, my future fiancé came to visit my family. My father invited him into the parlor, which nowadays would be the TV room. I went out on the porch, to sit on the swing. My fiancé went in all prepared to tell my father what his salary was, what increases he expected to get, and what books he meant to write. And Papa said, 'I understand you're a southerner.'

"He said, 'Yes, sir.'

" 'A Democrat?'

" 'Yes.'

" 'That's very good,' my father said. 'Similarity in politics and religion makes a good basis for marriage.'

"He *expected* him to make a living for me, of course. That was taken for granted.

"After I was engaged to be married, I didn't want to be a secretary at all anymore! No, I don't think we were driven in those days by desire to be a real career person. I think I just *thought* I wanted to be a secretary, but it all went out the window when I was to be happily married. In fact, the dean of the school called me in when I was being graduated and offered me a job as a research person and I said, 'Well, Dean Marshall, I'm going to marry your assistant dean. I don't want a job.' I wasn't interested at all. My new goal was to be a wife and run a home.

"The feeling of the times was that the marriage *was* the role of the woman. Not that I'd ever have married just to be married. I really thought highly of my husband from the first time I met him until the day he died in 1966. We were happily married.

"My husband was a lawyer, and he taught law and business and wrote books. I worked as a volunteer in the League of

Women Voters—that was what I liked best. It is a non-partisan organization that studies issues. You have to work and be really interested in what's going on in the world if you work in the League of Women Voters. I was president.

"I did some other volunteer work, too. When we moved to the suburbs, away from the university campus, I was asked to be a founder of the infant welfare group and I shocked my friends because I told them I was much more interested in the League of Women Voters. But, well, infant welfare was *the* thing to do in the community—if you wanted to have any friends or be socially acceptable. So I joined. And I was president of it. I was pretty good as an executive, if it doesn't sound as if I'm bragging. What I did best was preside at meetings and get other people to do the work.

"But one day after we'd lived in the suburbs for quite a while I was sitting with my husband before the fireplace and suddenly he looked at me and he said, 'Julia, when I married you, I considered you a very intelligent person, and I always have, up until recently. But now you're talking exactly like these women. Personalities. Gossip. Nothing else.' And it shocked me almost to death. I realized it was true.

"They were very narrow-minded people, most of those women I knew. There were lots of college graduates, but they had let it slip. They wanted to be sure they knew how to put the spoons on the table and how to serve things. And all they had on their coffee tables was *The Women's Home Companion* or something like that—not that I had anything against those, but that's not a very wide education. I said, 'For heaven's sake, I've got to do something.' And that's when I started volunteering to teach current-events classes in the neighborhood. I would take an issue of the day and I would present all sides of it. And I took *The New York Times, The Wall Street Journal, Harper's* magazine, and *The Atlantic* to get good literary points of view.

"I was able to do all that I did because I had a woman

living in who was a good cook and maid. She freed me up. She came during the Depression and she stayed on for years, until my husband died.

"I think your first obligation is to your husband. And motherhood. I loved it. I thought I did a good job with my dear children. We lost our son, but my daughter is a darling, wonderful girl. She's a talented artist. But this comes from her father's side of the family. I couldn't paint a box.

"My husband enjoyed my doing things. He taught me a lot, because he knew all about economics. He wanted me to use my brain, not just be a gossip. That's what started me, my own husband. When he wrote his business books, he would say, 'Now, you know this material. Come here. I'll read a chapter or a paragraph and you tell me if it's clear.' We'd go through the whole book that way. And if I said it wasn't clear, he'd rewrite it. And when the books were published the reviews said they were so well written. He gave me a lot of credit for it—not that I could have written it. Don't misunderstand me. He was a writer, I was a listener.

"In my day, the women had the babies and the men earned the living and that's just the way it was organized. And no one questioned that.

"I understand how women who want to work do feel they are impeded. Of course, there's a biological reason, because if a woman marries she is the one that has the child, and then she has to stop work. But it never worried me. I didn't want to be a career person. I had a father who worked for me and a husband who took care of me. Women of my time think of ourselves as having been very well taken care of, you know. It's just a different point of view, and from that point of view, I think I had a very good life.

"I know my daughter thinks that men have had it too good all these years and that they do keep women down, and I can't make her see. I don't try anymore.

"I wanted to be at home when my husband came home.

I never wanted to work. Why should I? I had plenty of ways to express myself through volunteer organizations.

"I'm eighty-five years old, and I'm the old-fashioned woman."

SARA AT THIRTEEN

Lounging on a couch after school, she pokes playfully at her cat and tells me her favorite way to spend a day is rummaging through the neighborhood shopping center with girlfriends, then a movie and lunch at McDonald's. In many ways, she is very much like the girls I knew at thirteen. And in many ways she is so very different.

"I'm in eighth grade. Science is my favorite subject. I like to do the lab work, where you make conclusions based on your experiments. I want to go to college. I'll look for a school based on the science they have. I might be a scientist someday. Sometimes I think about it. I thought I might be somebody who would work in a lab, with blood types.

"I'm pretty good at math, too. It's fun. It's another good subject of mine. Some people think girls aren't as good at math as boys. That's baloney. Every girl in my class is better at math than the boys 'cause the boys are into basketball teams and stuff and aren't studying.

"I think boys and girls are equal. I'm a girl and that's it. None of the boys open doors for us or anything like that. You're on your own feet. If anyone opened a door for me, I'd feel pretty out of place. Once a boy did it and it bothered me. Like, every time I dropped a book, he'd say 'Oh, Sara, here's your book.' And it aggravated me, because I could pick it up myself.

"Sometimes my father treats me and my brother differently. If I ask to do something, he won't say 'No, because you're a girl.' But once he took a five-mile bike ride and he took my brother. And then my sister and I asked to join them and he thought we couldn't do it. He said, 'Oh, it might be too long for you.' I told him that he was a male chauvinist and that I could do anything he could. He laughed. But I thought that was terrible, thinking that just men could bicycle-ride five miles. Later, when he wasn't with us, my sister and I did ride five miles.

"You have to live a little when you're living, I think. Not just be taken care of, but take care of yourself. Right now, my parents don't make all the decisions for me. I'm going to decide what high school I'll go to, as long as it's a good one. I do a lot of things myself. It gives you a good feeling that you can do something and that somebody else doesn't have to do it for you. But, you know, when you do something, it is nice to have someone to share it with, too.

"I will probably get married, I guess, because I've been brought up that way. But I would definitely want a job, too. I wouldn't stop work because I got married or anything, because if you study really hard and you go to school, and if you don't have a job, there's really no point in going to school or trying real hard. If you make an effort you should carry it all the way. After you have the skills, you should have fun with them. I don't think marriage is bad. But I don't think you should be the person who just cooks and takes care of the children. You should expand yourself.

"A job might be hard, but it would be worthwhile. I wouldn't want to just marry a rich man and forget everything else. That wouldn't be exciting. It'd be dull, 'cause life—taking risks, taking challenges, going for the extra job, taking the extra course—is fun. Then you don't say to yourself 'Well, I *could* have done it'; you *did* it.

"I'd probably want children, too. I might give up work till they went to school, but then I'd go back. If I found out stopping work would hold me back, it would irritate me. You'd just have to work around it. Maybe work part-time. But it is your job to take care of your children—yours and your husband's. He has to be in it just as much as me. I'd make sure he knew that. We'd have to share chores. I wouldn't let him sit there and read the newspaper while I made dinner. I think if a man wants to have children, then he should have the responsibility of them, too. I'll look for somebody who would share the same ideas. But he could have a career, too, just like me.

"My mother has a career. She teaches a course in psychology part-time. I think that's fine—it doesn't bother me and it doesn't seem odd. If she had to sit around the house all day it'd be very boring. She went to school and she studied, and she should do something with her knowledge, too.

"I think if you work very hard you deserve something in return. You should get a price back. I would want pay. I think it's nice that people do volunteer work—a lot of it is very good—but I don't know if I'd be that generous.

"I think women today are much better off. When my mom was growing up, I don't think there was as much opportunity for jobs, or other things. She also told me that the reason they went to college was to get married and that was it. Girls today have another thought—that they're going to get a job. It's not just marriage.

"There's pressures with being in charge, but I think it's neat. At school, I've directed plays. Sometimes people don't do their part or things don't come in on time or one person messes up and doesn't learn their lines. But I think it's fun that they're trusting you and asking your advice, because you're sort of on top, even though it's scary because everybody's looking towards you.

"I've always sort of fantasized about something—creating the cure for leukemia. Something nobody else can think of. I want to do the unsolvable. Then, after I solve it, I'll just keep on trying for something else. I'll go on from there."

Technical Appendix

This book is based on results of our exclusive nationally projectable mail survey. This survey was designed to determine attitudes and motivations of working and nonworking women relating to the work world, home environment, and themselves and their resulting behaviors.

Certainly a researcher or a writer alone could never have produced this book. The interaction of the creative and research team that did it has been uniquely productive; the whole is truly bigger than the sum of its parts.

The national representativeness of our sample is a highly significant point. Our survey can be projected to adult women nationwide, and each group that is discussed in depth in the book is representative of that segment of women on a national basis. In contrast, books based on such material as the author's interviews with acquaintances or people met on travels across the country, responses to newspaper ads asking for opinions, or responses to a questionnaire printed in a magazine—although some of these techniques may result in large sample sizes—are not nationally projectable. Such books represent only a limited group of people and are therefore not necessarily representative of more than the individuals interviewed. This is an important distinction.

Our data were obtained in the following manner.

I have had a working relationship with Market Facts, Inc., one of the world's largest research firms, for a number of years. When presented with the concept of using marketing research techniques to gather information for a book, they were enthusiastic and contracted to conduct a research study among their Consumer Mail Panel. This panel consists of more than 100,000 households who have agreed to participate in mail and telephone surveys. Samples drawn from these households have the same distributions as the U.S. Census of Population in terms of the key demographic variables of age, household income, population density, and geographic region. Thus these samples are representative of women nationally. Studies conducted by Market Facts in collaboration with several clients have demonstrated that in terms of attitude and behavior, Consumer Mail Panel samples are equivalent to independently drawn samples for most products and services.

I developed a four-page questionnaire to cover the information objectives agreed on by Nickles and myself. These information objectives, in turn, had been based on qualitative material generated in preliminary in-depth personal interviews.

The questionnaire contained the following elements:

- 14 semantic differentials on work attitudes.
- 46 six-point agreement/disagreement questions on attitudes toward self, home, and employment.

Plus open-end and multiple-choice questions to establish:

- Future plans for working outside the home.
- Preferences in spending time with women who work vs. those who do not.
- Mother's/father's occupations.
- Whether respondent had "ideal" as a child; if so, relationship of "ideal" to respondent and reason for choice.
- Whether respondent worked outside the home; number of hours, occupation, title, and responsibilities.
- Motivations for working outside the home.

• Aspects liked and disliked about the job.
• Indication of whether employment affects any of ten life areas, whether effect is positive or negative, and the nature of the effect.
• Whether special problems occur as a consequence of being a woman in the work force.
• Current salary.

In addition, demographic information on each respondent was pulled from the Market Facts data bank on the Consumer Mail Panel.

These self-administered questionnaires were mailed to 2,400 women, balanced on key U.S. Census characteristics, between the ages of twenty and fifty. Questionnaires were equally split between working and nonworking women. Usable completed returns numbered 1,885. The response rate of 79 percent allows us to assume that the questionnaires returned are representative of the original sample.

The quality of response was unusually good: The open-ended questions in which we asked respondents to write about such subjects as the impact of their jobs on their lives and aspects liked and disliked about their jobs were answered in much more depth than is usual for most self-administered questionnaires. Market Facts commented, "Our professional staff was impressed with the thoroughness of the answers in this survey. Evidently the topic and the specific questions were of great interest to most respondents."

The fact that questions on attitudes toward work, home, and self are very involving emotionally was also evident when the data were processed by computer. When these data were cross-tabulated according to women broken down into various groups (by degree of education, type of job, etc.) tremendous variations emerged in their answers to the questions. A less involving topic—such as attitudes toward paper clip usage, for example—would not produce such variations in responses.

All tabulations with the execption of those involving the three attitudinal groups utilized standard cross-tabulations. When figures from this study are cited as varying by segment from the cross-tabulations, these differences are significant at the 95 percent level of confidence.

The attitudinal groups (Go-Getters, Domestics, and Malcontents) were delineated by a statistical technique called Q analysis. This clustering technique groups people according to their answers to a series of questions. People with similar patterns of responses are placed by the computer in the same group. In order to insure that the groups are reliable (reproduceable), the sample was divided into halves and Q analysis was performed on each half. The computer was then programmed to divide respondents into two groups, then three groups, then four groups, and so on. Corresponding groups from each half were compared for significant differences using Chi-Square tests. The number of attitudinal groups was thus limited to three groups; respondents divided into more than three groups produced significant differences between the halves and were less reliable.

Further in-depth personal and telephone interviews were conducted to probe into findings developed by the national survey statistics. We went back to many of the mail survey respondents for interview by telephone. All in-depth interviews were recorded, with their permission, and were transcribed and provided the basis for further analysis and verbatim quotes.

In addition to analyzing the computer printouts, Nickles and I have read through each of the individual questionnaires. Our respondents ranged from an assembly line worker at a toothpaste factory to a symphony violinist to the president of a manufacturing company to a homemaker. Fascinating and varied stories emerged from each woman, and they bring the statistics vividly to life.

—Laura Ashcraft

Notes

Chapter 1

1. F. Y. Edgeworth, "Equal Pay to Men and Women for Equal Work," *Economic Journal* 32 (Dec. 1922): 439.
2. Basic data on women's participation in the work force were obtained from the Bureau of Labor Statistics of the U.S. Department of Labor—particularly the Women's Bureau, which makes available its *Handbook on Women Workers* and other publications on request—and the U.S. Bureau of the Census.
3. Courtnay Slater, "Statistics Reveal Three Distinct Phases of Growth of Women in Labor Force," *Business America* 2 (March 26, 1979): 20.
4. Nancy S. Barrett, "Women in the Job Market: Occupations, Earnings, and Career Opportunities," in *The Subtle Revolution: Women at Work*, ed. Ralph E. Smith (Washington, D.C.: The Urban Institute, 1979), p. 56.
5. "More Working, More Spending," *Marketing and Media Decisions* 14 (Dec. 1979): 131.
6. U.S. Department of Labor, Employment Standards Administration, Women's Bureau, *Working Mothers and Their Children* (Washington, D.C., 1977), p. 4.
7. Juanita Morris Kreps and Robert Clark, *Sex, Age, and Work: The Changing Composition of the Labor Force* (Baltimore: Johns Hopkins University Press, 1975), p. 78.
8. U.S. Bureau of Labor Statistics, *Employment and Earnings*, monthly, 1979.
9. Ibid.
10. Ann Marie Libinski, "Working Women Speak Out," *Chicago Tribune* (May 20, 1980), sec. 12, p. 1.
11. Barbara Brotman, "Working Mothers: What Science Really Knows," *Chicago Tribune* (May 11, 1980), sec. 12, p. 1.
12. U.S. Bureau of the Census, "Marital Status and Living Arrange-

ments: March 1978," *Current Population Reports: Population Characteristics,* series p–20, no. 338, 1979.

13. U.S. Bureau of the Census, *Current Population Reports,* series p–20, no. 327, and earlier issues as cited in U.S. Bureau of the Census, *Statistical Abstract of the U.S.: 1979,* 100th edition (Washington, D.C., 1979), p. 44.

14. Douglas Martin, "The Single Life," *Chicago Tribune* (Sept. 14, 1980), sec. 12, p. 4.

15. Kreps and Clark, *Sex, Age, and Work,* p. 78.

16. U.S. Bureau of the Census, "Marital Status," p. 20.

17. *Chicago Tribune* (Oct. 7, 1980), sec. 1, p. 14.

18. Ibid.

19. U.S. Department of Labor, *Working Mothers,* p. 1.

20. "The Superwoman Squeeze," *Newsweek* (May 19, 1980), p. 72.

21. U.S. Department of Labor, *Working Mothers,* p. 1.

22. *National Survey of Working Women: Perceptions, Problems, and Prospects,* report of a national survey of working women, National Commission on Working Women (Washington, D.C.: Center for Women and Work, June 1979). Available by writing the Women's Bureau of the Department of Labor.

23. Gail Sheehy, *Passages: Predictable Crises of Adult Life* (New York: Bantam, 1977), p. 531.

24. U.S. Bureau of the Census, "Marital Status and Living Arrangements: March 1978," *Current Population Reports: Population Characteristics,* series p–20, no. 349, 1980.

25. Ibid.

26. "Marital Status, March 1979."

27. Speech by the Hon. Vincent Barabba, U.S. Bureau of the Census, U.S. Department of Commerce, March 26, 1980, to the American Marketing Association.

28. Ibid.

29. "Women, the Emerging Marketing Majority," *Madison Avenue* 22 (Nov. 1980): 52.

30. "More Working, More Spending," p. 132.

31. "Women's Buying Power Is Fueling the Small-Car Revolution," *Chicago Sun-Times* (March 30, 1980), p. 7.

32. Robert L. Skrabanek, "The Growing Power of Women," *American Demographics* 2 (Sept. 1980): 24.

33. "It'll Be Tough All Over Until 2050, Experts Say," *Chicago Tribune* (Nov. 10, 1980): 1.

34. David Ignatius, "The Rich Get Richer as Well-to-Do Wives Enter the Labor Force," *Wall Street Journal* (Sept. 8, 1978): 1.

Chapter 2

1. Gloria Norris and Jo Ann Miller, *The Working Mother's Complete Handbook* (New York: A Sunrise Book, E. P. Dutton, 1979), p. 217. Citing a *Redbook* magazine survey of 10,000 women.
2. Caroline Bird, *The Two-Paycheck Marriage* (New York: Rawson, Wade, 1979), p. 13.
3. From a report of a national survey by Joan Huber and Glenna Spitze reported in *American Demographics* 2 (Sept. 1980): 11.
4. Bird, *Two-Paycheck Marriage*, p. 13.

Chapter 5

1. The number of women earning $20,000 a year and up increased from 154,941 in 1970 to 2,305,000 in 1977—U.S. Bureau of the Census, "Money, Income and Poverty Status of Families and Persons in the United States: Advance Report," *Current Population Reports: Consumer Income*, series p–60, no. 125 (Washington, D.C., 1980), pp. 22–24.

Chapter 6

1. U.S. National Center for Education Statistics, *Digest of Education Statistics*, Annual, cited in U.S. Bureau of the Census, *Statistical Abstract of the U.S.: 1979*, 100th edition (Washington, D.C., 1979), p. 44.
2. U.S. Department of Health, Education and Welfare, Educational Division, U.S. National Center for Education Statistics, *Fall Enrollment in Higher Education*, Annual, 1978, NCES, 79–317.
3. U.S. Bureau of the Census, "School Enrollment: Social and Economic Characteristics of Students," *Current Population Reports*, series p–20, no. 346, 1978.

4. U.S. Department of Commerce, Bureau of the Census, *Data User News* 15, no. 8 (Aug. 1980), p. 7.
5. Helen J. McLane, *Selecting, Developing, and Retaining Women Executives: A Corporate Strategy for the Eighties* (New York: Van Nostrand Reinhold, 1980), p. 8.
6. *Data User News*, p. 7.
7. Roger D. Blackwell, "Eight Campus Trends Will Change Marketing Managers, Management," *Marketing News* (May 30, 1980), p. 7.
8. Ibid.
9. *National Survey of Working Women: Perceptions, Problems, and Prospects*, p. 1.
10. "The Women in the Office: The Economic Status of Clerical Workers," prepared by Women Employed Institute, Chicago.
11. Rosabeth Moss Kanter, *Men and Women of the Corporation* (New York: Basic Books, 1977), p. 140, citing Eli Chinoy, *Automobile Workers and the American Dream* (New York: Doubleday, 1955); Robert Guest, "Work Careers and Aspirations of Automobile Workers," *American Sociological Review* 19 (1954): 155–163.
12. Kanter, *Men and Women of the Corporation*, p. 249.
13. Ibid., p. 266.
14. Ibid., pp. 153–155.
15. Ibid., p. 161.
16. Heidrick & Struggles, Inc., *Profile of a Woman Officer* (Chicago, 1979).
17. Ibid., 1978.
18. Ibid., 1979.
19. U.S. Department of Labor, *The Occupational Outlook Handbook* (1978–1979), (Washington, D.C., 1979).
20. Kreps and Clark, *Sex, Age, and Work*, p. 55.
21. Bird, *Two-Paycheck Marriage*, p. 258.

Chapter 7

1. Sandra L. Hofferth and Kristin A. Moore, "Women and Their Children," in Smith, *Subtle Revolution*, p. 149; Norris and Miller, *Working Mother's Handbook*, pp. 274–275.

Chapter 8

1. U.S. Department of Labor, Women's Bureau, from 1978 annual averages of data.
2. Ibid.
3. U.S. Department of Labor, Office of the Secretary, Women's Bureau, *The Earnings Gap Between Women and Men* (Washington, D.C., 1979).
4. A study made for the National Commission on the Observance of International Women's Year, reported in Caroline Bird, *What Women Want* (New York: Simon and Schuster, 1979), p. 88.
5. Doreen Managan, "Financial Advertising to Women," *Madison Avenue 22* (Nov. 1980): 52.
6. Bird, *Two-Paycheck Marriage*, pp. 87–93; Hofferth and Moore, "Women's Employment and Marriage," in Smith, *Subtle Revolution*, p. 113; and Clair Vickery, "Women's Economic Contributions to the Family," in *Subtle Revolution*, p. 188.
7. Kanter, *Men and Women of the Corporation*, p. 285.
8. U.S. Bureau of Labor Statistics, *Employment and Earnings*, monthly, cited in U.S. Bureau of the Census, *Statistical Abstract of the U.S.: 1979*, 100th edition (Washington, D.C., 1979), p. 4.
9. Norris and Miller, *Working Mother's Handbook*, p. 192.
10. Nancy Chodorow, *The Reproduction of Mothering: Psychoanalysis and the Sociology of Gender* (Berkeley and Los Angeles: University of California Press, 1978), p. 196.
11. Nadine Brozan, "Number of Women with Two Jobs Doubles in Decade," *Chicago Tribune* (July 1, 1980), sec. 4, p. 10.
12. U.S. Department of Labor, Office of the Secretary, Women's Bureau, *Economic Responsibilities of Working Women* (Washington, D.C., 1979).
13. Managan, "Financial Advertising to Women," p. 52.
14. Eli S. Belil, "Men Adopting New Attitudes, Values, Goals, and Life-styles," *Marketing News 14* (Jan. 9, 1981): 27.
15. "Coporate Women: Now Eager to Accept Transfers," *Business Week* (May 26, 1980): 156.
16. Barrett, "Women in the Job Market," in Smith, *Subtle Revolution*, p. 52.
17. Bailey Morris, "Women Are Victims of a 'Double-Day' Syndrome," *Chicago Sun-Times* (June 29, 1980), p. 22.

18. Ibid.
19. Sandra L. Hofferth and Kristin A. Moore, "Women's Employment and Marriage," in Smith, *Subtle Revolution*, citing Kathryn E. Walker, "Household Work Time: Its Implications for Family Decisions," *Journal of Home Economics* 65 (Oct. 1973): 7–11.
20. Clair Vickery, "Women's Economic Contribution to the Family," in Smith, *Subtle Revolution*, p. 184.
21. Bird, *Two-Paycheck Marriage*, p. 87.
22. Hofferth and Moore, in Smith, *Subtle Revolution*, pp. 120–121, citing J. Burke and Tamara Weir, "Relationship of Wives' Employment Status to Husband, Wife, and Pair Satisfaction and Performance," *Journal of Marriage and the Family* 38 (May 1971): 278–287.
23. Ibid. p. 121.
24. Hofferth and Moore, in Smith, *Subtle Revolution*, p. 115, citing Martin Meissner, Elizabeth Humphreys, Scott M. Meis and William J. Scheu, "No Exit for Wives: Sexual Division of Labour in the Culmination of Household Demands," *Canadian Review of Sociology and Anthropology* 12 (1975): 424–439.
25. Glenn Collins, "Charting the Trailblazers: First-Time Mothers Over 40," *Chicago Tribune* (Nov. 9, 1980), sec. 12, p. 10.
26. *National Survey of Working Women: Perceptions, Problems, and Prospects* (Washington, D.C.: Center for Women and Work, June 1979), p. 13.
27. "Job and Family: The Walls Come Down," *U.S. News and World Report* (June 16, 1980), p. 58.
28. Louis A. Fanelli, "Gas Crisis Fuels Catalog Sales," *Advertising Age* 50 (Aug. 6, 1979): 34.
29. Heidrick & Struggles, Inc., *Profile of a Woman Officer*, 1979, p. 4.
30. Robert L. Skrabanek, "The Growing Power of Women," *American Demographics* 2 (Sept. 1980): 24.
31. Ibid., p. 23.
32. Diane Rothbard Margolis, "The Invisible Hands: Sex Roles and the Division of Labor in Two Local Political Parties," from *Women and Work: Problems and Perspectives*, ed. Rachel Hut-Kahn, Arlene Kaplan Daniels, and Richard Colvard. Unpublished ms., Society for the Study of Social Problems.
33. Skrabanek, "Power of Women," p. 24.
34. Nancy M. Gordon, "Institutional Responses: The Federal Income

Tax System," in Smith, *Subtle Revolution*, p. 203; U.S. life tables and actuarial tables, National Center for Health Statistics, 1977.
35. Study by Deborah L. Wingard, University of California, School of Medicine, San Diego.
36. Chodorow, *Reproduction of Mothering*, p. 185.
37. Chris Stoehr, "A New Generation Gap—Kids Are More Traditional," *Chicago Tribune* (Nov. 23, 1980), sec. 12, p. 1.

Chapter 9

1. Chodorow, *Reproduction of Mothering*, p. 122.
2. Ibid., p. 185.
3. Ibid., p. 212.
4. Norris and Miller, *Working Mother's Handbook*, p. 122.
5. Ruth E. Zambrana, Marcia Hurst, and Rodney L. Hite, "The Working Mother in Contemporary Perspective: A Review of the Literature," *Pediatrics* 64 (Dec. 1979): 865–867.
6. Norris and Hofferth, "Women and Their Children," in Smith, *Subtle Revolution*, p. 149.
7. Ibid.
8. Bird, *Two-Paycheck Marriage*, p. 74.
9. Channing Stowell III, "Where, What, and How We Eat," *Advertising Age* 50 (April 30, 1979): S5–S14.

Bibliography

Articles

Ames, Elizabeth. "Test Your Ambition Temperature." *Self*, May 1980, p. 67.

Baillyn, Lotte. "Taking Off for the Top—How Much Acceleration for Career Success?" *Management Review* 68 (1979): 18–23.

Balsley, Dr. Irol. "Should Machines Replace the Steno Pad?" *Management World* 8 (1979): 25–26.

Bartol, Kathryn M.; Anderson, Carl R.; and Schneier, Craig Eric. "Motivation to Manage Among College Business Students: A Reassessment." *Journal of Vocational Behavior* 17 (1980): 22–32.

Bartol, Kathryn M., and Manhardt, P. J. "Sex Differences in Job Outcome Preparedness: Trends Among Newly Hired College Graduates." *Journal of Applied Psychology* 64 (1979): 477–482.

Belil, Eli S. "Men Adopting New Attitudes, Values, Goals, and Lifestyles." *Marketing News* 14 (1981): 27.

Bennetts, Leslie. "Women in Office: How Have They Affected Women's Issues?" *New York Times*, 4 Nov. 1980, p. 8.

Bensahel, Jane G. "How Much Longer Will Managers Have Secretaries?" *International Management* 33 (1978): 37–42.

Biggins, J. Veronica. "Banks Show Significant Progress for Women and Minorities." *ABA Banking Journal* 71 (1979): 22–26.

Biles, George E., and Pryatel, Holly A. "Myths, Management, and Women." *Personnel Journal* 57 (1978): 572–577.

Blackwell, Roger D. "Eight Campus Trends Will Change Marketing Managers, Management." *Marketing News* 13 (30 May 1980): 1–19.

"Brands Switched When Mom Works." *Advertising Age* 50 (1979): sec. 2, S18–S20.

Brenner, O. C., and Tomkiewicz, Joseph. "Job Orientation of Males and Females: Are Sex Differences Declining?" *Personnel Psychology* 32 (1979): 741–750.

Briggs, Jean A. "How You Going to Get 'em Back in the Kitchen? (You Aren't.)" *Forbes* 120 (1977): 177.

Brotman, Barbara. "Working Mothers: What Science Really Knows." *Chicago Tribune*, 11 May 1980, pp. 1–4.

Brown, David L. "Women in the Labor Force." *Journal of Home Economics* 69 (1977): 21.

Brozan, Nadine. "Number of Women with Two Jobs Doubles in Decade." *Chicago Tribune*, 1 July 1980, p. 10.

Castor, Arnold. "A New Role and Opportunity Is Seen for Today's Super Secretary." *Administrative Management* 40 (1979): 92–102.

Cavanaugh, H. A. "Work: Tomorrow Isn't What It Used to Be." *Electrical World, The Management Report* 191 (1979): 27–30.

Cimons, Marlene. "Feminists Pessimistic About ERA." *Chicago Sun-Times*, 7 Nov. 1980, p. 42.

Collins, Glenn. "Charting the Trailblazers: First-Time Mothers Over 40." *Chicago Tribune*, 9 Nov. 1980, p. 10.

Cook, Mary F. "Is the Mentor Relationship Primarily a Male Experience?" *The Personnel Administrator* 24 (1979): 82–84.

"Corporate Woman: Now Eager to Accept Transfers." *Business Week*, 26 May 1980, pp. 153–156.

"Degree Combo: It's New Key to Top for Women." *Chicago Sun-Times*, 15 Sept. 1980, pp. 60–62.

"Divorce Doubles" *American Demographics* 2 (1980): 9.

Dullea, Georgia. "Vast Changes in Society Traced to the Rise of Working Women." *New York Times*, 29 Nov. 1977, p. 28.

Edgeworth, F. Y. "Equal Pay to Men and Women for Equal Work." *Economic Journal* 32, no. 4 (1922): 439.

Fanelli, Louis A. "Gas Crisis Fuels Catalog Sales." *Advertising Age* 50 (6 Aug. 1979): 34.

Felsenthal, Carol. "Women Far from the Top in Unions." *Chicago Tribune*, 20 July 1980, sec. 12, p. 9.

Ferber, Marianne A., and McMahon, Walter W. "Women's Expected Earnings and Their Investment in Higher Education." *The Journal of Human Resources* 14 (1979): 405–420.

Glick, Paul C. "Updating the Life Cycle of the Family." *Journal of Marriage and the Family* 39 (1977): 3–15.

Goodman, John, Jr. "People of the City." *American Demographics* 2 (1980): 16.

Gottschalk, Earl C., Jr. "Day-Care Is Booming, but Experts Are Split over Its Effects on Kids." *Wall Street Journal*, 15 Sept. 1978, p. 1.

Grossman, Allyson Sherman. "Labor Force Patterns of Single Women." *Monthly Labor Review* 102 (Aug. 1979): 46–49.

Guest, Robert. "Work Careers and Aspirations of Automobile Workers." *American Sociological Review* 19 (1954): 155–163.

Hungerford, Nancy, and Paolucci, Beatrice. "The Employed Female Single Parent." *Journal of Home Economics* 69 (Nov. 1977): 10–13.

Ignatius, David. "The Rich Get Richer as Well-to-Do Wives Enter the Labor Force." *Wall Street Journal*, 8 Sept. 1978, p. 1.

"It'll Be Tough All Over Until 2050, Experts Say." *Chicago Tribune*, 10 Nov. 1980, sec. 1, p. 1.

"Job and Family: The Walls Come Down." *U.S. News and World Report*, 16 June 1980, p. 58.

Kotulak, Ronald. "More Singles, Divorces, and Fewer Kids." *Chicago Tribune*, 26 April 1981, sec. 1, p. 1.

Lazer, William, and Smallwood, John E. "The Changing Demographics of Women." *Journal of Marketing* 41 (July 1977): 18–22.

Lipinski, Ann Marie. "Working Women Speak Out." *Chicago Tribune*, 20 May 1979, sec. 12, pp. 1–4.

Malabre, Alfred L., Jr. "As Their Ranks Swell, Women Holding Jobs Reshape U.S. Society." *Wall Street Journal*, 21 Sept. 1978, p. 1.

Managan, Doreen. "Financial Advertising to Women." *Madison Avenue* 22 (Nov. 1980): 49–54.

Martin, Douglas. "The Single Life." *Chicago Tribune*, 14 Sept. 1980, sec. 12, pp. 1–3.

Mason, Karen Oppenheim; Czajka, J. L.; and Arber, S. "Change in U.S. Women's Sex-Role Attitudes (1964–1974)." *American Sociological Review* 41 (1976): 573–596.

McBrearty, James C. "The Kitchen Revolution: New Careers for American Women." *Arizona Review* 21 (1972): 10–14.

McCall, Suzanne H. "Meet the Workwife." *Journal of Marketing* 41 (1977): 55–65.

Miner, J. B. "Motivation to Manage Among Women: Studies of Business Managers and Educational Administrators." *Journal of Vocational Behavior* 5 (1974): 197–208.

———. "Motivation to Manage Among Women: Studies of College Students." *Journal of Vocational Behavior* 5 (1974): 241–250.

"More Americans Delay Tying Marriage Knot." *Wall Street Journal*, 27 June 1979, p. 6.

"More Working, More Spending." Special Report on Women. *Marketing and Media Decisions* 14 (1979): 68–69.

Morris, Bailey. "Women Are Victims of a 'Double Day' Syndrome." *Chicago Sun-Times,* 29 June 1980, sec. 5, p. 21.

———. "Women Cash in on Bank Careers." *Chicago Sun-Times,* 22 June 1980, sec. 5, p. 12.

Nemy, Enid. "Leadership 'Crisis' Could Use a Bit More Beta, Panel Told." *Chicago Tribune,* 7 Dec. 1980, sec. 12, p. 9.

Porter, Sylvia. "Last-In, First-Out Job Myth Shattered." *Chicago Sun-Times,* 3 Dec. 1980, p. 81.

Renshaw, Domeena C., M.D. "Sex and the Female Psyche." *Comprehensive Therapy* 4 (1978): 17–21.

Russell, Cheryl. "Portrait of Women." *American Demographics* 2 (1980): 40–41.

Safran, Claire. "Inflation: How the Money Pinch Hurts Young Couples." *Redbook* (Sept. 1979): 31.

Schumer, Fern. "I Love You, Honey—Sign Here." *Chicago Tribune,* 2 Sept. 1980, sec. 5, p. 1.

"Shopping Services for Working Women." *Stores* 61 (1979): 44.

Skrabanek, Robert L. "The Growing Power of Women." *American Demographics* 2 (1980): 23–25.

Slater, Courtenay, and Carson, Joseph G. "Job Data Show Growing, Changing Role for Women in U.S. Economy." *Commerce America* 3 (1978): 20–21.

Slater, Courtenay, and Kraseman, Thomas. "Statistics Reveal Three Distinct Phases in Growth of Women in Labor Force." *Business America* 2 (1979): 20–21.

Smith, Catherine Begnoche. "Influence of Internal Opportunity Structure and Sex of Worker on Turnover Patterns." *Administrative Science Quarterly* 24 (1979): 362–381.

Stoehr, Chris. "A New Generation Gap—Kids Are More Traditional." *Chicago Tribune,* 23 Nov. 1980, sec. 12, p. 1.

Stowell, Channing III. "Where, What, and How We Eat." *Advertising Age* 50 (30 April 1979):sec. 2, S1–S14.

Szilagy, Andrew D. "Reward Behavior by Male and Female Leaders: A Causal Inference Analysis." *Journal of Vocational Behavior* 16 (1980): 59–72.

"The American Family: Bent—but Not Broken." *U.S. News and World Report,* 16 June 1980, pp. 48–54.

"The Superwoman Squeeze." *Newsweek,* 19 May 1980, pp. 72–79.

Varro, Barbara. "Sexual Blackmail: Female Workers Are Refusing to Pay Up." *Chicago Sun-Times*, 23 March 1980, p. 3.

———. "The State of Single America." *Chicago Sun-Times*, 18 Sept. 1980, p. 81.

"Women, the Emerging Marketing Majority." *Madison Avenue* 22 (1980): 52.

"Women's Buying Power Is Fueling the Small-Car Revolution." *Chicago Sun-Times*, 30 March 1980, p. 7.

Woodworth, Margaret, and Woodworth, Warner. "The Female Takeover: Threat or Opportunity?" *The Personnel Administrator* 24 (1979): 19–28.

Zambrana, Ruth E.; Hurst, Marcia; and Hite, Rodney L. "The Working Mother in Contemporary Perspective: A Review of the Literature." *Pediatrics* 64 (1979): 862–870.

Books

Adams, Jane. *Women on Top: Success Patterns and Personal Growth.* New York: Hawthorn Books, 1980.

Bird, Caroline. *The Two-Paycheck Marriage.* New York: Rawson, Wade, 1979.

Butler, Matilda, and Paisley, William. *Women and the Mass Media: Sourcebook for Research and Action.* New York: Human Sciences Press, 1980.

Chafe, William H. *Women and Equality: Changing Patterns in American Culture.* New York: Oxford University Press, 1977.

Chodorow, Nancy. *The Reproduction of Mothering: Psychoanalysis and the Sociology of Gender.* Berkeley and Los Angeles: University of California Press, 1978.

Colvard, Richard; Daniels, Arlene Kaplan; and Hut-Kahn, Rachel, eds. *Women and Work: Problems and Perspectives.* Unpublished manuscript. Society for the Study of Social Problems.

Engels, Friedrich. *The Origin of the Family, Private Property, and the State.* 1884. New York: International Publishers, 1942.

Farley, Lin. *Sexual Shakedown: The Sexual Harassment of Women on the Job.* New York: Warner Books, 1978.

Friday, Nancy. *My Mother, Myself.* New York: Delacorte Press, 1977.

Gilman, Charlotte Perkins. *Women and Economics.* New York: Harper and Row, 1966.

Harragan, Betty Lehan. *Games Mother Never Taught You: Corporate Gamesmanship for Women.* New York: Warner Books, 1977.

Henley, Nancy M. *Body Politics (Power, Sex, and Nonverbal Communication).* Englewood Cliffs, N.J.: Prentice-Hall, 1977.

Hennig, Margaret, and Jardim, Anne. *The Managerial Woman.* New York: Pocket Books, 1977.

Howe, Louise Kapp. *Pink-Collar Workers (Inside the World of Women's Work).* New York: Avon, 1978.

Kanter, Rosabeth Moss. *Men and Women of the Corporation.* New York: Basic Books, 1977.

Kennedy, Marilyn Moats. *Office Politics: Seizing Power, Wielding Clout.* Chicago: Follett Publishing Co., 1980.

Kreps, Juanita Morris, and Clark, Robert. *Sex, Age, and Work: The Changing Composition of the Labor Force.* Baltimore: Johns Hopkins University Press, 1975.

Kupinsky, Stanley, ed. *The Fertility of Working Women: A Synthesis of International Research.* New York: Praeger, 1977.

McLane, Helen J. *Selecting, Developing, and Retaining Women Executives: A Corporate Strategy for the Eighties.* New York: Van Nostrand Reinhold Co., 1980.

Miller, Jean Baker, M.D. *Towards a New Psychology of Women.* Boston: Beacon Press, 1977.

Montagu, Ashley. *The Natural Superiority of Women.* New revised edition. New York: Collier Books (Division of Macmillan Publishing Co.), 1974.

Norris, Gloria, and Miller, Jo Ann. *The Working Mother's Complete Handbook.* New York: E. P. Dutton (A Sunrise Book), 1979.

Pincus, Cynthia, Ph.D.; Elliott, Leslie; and Schlachtes, Trudy. *The Roots of Success.* Englewood Cliffs, N.J.: Prentice-Hall, 1980.

Rossi, Alice. *The Feminist Papers from Adams to de Beauvoir.* New York: Bantam Books, 1974.

Sheehy, Gail. *Passages: Predictable Crises of Adult Life.* New York: Bantam Books, 1977.

Smith, Ralph E., ed. *The Subtle Revolution: Women at Work.* Washington, D.C.: The Urban Institute, 1979.

Toffler, Alvin. *The Third Wave.* New York: William Morrow and Co., 1980.

Other

Heidrick & Struggles, Inc. *Profile of a Woman Officer.* Chicago: 1977, 1978 and 1979.

"Labor Force Participation of Women." *Consumer Prospects.* Glastonbury, Conn.: The Futures Group, March 1978.

National Survey of Working Women: Perceptions, Problems and Prospects. National Commission on Working Women, Center for Women and Work. Washington, D.C.: Center for Women and Work, June 1979.

U.S. Department of Commerce, Bureau of the Census. *Data User News* 15 (1981).

————. "Marital Status and Living Arrangements: March 1978." *Current Population Reports: Population Characteristics,* series p–20, no. 338, 1979.

————. "Marital Status and Living Arrangements: March 1979." *Current Population Reports: Population Characteristics,* series p–20, no. 349, 1980.

————. "Money, Income, and Poverty Status of Families and Persons in the United States." Advance report. *Current Population Reports: Consumer Income,* series p–60, no. 125, Oct. 1980.

————. *Statistical Abstract of the U.S.: 1979,* 100th edition. Washington, D.C.: U.S. Government Printing Office, 1979.

————. *A Statistical Portrait of Women in the U.S.,* no. 100. Washington, D.C.: U.S. Government Printing Office, 1978.

U.S. Department of Health, Education and Welfare. *Social Security and the Changing Roles of Men and Women.* Washington, D.C.: U.S. Government Printing Office, Feb. 1979.

————. "School Enrollment: Social and Economic Characteristics of Students." *Current Population Reports,* series p–20, no. 346, 1978.

U.S. Department of Health, Education and Welfare, Educational Division, U.S. National Center for Education Statistics. *Fall Enrollment in Higher Education, 1978.* Washington, D.C.: U.S. Government Printing Office, 1980.

U.S. Department of Labor, Bureau of Labor Statistics. *Employment and Earnings,* monthly, 1977, 1978, and 1979.

U.S. Department of Labor, Women's Bureau. *The Earnings Gap Between Women and Men.* Washington, D.C.: U.S. Government Printing Office, 1979.

252   *Bibliography*

———. *Economic Responsibilities of Working Women.* Washington, D.C.: U.S. Government Printing Office, 1979.

———. *The Myth and the Reality.* Washington, D.C.: U.S. Government Printing Office, 1979.

———. *Women Workers Today.* Washington, D.C.: U.S. Government Printing Office, 1976.

———. *Working Mothers and Their Children.* Washington, D.C.: U.S. Government Printing Office, 1977.

———. *The Occupational Outlook Handbook* (1978–1979). Washington, D.C.: U.S. Government Printing Office, 1979.

Weinstock, E. C.; Tietze, F.; and Jaffe, J.G. "Abortion Need and Services in the U.S., 1974–1975." In Alan Guttmacher Institute, "Family Planning Perspectives," vol. 9, no. 3. The Alan Guttmacher Institute, 1977.

Women Employed Institute. *Closing the Wage Gap: A National Imperative.* Chicago, 1979.

———. *The Women in the Office: The Economic Status of Clerical Workers.* Chicago, 1979.